CANNING FOR A NEW GENERATION

CANNING FOR A NEW GENERATION

BOLD, FRESH FLAVORS FOR THE MODERN PANTRY

Liana Krissoff

photographs by Rinne Allen

STEWART, TABORI & CHANG   NEW YORK

The recipes in this book have been developed and tested in a home kitchen. Canning and preserving, as is true of any other kind of cooking, carry risks. Please follow the recipes and instructions carefully, and if there is any confusion about the ingredients or the process, please consult an up-to-date U.S. government source for clarification. The author and publisher assume no responsibility for damages associated with the use of this book.

Published in 2010 by Stewart, Tabori & Chang
An imprint of ABRAMS

Text copyright © 2010 Liana Krissoff
Photographs © 2010 Rinne Allen

Library of Congress Cataloging-in-Publication Data

Krissoff, Liana.
  Canning for a new generation / by Liana Krissoff ; photographs by Rinne Allen.
    p. cm.
  Includes index.
  ISBN 978-1-58479-864-4
  1. Canning and preserving. 2. Fruit--Preservation. 3. Vegetables--Preservation. I. Title.
  TX601.K823 2010
  664'.0282--dc22
                        2009049111

Editors: Luisa Weiss and Kate Norment
Designer: Alissa Faden
Production Manager: Tina Cameron

The text of this book was composed in Archer and Gotham.

Printed and bound in the United States
10

Stewart, Tabori & Chang books are available at special discounts when purchased in quantity for premiums and promotions as well as fundraising or educational use. Special editions can also be created to specification. For details, contact specialsales@abramsbooks.com or the address below.

THE ART OF BOOKS SINCE 1949
115 West 18th Street
New York, NY 10011
www.abramsbooks.com

For Thalia

CONTENTS

Introduction

When I was growing up, canning was for old folks and cranks and separatists—oh, and for my parents, who spent every summer of my Virginia childhood scrambling to convert overflowing bushel baskets of fruits and vegetables from their garden into a pantry lined with shelf upon shelf of colorful canning jars, not to mention a stuffed-to-the-rim chest freezer or two. Not for me. I had better, far more important things to do. I can't remember what they were.

When I left home and moved to New York, I happily immersed myself in a project of experiencing every new food I possibly could: seeking out Malaysian braised frog's legs in Jackson Heights, buying armloads of vegetables and unfamiliar species of seafood in Chinatown and coming home to figure out what to do with it all, pestering kielbasa makers in Greenpoint for detailed explanations of the different varieties of smoked sausage hanging above their heads.

But as I started to miss the rosy homemade applesauce and the salsa that was just as hot as I liked it and the spicy-tangy pickled beans I'd snacked on blithely every day after school, I thought maybe I should try canning something myself. I flipped through some canning books at Barnes & Noble (public libraries also being the domain of old folks and cranks—though not separatists so much), and found that the common thread running through them all, from the classic *Ball Blue Book* to the newer, prettier books on jams and jellies, is the notion that Canning Is Hard: tedious work, complicated, deadly. I somehow got the impression that I would die if I tried this without three thermometers calibrated monthly, a hundred-foot roll of litmus paper, and a topographical map that pinpointed my location and its exact elevation.

Then several years later, living in a comically narrow railroad apartment in Hell's Kitchen in Manhattan, I found myself with a few baskets of apples I'd picked at an orchard somewhere north of the city with the man who would in a couple of weeks ask me to marry him. Something was in the air—fall, of course, and fast-declining Pink Ladies, and the beginnings of the eat-local movement swirling around—but also I was in love. I was about to become an honest-to-god wife. I called my mom and asked her how to make applesauce (now it seems so simple, second nature). I started canning in my tiny galley kitchen, in a stockpot with empty upside-down tuna cans in the bottom, using spring-loaded tongs with rubber bands wrapped around the ends to pull hot jars out of boiling water.

Nobody having died after eating (or at least being ceremoniously presented with) my applesauce, I went back to the bookstore and began a years-long search for a good, modern, clear, easy-to-follow

canning book with delicious-looking recipes I wanted to make and eat. Finally I gave up and decided to simply learn as much as I could on my own—reading all the bad books, canning lots of stuff all year round, asking Mom and Dad and friends and neighbors and relatives and neighbors of strangers for advice—and write one myself.

The recipes here are for people a little bit like me. For those of us who upon hearing "pickle" remember Mom's sweet watermelon-rind pickles ice-cold out of the fridge, but also think of the dollop of goodness that goes on top of a bowl of curried lentils, or the dainty dish of *tsukemono* pickles that might come with the sashimi at a good sushi bar. Those people for whom "ferment" means not just full-sour dills bobbing about in a crock of cloudy brine on the Lower East Side but also spicy red kimchi. And those of us who, while thoroughly enjoying

a sweet, thick slather of classic peach preserves on toast every now and then (or, okay, often), might prefer a tart-sweet black plum jam spiked with fragrant cardamom, or a small spoonful of fig preserves with port and rosemary alongside a wedge of veiny blue cheese and a thick slice of dark bread.

This book reflects what I, a person with tastes and interests that run to bread-and-butter pickles and strawberry jam and far beyond, like to cook and eat throughout the year, and how I in my small way extend the seasons of my favorite ingredients—and the memories that those foods invoke. I want you to find a way to do something similar, using this book as a starting point and inspiration. You'd be surprised how tomatoes, perhaps put up one hot Saturday with friends who've come over to spend an afternoon drinking frosty beers and filling the countertop with bright red pint jars, can comfort

and nourish on a cold night in January in a simple pasta dish. How an early-morning spoonful of perfect blueberry marmalade, made by a good friend you might know only via email and your respective blogs, can help you make it through a busy day of office work. How a hot wokful of diced pickled yard-long beans and spicy minced pork, while cooked in a kitchen in the rural South, can bring back that Chinese-takeout favorite you've been craving since you left the city.

Folks nowadays can for many reasons. Sure, it could be that they're preparing for the apocalypse or, just as bad, a government takeover. (Ask me about the time I was standing in line at a grocery store with a cartful of canning jars and the guy behind me gave me a knowing look and started talking about how—soon—we're *all* going to have to start canning.) Maybe they've found a way to can in a truly

frugal way, or they have access to a lot of produce and can't stand for any of it to go to waste. Maybe they're sensitive types who put summer produce up in jars because otherwise they'd miss it during winter. Maybe they just like to make a few batches of special jam to give to friends as holiday gifts that won't go bad before the New Year. Some do it to reconnect with the past, or to satisfy some deep do-it-yourself urge. And some surely do it just because it's . . . something to do.

For me, putting up the very best produce I can find in season—especially if it's homegrown or from a nearby farm—is quite simply a way to spend some marginally productive time in the kitchen, preferably with my family and friends. Opening the jars and enjoying them later, I'm reminded of those fun times of tasting and talking, usually about food but also about music and politics and everything else that matters. In addition, taking on a kitchen project of a certain complexity, like canning or pickling or fermenting (or smoking meat or stuffing sausage or aging cheese), helps me remember what food was like when I was a kid and my mom and dad did these things, and what it might have been like when they were kids.

I don't *have* to can things to keep my family in food—the power never goes out at my house for more than a couple days at a time, the winters are pretty darn temperate, and we can always just run out to a grocery store and get anything we need. I understand that canning isn't really economical in most cases. If I didn't put up a dozen jars of strawberry jam each spring, I don't think I'd end up buying a dozen jars throughout the year to fill the void; I'd just eat something else. The point is, preserving food—and thinking of delicious ways to use those preserves—is fun.

What You Can Preserve

Lower-sugar jams and preserves: The jams and fruit preserves in this book are all quite low in sugar, simply because I think looser, less-sweet spreads taste better than sticky, cloying ones. Most contain fresh lemon juice, which is added primarily for flavor but also to up the acid content a bit. The jams and preserves have a remarkably intense fruit flavor because excess water is cooked out rather than gelled with store-bought pectin.

Easygoing, naturally gelled jellies: My own home-made jellies would never win any awards, that's for sure, unless the judges were tasting blindfolded. Most of the time I can't be bothered with using a jelly bag to strain the cooked fruit juice slowly (I use a very fine sieve), or letting the strained juice sit overnight in the refrigerator to let it clear up. So my jellies tend to be a little cloudy. I think they're pretty enough, and they taste great, so who cares if they're not absolutely sparkling clear? Because I don't use store-bought pectin, all the gelling action comes from the fruit itself or from tart Granny Smith apples, which do need a fair amount of sugar to gel properly. Banning pectin limits jelly options some-what, yes, but I consider jelly to be an occasional luxury anyway, unlike everyday jams and preserves.

Real pickles: Here you'll find everything from refrigerator pickles in vinegar brines that will last a few weeks or months in the fridge and don't need any processing, to canned quickly brined pickles that will last a year in the pantry, to long-fermented pickles made sour by fermentation, to Indian and Middle Eastern–style "pickles" such as citrus preserved in salt. Most pickles are low in sugar, but not low in salt (which I fervently adore) or delicious tanginess, whether it's that sharp bite of the acetic acid in vinegar or the mellow tang of fermentation-produced lactic acid.

Eminently useful frozen ingredients: As opposed to stuff you've just stashed in the freezer for no reason. (It's okay. I do that too—all the time.)

A Few Words about Ingredients

Vinegar: Be sure to use the type of vinegar called for in the recipe, or at least one with the same percentage of acidity, so that the finished pickle ends up with a pH below 4.6 and is safe to can in a boiling-water bath. Most of the pickle recipes specify cider vinegar or distilled white vinegar, both of which are generally 5 percent acidity—look on the bottle label to confirm the acidity before you use it—and so can be substituted for one another if necessary. (Cider vinegar, which I think tastes better than distilled white vinegar in most cases, may darken light-colored vegetables a bit.) If the recipe says to use a wine vinegar, again, check the label. Don't use homemade vinegar for canned

---

TERMINOLOGY SCHMERMINOLOGY

In standard (read: USDA and *Ball Blue Book*) usage, a "jam" is a softly gelled spread containing crushed or diced fruit; a "preserve" contains whole small fruits or large pieces of larger fruits (got that?) in a thickish syrup that may or may not be gelled; a "conserve" usually contains nuts and/or dried fruit; a "marmalade" usually contains citrus zest or rind and pulp suspended in jelly; a fruit "butter" is smooth-textured and thick; and a "jelly" is a firmly gelled clear fruit juice. I use "preserve" in two ways here, both to denote the whole-fruit/large-piece spread and to describe all the preserving recipes in this book, since even the pickles and frozen foods are, of course, preserved foods.

pickles, since it's hard to know exactly how much acid it contains. Also, when a recipe says to boil the vinegar mixture, boil only for the amount of time specified and no longer; acetic acid evaporates more quickly than water does, and excess boiling can throw off the acidity of the brine.

Lemon juice: I use exclusively fresh lemon juice in fruit preserves, where its presence is needed mostly for flavor—fresh simply tastes better to me than bottled. In fig preserves, canned tomato products, and in vegetable pickles like the Baby Artichokes with Lemon and Olive Oil on page 50 and the Roasted Red Peppers with Lemon Juice on page 149, lemon juice is added not primarily for its flavor but for its acidity. Because the acidity of fresh lemon juice varies somewhat (in my testing from a pH of around 2.8 to 3.0), to be absolutely safe you should use bottled lemon juice (whose pH is usually lower and more consistent than fresh, coming in at around 2.75 in my tests).

Pure kosher salt: The pickle recipes here call for pure kosher salt, which contains no additives like caking agents or iodine, which can result in a cloudy brine. There should be only one ingredient listed on the salt container: salt. You can certainly use canning and pickling salt instead—it's also pure—but because it's finer-grained than kosher, use scant measures. If you don't care about cloudiness, any old salt is fine.

Sugar: You'll get the best results with white granulated pure cane sugar. You can try substituting unprocessed sugar, or artificial sweeteners, but expect quite different preserves from the ones I describe. Some recipes use honey as a sweetener; this is done because the flavor of the honey is welcome in those particular foods. Agave nectar makes a decent low-glycemic alternative to honey, so use that if you wish. Folks trying to limit their refined-sugar intake should check out books specifi-

cally written for them; a great one is *Canning and Preserving without Sugar*, by Norma MacRae (see Further Reading, page 292).

Produce: Use only top-quality fruit and vegetables. Canning and preserving will do absolutely nothing to improve sub-par produce. Don't use any produce that exhibits signs of spoilage or disease. Imperfections are fine—just trim them off.

A Few Words about Pectin

Pectin is a natural substance found in the cell walls of fruits and vegetables in varying amounts. Pectin comes into play when making jams, preserves, and jellies because without sufficient pectin (and enough sugar and acid to react with it), the liquid won't thicken and gel. This is fine if you don't mind thin, syrupy preserves and liquid jellies, but if you want a nice, spreadable preserve, you'll need to consider the pectin content of the fruit or fruits you're using. Fruits with very high pectin content include green apples (used extensively in this book, in several ways), citrus, quince, cranberries, some blackberries, and some plums. Fruits that are underripe and a little hard have more pectin than ripe fruit; in most jams, preserves, and jellies, a combination of about a quarter underripe fruit (for the pectin) and three quarters ripe fruit (for flavor and natural sweetness) is ideal. Pectin is most concentrated in the cores and seeds, rinds and peels, and membranes of fruit, so wherever possible I find ways to use whole fruit. Sometimes that means including thin slices of lemon, or putting apple or citrus trimmings in a jelly bag or cheesecloth to cook with the fruit mixture to extract their precious pectin without actually including them in the preserve.

There are many kinds of commercially produced pectin, most of them derived from apples or citrus fruit (which are naturally high in pectin), that can be added to preserves made with fruits that are too low in pectin to gel on their own, and they all are reliable, albeit in a standardized way. If I were to recommend one over the others, it would be Pomona's Universal pectin, which is activated by calcium (included in the box) rather than sugar, so with it you can make thick, spreadable jams with just a little sweetener or none at all. The Quick, High-Yield Strawberry Jam on page 29 relies on Pomona's, which will give you some idea of how it is used.

That said, I don't tend to use commercial pectin in my preserves, for a few reasons: First, I prefer the consistency of preserves that have set with home-made apple pectin or from the fruits themselves. These preserves are not rubbery or stiff or grainy. Second, simply because it is *possible* to make excellent, not-too-sweet fruit spreads without it. In fact, the method I describe here for making jams and preserves—in which the fruit and sugar are cooked briefly and then drained so that the syrup they produce can be cooked down and thickened (sometimes with chunks of green apple added) before the fruit is returned to the pan—results in preserves that have much more fruit flavor than in typical fruit products because there is no commercial pectin gelling excess water. They do not taste caramelized or sticky or heavy the way traditional long-boil preserves do, because the fruit solids themselves have not been cooked for long periods and because they contain less sugar.

How Preserving Works
◇◇◇◇◇◇◇◇◇◇◇◇◇◇◇◇◇◇◇◇◇◇

How canning preserves food: The microorganisms that lead to food spoilage need certain conditions to survive: They need water, they need temperatures between about 40°F and 139°F, they need oxygen, and they need a low-acid environment. Most canned preserves and pickles have a water content

sufficient to support the growth of microorganisms. So we can't meet the first condition. Sterilizing the jars and heating the food to boiling for a certain length of time before it's put into jars kills existing microorganisms, but of course canned foods are meant to be stored at room temperature, which is smack in the middle of the zone most conducive to the growth of new bacteria. So the second condition can't be met if we want to line up our pretty jars in the pantry. That leaves the last two conditions, which, happily, can be dealt with.

Processing the filled jars—sealing them by means of a boiling-water bath—creates an anaerobic (airless) environment, a vacuum, in which microorganisms that might have found their way into the jars as they were being filled cannot survive. How is the vacuum formed? When the jars are put in the boiling-water bath and the food inside heats up, the food expands, forcing the air out the as-yet-unsealed lids. When the jars are removed from the canning pot and begin to cool, the food contracts, forming a vacuum as the lid contracts and seals tightly onto the rim of the jar. (Those popping sounds you sometimes hear as the jars are cooling are made by the dome-style lids contracting.) This not only prevents microorganisms from entering the jar, but also creates an inhospitable climate for any that are somehow still there: There's no air in the jars.

Now, if it weren't for the fact that the *spores* of certain microorganisms are both resistant to heat at the level that can be achieved in a boiling-water bath (212°F at sea level) and also thrive in anaerobic situations, we'd be all set. But there's one more condition that even these spores need to survive: a low-acid environment, and here we take care of that, too. All of the canning recipes in this book are for high-acid foods—that is, foods that have a pH level *below* 4.6 (actually they're all below 4.0), which is sufficient to prevent the growth of microorganisms as well as the activation of their spores. Most fruits are naturally acidic, with the exception of some tropical fruits, like figs, and some tomatoes (see page 16), so preserves made almost exclusively with fruit—jams, preserves, jellies, juices, and so on—will be high-acid foods. Vegetables are low in acid, but if acid is added in the correct amounts (as in pickles), they become acidic enough to preserve safely in a boiling-water bath.

Vegetables can be acidulated—pickled—in two ways: (1) acid can be added in the form of vinegar or a combination of vinegar (which contains acetic acid in varying percentages) and lemon juice (which contains citric acid), or (2) the vegetables can be fermented to the point where beneficial bacteria (primarily *Lactobacillus*) have converted the natural sugars present in the vegetables to lactic acid, thus lowering the pH to an acceptable level, below 4.6. This is why it's important that for pickled foods you do not change the proportions of vinegar to the other ingredients. Foods that ferment in salt or salt water are still preserved by means of the acid that's created, but you need to use the amount of salt called for in the recipes to keep away harmful bacteria (which happen to dislike salty environments as well as acidic ones), making room for good bacteria to acidify and therefore preserve the food.

So there you go. Heating to kill off existing microorganisms, processing to create a vacuum and prevent introduction and growth of microorganisms, and using high-acid foods or acidulating those that are not in order to create an acidic environment that's inhospitable to microorganisms.

How sugar preserves food: You might notice I didn't say anything about sugar above. Sugar can act as a preservative if used in quantities high enough that the sugar replaces the microorganism-sustaining water in the food. Standard fruit preserves, jams, and jellies often contain enough sugar

BOTULISM

Botulism poisoning, a very serious and sometimes deadly illness, is most commonly the result of ingesting improperly canned *low-acid* foods like plain unpickled green beans. All the canned foods here are high-acid fruits or acidulated vegetables, so botulism isn't really an issue, but let's discuss the bacterium that causes it, *Clostridium botulinum*, in a bit more detail anyway. While the bacterium itself is killed by boiling temperatures, its spores survive much higher temperatures than can be achieved in a boiling-water bath and are actually activated in oxygenless environments like the inside of a canning jar. This means that even though a food has been boiled, processed, and sealed, it may still contain the spores whose activation and growth produce a toxin that can cause botulism poisoning. The spores cannot, however, survive in high-acid environments—that is, in foods that have a pH lower than 4.6. All of the canning recipes in this book result in foods with pH levels that are well below 4.6; for the pickling recipes using vinegar, it's important that you use the vinegar called for in the recipe, with the acidity percentage specified.

Low-acid foods, or vegetables that have *not* been acidulated (pickled) to a proper degree, must be canned in a pressure canner, which can process jars at temperatures higher than that of boiling water, high enough to kill bacteria as well as the spores of *Clostridium botulinum. Do not process nonacidulated vegetables or meats in anything other than a pressure canner.* None of the canning recipes in this book requires a pressure canner because they are all for high-acid foods.

to at least slow the spoilage of opened jars, but not enough to stop it completely. Sugar is not, however, absolutely necessary in preserving fruit products in jars (despite what many sources imply). It is possible, for example, to can plain fruit in nothing but water or its own juice: The acid in the fruit, heat-processing, and an anaerobic environment are together sufficient to prevent spoilage. Fruit and fruit spreads canned without a lot of sugar tend to taste a little lifeless, it's true, and will spoil more quickly after the jars are opened, so I recommend using at least some sugar in every fruit recipe here. Sugar is needed only to enhance the flavor of fruit preserves, to increase the quality of preserves (it helps fruit keep its shape in liquid), and to react with the natural pectins in fruit to create a gel.

There are a few recipes in the book in which sugar does act as a primary means of preservation: Candied Citrus Rind on page 259, Crystallized Ginger on page 70 (the spice ginger is a rhizome and, like a vegetable, has a pH higher than 4.6, so it can't be preserved without removing the water by drying or saturating it with sugar), and Pumpkin Chips on page 228 (pumpkin, too, is a vegetable).

How refrigerating preserves food: At temperatures of 40°F and below, as in a properly set refrigerator, growth of microorganisms that cause spoilage slows, though it doesn't stop altogether. Refrigerator pickles—that is, vegetables that are acidulated but not processed and sealed in a jar in a canning pot—can last longer in the refrigerator than fresh refrigerated vegetables, simply because they are submerged in an acidic liquid in which spoilers won't thrive.

How freezing preserves food: Growth of almost all microorganisms slows dramatically at temperatures below freezing, or 32°F, and stops at temperatures below that—0°F or lower is optimal for freezing food. That said, microorganisms are not actually killed by freezing, and any microorganisms that are present in frozen food can reactivate upon thawing. In addition, enzymes that are naturally present in foods can continue to break them down, if very slowly, at freezing temperatures. Blanching or cooking foods before freezing them will inactivate most of the enzymes and kill other spoilers.

How drying preserves food: This one's easy: Microorganisms need water. Remove the water, and they meet a horrible end.

THE TOMATO: FRUIT OR VEGETABLE?

Everyone knows that the tomato is a fruit, and indeed most tomatoes are acidic enough to can in a boiling-water bath without any added acid. However, some tomato varieties, including some San Marzano–type plum tomatoes, are not acid enough to be safely canned on their own. Also, the acidity of tomatoes has been found to vary according to the particular conditions in which they were grown and when in the season they were harvested. For these reasons, it is strongly recommended that acid be added to each jar of canned tomatoes, tomato juice, tomato sauce, and the like, to lower the pH of the jar's contents enough to prevent the growth of microorganisms. In the tomato recipes here, and in those from any reputable source, citric acid or bottled lemon juice is added to each jar. Don't forget to add it; otherwise you can't be certain of the safety of your tomato-based foods. The Charred Tomato and Chile Salsa on page 169 contains vinegar to ensure that it's acidic enough; don't leave it out, and don't use vinegar of a different acidity.

What You Need

◇◇◇◇◇◇◇◇◇◇◇◇◇◇◇

All you really need for canning is a wide pan, a large pot, and a jar lifter. This is oversimplifying a bit, but it *is* true that you don't need a lot of specialized equipment to make good preserves and pickles, and much of what you do need you probably already have.

Wide, 6- to 8-quart preserving pan: This is the pan you put your jams, jellies, and other preserves in to cook them. It should be wide so that the liquid has the maximum surface area for quick evaporation as it boils. If you must use a deeper, narrower pot, it will take longer for the preserves to thicken, and the fruit may overcook a bit and break down more than is ideal. It will still taste delicious, though, and I've made plenty of very good preserves in a deep pot, so if you don't have the perfect pan, don't let that stop you.

Your preserving pan should hold 6 to 8 quarts—any smaller and you run the risk of sticky, super-hot preserves boiling over. Never fill the pan more than about one third, as some preserves will boil up more than you might expect. (Don't even ask how I learned this.)

Finally, the pot should be nonreactive, because every preserve you're going to put in it will be acidic. Nonreactive means, preferably, heavy-bottomed stainless steel (shiny) or enameled cast iron (opaque white or cream). Don't use aluminum, which can darken your preserves and impart an off taste. Some books recommend copper preserving pans, which conduct heat very well, but those will react with the acids in any fruit left in the pan for very long, so I'd avoid them.

The preserving pan I used to test all of these recipes is a 6-inch-tall, 9½-inch-diameter Vollrath 7-quart stainless-steel pot, with a very thick, heavy base and stainless-steel handles that only rarely get too hot to touch. It has a mirror finish that's easy to clean, and the heavy bottom heats evenly, so preserves don't stick or burn (unless I forget to stir them). It set me back sixty-six dollars at a restaurant-supply store, and it has been well worth the expense. Cheaper pots will do fine, of course, but if they're lightweight, beware of hot spots and stir vigilantly to keep your preserves from burning.

Big pot for boiling-water-bath canning: In just about any hardware store or big-box emporium you can find one of those huge blue- or black-and-white-speckled enamelware pots with a rack that fits inside to hold jars, but for most of the recipes in this book *you don't need one*, and in fact I use mine only when I'm canning batches of more than four or five pint jars.

Instead, I use an 8½-inch-tall, 9-inch-diameter Lincoln Wear-Ever (read: inexpensive) aluminum 9-quart stock pot with a mismatched lid, and a rack made out of extra jar lid rings that I've lashed together with little pieces of kitchen string (if you have a round stainless-steel cooling rack or trivet that fits in the bottom of the pot, that would be even better than jar lids). You don't need a rack that you can lift up and down and hook onto the sides of the pot, like the ones that come with dedicated canning pots; it's fine just to put the jars directly in the water on a rack on the bottom of the pot.

I can fit three standard quart jars, four pint jars, six half-pint jars, or seven 4-ounce jars in it, and various combinations of sizes. This smallish pot requires less water—and thus less heating time and energy—than those monster enamelware pots, and the stay-in-place rack is much easier to use than the awkward rack that comes with most canning pots.

The pot you use must be deep enough so that water will cover your filled jars by at least an inch, boil, and not overflow. When I lived in a minuscule apartment in Manhattan, I would water-bath my filled cans in a stock pot so short that when the water was deep enough to cover the lids of the jars it came to the very top of the pot, which meant I had to watch it every second so that it wouldn't splash over and extinguish the gas flame. I don't recommend this. It's unsafe in myriad ways.

Candy thermometer: Any kind will do for jam and jelly making, but after you've made a few batches you probably won't even need it. Before you use it for the first time, put the tip in water at a full rolling boil and take the reading. If it's not 212°F, the temperature at which water boils at sea level, note how many degrees off it is, and take that into account as you follow a recipe. Jelly cooked to 8°F above the boiling temperature of water will gel, so, for example, if your thermometer reads 208°F at boiling, your jelly will be ready at 216°F rather than 220°F at sea level.

For pasteurizing cucumber pickles, in which the water in the canning pot is maintained at 180°F for 30 minutes, you'll definitely need a thermometer—the water gives no outward signs that it's at that temperature.

Scale: In the canning and preserving recipes here, where it's important that you use precise quantities (not only for safety but also so your preserves taste and look the way I've so evocatively described them), I've listed amounts for the main fruit or vegetable by weight rather than by volume. One person (say, my mom) can dice 3 pounds of strawberries and end up with 10 cups, while another person (me) can do it and get 9 cups. And one person can pick 5 oranges off their tree to get 3 pounds, then go next door and have to steal 7 of the neighbor's oranges to get 3 pounds. It just makes more sense to weigh these things, and for that you'll need a scale. Of course, if you're buying your produce at a

place where there are scales, you can just keep track of how much you buy and calculate from there to determine how much of it you'll need for a particular recipe. The weights I provide are for uncut fruit.

Jar lifter: For a long time, I just used a pair of stainless-steel tongs with rubber bands wrapped around the ends to move the hot jars around. This works fine, but certainly not as well as a tool specifically designed to lift jars. For my part, the recent purchase of a jar lifter has made me a happier and more content individual, and I'd highly recommend you make the three-dollar investment yourself. You can find jar lifters in hardware stores and big-box stores that stock canning supplies. Note that if you're using Weck jars (see Sources, page 291), you might consider getting one of the Weck jar lifters that fit them just right.

Wide-mouth funnel: These too are sold wherever you can buy canning supplies, and it's another tool I did without for a long time. It's not absolutely necessary, but like a jar lifter, it will make your canning adventures brighter and more cheerful.

Very-fine-mesh sieve, bouillon strainer, or jelly bag: You'll need one of these only if you're making jelly or juice. I use a lower-end bouillon strainer, which looks like a conical colander or *chinois* made of an extremely fine wire mesh that keeps all but the tiniest bits from draining through. I got it at a restaurant-supply store for around twenty-five dollars—not cheap, but it's made a huge difference in the ease with which I can now drain cooked fruit to get juice for jelly. Just set it over a deep bowl (I prop mine up between two chairs, and position the bowl on the floor underneath it), pour in the cooked fruit, and let it sit. You can stir the fruit gently to speed up the draining, but don't press so hard as to push any solids through. The strainer works just as well as a jelly bag and is easier to use and clean.

If you use a jelly bag, hang it on a dowel or broom handle and suspend it (between two chairs again) over a deep bowl, then carefully ladle in the fruit and liquid. Let it hang and drip for at least half an hour, and don't squeeze it if you plan to enter that jelly in the county fair, where the good judges tend to frown upon cloudy product. I've actually never seen a jelly bag for sale in a brick-and-mortar operation, so I sewed my own out of four layers of cheesecloth—I bound the seams and top opening with bias tape to keep the little bits of cheesecloth thread contained. The one I made is too small to be of much use; if you make one yourself, make sure it's nice and big.

Other tools: You'll need a wooden spoon or heat-proof spatula for stirring the preserves, a chopstick or thin plastic spatula for removing air bubbles when you fill the jars, a small heatproof container to put the jar lids and boiling water in, and a ladle (or measuring cup) for scooping preserves into jars.

If you're making long-fermented pickles, *nuka*, or sauerkraut, you'll need a crock or other nonreactive container big enough to hold the vegetables submerged in brine. Don't use very old stoneware crocks, as the glaze could contain lead. I've seen new food-safe crocks at hardware and kitchenware stores, but if you rummage around in your cupboard you'll probably come across something you can use. My best sauerkraut-fermenting vessel, for example, is a plastic bucket that originally contained seven pounds of rendered duck fat (don't ask).

Canning jars, new lids, and metal rings (screw bands): I use almost exclusively Ball, Kerr, and Mason canning jars with two-piece lids—that is, jars specifically designed for home canning, with flat dome-style lids that are held in place during processing by metal rings. The jars are sturdy and made to withstand the heat of processing. (I've poured fully boiling water into room-temperature canning jars without incident, and have never had one break in the pot—or, come to think of it, *anywhere*.) Do not use old mayonnaise or other jars if you intend to process in boiling water, and it's always a good idea to heat glass jars by submerging in hot water before adding hot liquids or preserves.

Canning-jar lids are coated on the underside to resist corrosion from the acidic foods inside, and the underside has a ring of rubberized sealing compound around the edge, which is what adheres to the jar rim. Use brand-new, clean flat lids every

> ### FANCY JARS
>
> All the canning recipes in this book assume you're using standard Mason-style canning jars, since those are easy, cheap, and extremely reliable. They're the only kind officially approved for home canning by the USDA. Unofficially, there's one—and as far as I know *only* one—other kind of canning jar that's perfectly acceptable and, for me, 100 percent reliable. They're not inexpensive, and they require a bit more effort to use, but on special occasions I'll break out the Weck jars (see Sources, page 291), which come in various shapes and sizes, each more elegant than the last. Carefully follow the instructions that come with the jars. Basically, you heat or sterilize both the glass jar and the glass lid in boiling water, fit a rubber gasket onto the lid, and keep the lid in hot water until the jars are filled. Fill the jars, then put the lids on, gasket side down, and attach two metal clamps to the jar to hold the lid onto the jar during processing. Put the jars in the water, boil for the time specified in the recipe, and then remove the jars and let them cool. Then remove the clamps and check the seal by holding on to the lid and lifting carefully.

time; they're cheap and are sold separate from the jars, in little boxes. *Don't reuse previously sealed lids, as the sealing compound has been compromised.* The screw-band rings come with new jars and are reusable.

Canning Step by Step

1. Prepare for water-bath canning: It will probably take half an hour or so to bring the water in your canning pot to a boil, so fill it up and put it on the heat well in advance (when the recipe says "Prepare for water-bath canning" is a good time). Wash the jars well, then submerge them in the water as it heats up. If the recipe says to sterilize the jars, make sure the water covering the jars has been at a full boil for at least 10 minutes before pulling them out and filling them. If the filled jars will be processed for 10 minutes or longer, there's no need to sterilize them first, as they'll be sterilized during processing.

Clear off some counter or table space by the stovetop and set two folded towels nearby: one to put hot empty jars on for filling, and one to put the filled jars on when they come out of the canning pot (the latter should be in an out-of-the-way spot, if possible, where the jars can remain undisturbed for 12 hours). The towels will absorb heat from the jars and protect the counter surfaces. I also put a hot pad near the stovetop to put the preserving pan on when I'm ladling preserves or hot vinegar brine into the jars.

Gather everything you'll need:
* a jar lifter or tongs with rubber bands wrapped around the ends
* a small heatproof bowl or saucepan (put new, clean flat jar lids in it, and pile the clean metal jar rings next to it)
* a ladle or 1-cup measure for ladling preserves or brine into the jars

* a wide-mouth funnel for filling the jars (this is optional, but it helps prevent mishaps)
* a wooden or plastic chopstick or small, thin plastic spatula for removing air bubbles around the inside of each jar
* a clean paper towel for wiping the jar rims after filling

2. Make the preserve or pickle as described in the recipe.

3. Fill the jars: When the preserve is ready or the pickle brine has come to a boil, remove it from the heat.

Use the jar lifter to lift the hot jars out of the boiling or simmering water, empty the water back into the pot, and set the jars upright on one of the folded towels. Ladle hot water from the canning pot into the bowl with the jar lids. (I usually just pour in the hot water from the first jar I remove from the canning pot.) This will soften the rubberized ring of sealing compound around the underside of each lid so that it adheres to the jars and seals properly. Make sure that the lids aren't stacked tightly together, which can prevent water from coming into contact with the seal. You don't have to actually simmer the lids on the stovetop, and you shouldn't boil them (this could damage the sealing compound); as long as the water is about at a simmer when you ladle it in, they'll be fine.

If filling with fruit preserves, put the funnel in the first hot jar and ladle in the hot preserves, keeping the ladle as low and close to the funnel as possible to prevent too many bubbles from forming in the jar. Fill to ¼ inch from the top. Repeat with the remaining jars, then put the lids on and process as below.

If filling with uncooked room-temperature vegetables or fruit (what's known as "raw pack"), just pack them in the jars, not too tightly unless the

recipe says to pack tightly. There should be enough space between the solids for the brine or syrup to flow around them to heat them up evenly as they're processed. Put the funnel in the mouth of the first jar and ladle in the syrup or brine. Repeat with the remaining jars, then put the lids on and process as below.

If filling with hot cooked solid fruit or vegetables, use a slotted spoon to transfer them from the cooking liquid to the jars, then ladle in the hot cooking liquid. Put the lids on and process as below.

4. Put the lids on and process the jars: Run the chopstick around the inside of each jar to pop any large-ish bubbles (tiny ones are okay). Dip the paper towel in hot water and use it to wipe the rims and outside threads of the jars clean of any dripped preserves, syrup, or brine—these can prevent a seal from forming between the sealing compound and the jar. Put the flat lids on the jars, white side down, then put the rings on, tightening them just finger-tight—don't force them at all. (I hold the flat lid down gently with one finger and screw on the rings with the fingertips of my other hand.) You don't want the rings to be screwed too tight, because the air in the jar needs to escape as the contents are heated in the canning pot. When all the lids and rings are on, use the jar lifter to carefully return the jars to the hot water in the canning pot, making sure they're standing upright on the rack and not touching one another or the sides of the pot and that the water covers them by at least 1 inch. Turn up the heat, cover the pot, and bring the water in the canning pot to a full boil. Boil for the time indicated in the recipe *plus additional time if you live more than 1,000 feet above sea level* (see right). Remove the jars to the second, out-of-the-way towel on the countertop to cool. It's most important that jellies be allowed to cool for 12 hours before the jars are disturbed at all—moving them could break the gel.

5. Turn off the burner and pop open a cold beer, 'cause you're done. Well, almost. Remember to check, after the jars have cooled for about an hour, that the lids have sealed properly. This is easy to do: Press down in the center of the flat lid. If it doesn't move, the jar has sealed. If it pops down and then up again, it has not sealed; refrigerate the jar immediately and use the contents. Another way to check that a lid has sealed is to remove the ring, grip the lid with your thumb and middle finger, and slowly lift it straight up. If the lid comes off, obviously it hasn't sealed. Label the cooled jars and store them in a cool, dark spot. Then, for goodness sake, *use them!*

ADJUSTING FOR ALTITUDE

Because of lower atmospheric pressure at higher elevations, water boils at lower temperatures, and this means it will take longer to kill off spoilers. So find your approximate elevation (see Further Reading, page 292, for an easy-to-find source of that information online), and make the following adjustments as necessary:

✳ To sterilize jars, boil for 10 minutes, plus 1 minute for every 1,000 feet above sea level you live.

✳ If the recipe specifies processing in boiling water for 20 minutes or less, increase the processing time by 1 minute for every 1,000 feet above sea level you live.

✳ If the recipe specifies processing in boiling water for more than 20 minutes, increase the processing time by 2 minutes for every 1,000 feet above sea level you live.

Spring

Early spring is a horrible tease. As the first warm rains move in, we want to be eating nothing but fresh food. No frozen vegetables, no stews, no heavy meats (all right, for Easter the Krissoffs have been known to roast a leg of lamb and a ham—on the same day). But of course in most parts of the country very little "springtime" produce is actually ready in spring, and small-town farmers' markets, where growers are offering another few bunches of chard, some root vegetables from last year, and maybe some nice spring onions, can be depressingly sparse.

And then the asparagus hits. Then strawberries . . . and more strawberries, so easy to pluck from their lush, leafy hiding spots. My daughter, Thalia, and I make several trips to the local U-pick place every year, and we preserve most of them as soon as we get home, saving plenty of the firm, juicy berries to enjoy fresh at every meal for the next few days. It's so tempting to pick and buy more than I need right away because it's still cold enough during the day to leave pails and boxes of fruit on the porch rather than trying to find space in the fridge. Thalia's first year, she ate so many strawberries in the five or six weeks they were in season that she wouldn't touch another one in any form for the next eleven months.

Thankfully, by the time you're all strawberried out, it's summer, and the rest of the bounty is starting to arrive.

SPRING FRUITS

Strawberry Jam

MAKES ABOUT 4 HALF-PINT JARS

◇◇

YOU DON'T NEED TO USE AS MUCH (OR ANY) LEMON ZEST HERE. But I think its fresh, puckery tartness makes the strawberries taste more like strawberries, and if you have a lemon or two on hand for the juice, you might as well use the zest, too.

3 pounds rinsed and hulled strawberries, diced (about 9 cups)
1½ cups sugar
3 tablespoons strained fresh lemon juice
Grated zest of 2 lemons (optional)

Prepare for water-bath canning: Sterilize the jars and keep them hot in the canning pot, put a small plate in the freezer, and put the flat lids in a heat-proof bowl. (See page 21 for details.)

Put the strawberries and sugar in a wide, 6- to 8-quart preserving pan. Bring to a simmer, stirring frequently, then continue to cook for 5 minutes. Pour into a colander set over a large bowl and stir the berries gently to drain off the juice. Return the juice to the pan and bring to a boil over high heat. Boil, stirring occasionally, until the syrup is reduced to about 1½ cups, about 20 minutes.

Return the strawberries and any accumulated juice to the pan, along with the lemon juice and the zest (if using), and bring to a simmer. Simmer, stirring frequently, until a small dab of the jam spooned onto the chilled plate and returned to the freezer for a minute becomes somewhat firm (it will not gel), about 15 minutes. Skim off as much foam as you can, then remove from the heat and stir gently for a few seconds to distribute the fruit in the liquid.

Ladle boiling water from the canning pot into the bowl with the lids. Using a jar lifter, remove the sterilized jars from the canning pot, carefully pouring the water from each one back into the pot, and place them upright on a folded towel. Drain the water off the jar lids.

Ladle the hot jam into the jars, leaving ¼ inch headspace at the top. Use a damp paper towel to wipe the rims of the jars, then put a flat lid and ring on each jar, adjusting the ring so that it's just finger-tight. Return the jars to the water in the canning pot, making sure the water covers the jars by at least 1 inch. Bring to a boil, and boil for 5 minutes to process. Remove the jars to a folded towel and do not disturb for 12 hours. After 1 hour, check that the lids have sealed by pressing down on the center of each; if it can be pushed down, it hasn't sealed, and the jar should be refrigerated immediately. Label the sealed jars and store.

NONSENSE

In midwinter especially, I find myself needing a little taste of something sweet after supper. It's dark and frigid, our house is—well, *drafty* would be generous, and while a sunny and cheerful strawberry shortcake would be ideal, I have to ration the amount of time I spend out from under the cozy blankets on the couch. Just this spring I discovered the dessert that for unknown reasons is called "nonsense." It's part of an esteemed group of fruity, insubstantial concoctions that also includes "trifle" and "fool," and is perhaps called nonsense because the other synonyms were already taken. This version, adapted from *How to Cook Well* by Rosalie J. Benton, published in 1886 (a year after our house was built), has only two ingredients. With an electric mixer, beat 1 good fresh egg white until foamy and white. A little at a time, add 3 tablespoons mashed Strawberry Preserves (page 30) or Strawberry Jam (page 27), and whip until the mixture holds firm peaks. Spoon into old-fashioned Champagne glasses or small dessert bowls, drizzle with a little of the syrup from the preserves, and serve with a simple sugar cookie or cracker on the side. This will serve 2 or 3.

Quick, High-Yield Strawberry Jam

MAKES ABOUT 7 HALF-PINT JARS

HERE'S A BASIC JAM RECIPE THAT USES POMONA'S UNIVERSAL, A COMMERCIAL SUGAR-FREE LOW-METHOXYL NATURAL PECTIN DERIVED FROM CITRUS RINDS. It can be used in low- or even no-sugar recipes because it's activated by calcium rather than sugar. You can adapt it to just about any fruit. If what you want is a lot of jam from not a lot of fruit (say, if you're making a big batch to give as gifts), and if you want to cut back dramatically on the sugar content, this is the way to go. This jam, while not as intensely fruit-flavored as the no-commercial-pectin preserves in this book (here you're essentially gelling the water that in other recipes is cooked off), will be thick, semi-firm, and light—a refreshing jam, if you will allow that such things exist. Pomona's Universal can be found at health-food stores or online (see Sources, page 291).

Here you must crush the strawberries—with your hands, a potato masher, or a food processor—rather than dice them. Diced fruit will simply float to the top of the jar and look kind of—well, dicey. The mashed pulp will meld with the gelling liquid nicely.

½ to 1½ cups sugar, honey, or other sweetener
4 teaspoons Pomona's Universal pectin powder
   3 pounds rinsed and hulled strawberries, crushed, not diced (about 8 cups)
3 tablespoons strained fresh lemon juice
Grated zest of 2 lemons (optional)
4 teaspoons calcium solution (included in the box of pectin)

Prepare for water-bath canning: Sterilize the jars and keep them hot in the canning pot, and put the flat lids in a heatproof bowl. (See page 21 for details.)

In a medium bowl, stir the sugar and pectin powder together thoroughly. (If using a liquid sweetener, add it directly to the strawberries.) Put the strawberries, lemon juice, lemon zest (if using), and calcium solution in a wide, 6- to 8-quart preserving pan. Bring to a boil over high heat, stir in the sugar-pectin mixture, and stir until the sugar is dissolved, 1 to 2 minutes. Return to a boil, then remove from the heat.

Ladle boiling water from the canning pot into the bowl with the lids. Using a jar lifter, remove the sterilized jars from the canning pot, carefully pouring the water from each one back into the pot, and place them upright on a folded towel. Drain the water off the jar lids.

Ladle the hot jam into the jars, leaving ¼ inch headspace at the top. Use a damp paper towel to wipe the rims of the jars, then put a flat lid and ring on each jar, adjusting the ring so that it's just finger-tight. Return the jars to the water in the canning pot, making sure the water covers the jars by at least 1 inch. Bring to a boil, and boil for 5 minutes to process. Remove the jars to a folded towel and do not disturb for 12 hours. After 1 hour, check that the lids have sealed by pressing down on the center of each; if it can be pushed down, it hasn't sealed, and the jar should be refrigerated immediately. Label the sealed jars and store.

Classic Strawberry Preserves

MAKES ABOUT 4 HALF-PINT JARS

WHOLE STRAWBERRIES IN A THICK BUT NOT GELLED SYRUP CAN BE GENTLY FLATTENED ONTO SPLIT BISCUITS OR SPOONED OVER ANY NUMBER OF CREAMY THINGS. The berries' overnight stay in sugar encourages their slow, gradual absorption of the sugar, which helps them hold their shape and stay a little plump as they cook.

3 pounds rinsed and hulled strawberries
1½ cups sugar
3 tablespoons strained fresh lemon juice

Layer the strawberries and sugar in a large bowl. Cover and refrigerate overnight.

Prepare for water-bath canning: Sterilize the jars and keep them hot in the canning pot, and put the flat lids in a heatproof bowl. (See page 21 for details.)

Using care not to damage the strawberries, gently transfer them with the sugar to a wide, 6- to 8-quart preserving pan. Bring to a simmer, gently stirring, then continue to cook for 5 minutes. Pour into a colander set over a large bowl. Return the juice to the pan and bring to a boil over high heat. Boil, stirring occasionally, until the syrup is reduced to 1½ cups, about 15 minutes.

Return the strawberries and any accumulated juice to the pan, along with the lemon juice, and bring to a simmer. Simmer, stirring frequently, until the strawberries are glossy and very tender but still hold their shape, about 20 minutes. Skim off as much foam as you can, then remove from the heat and stir gently for a few seconds to distribute the fruit in the liquid.

Ladle boiling water from the canning pot into the bowl with the lids. Using a jar lifter, remove the sterilized jars from the canning pot, carefully pouring the water from each one back into the pot, and place them upright on a folded towel. Drain the water off the jar lids.

Ladle the hot preserves into the jars, leaving ¼ inch headspace at the top. Use a damp paper towel to wipe the rims of the jars, then put a flat lid and ring on each jar, adjusting the ring so that it's just finger-tight. Return the jars to the water in the canning pot, making sure the water covers the jars by at least 1 inch. Bring to a boil, and boil for 5 minutes to process. Remove the jars to a folded towel and do not disturb for 12 hours. After 1 hour, check that the lids have sealed by pressing down on the center of each; if it can be pushed down, it hasn't sealed, and the jar should be refrigerated immediately. Label the sealed jars and store.

Strawberry and Lemon Preserves

MAKES ABOUT 4 HALF-PINT JARS

IN THIS PRESERVE, SLICES OF WHOLE LEMONS ARE SIMMERED IN THE JUICES OF THE STRAWBERRIES UNTIL TRANSLUCENT. Preserves like this appeal to the side of me that craves variety even at the micro level. Spooned onto toast or a biscuit, each bite may be a little different, depending on whether you get a soft mound of sweet berry or a tender wedge of tart lemon.

2 lemons
3 pounds rinsed and hulled strawberries
1½ cups sugar

Scrub and quarter the lemons, removing the seeds. Slice the lemon quarters crosswise into ⅛-inch-thick pieces. Layer the strawberries, lemons, and sugar in a large bowl. Cover and refrigerate overnight.

Prepare for water-bath canning: Sterilize the jars and keep them hot in the canning pot, and put the flat lids in a heatproof bowl. (See page 21 for details.)

Using care not to damage the strawberries, gently transfer the strawberries, lemons, sugar, and ½ cup water to a wide, 6- to 8-quart preserving pan. Bring to a simmer, gently stirring, then continue to cook for 5 minutes. Pour into a colander set over a large bowl. Return the juice to the pan and bring to a boil over high heat. Boil, stirring occasionally, until the syrup is reduced to about 1½ cups, about 15 minutes.

Return the strawberries, lemons, and any accumulated juice to the pan and bring to a simmer. Simmer, stirring frequently, until the strawberries are glossy and very tender but still hold their shape, about 20 minutes. Skim off as much foam as you can, then remove from the heat and stir gently for a few seconds to distribute the fruit in the liquid.

Ladle boiling water from the canning pot into the bowl with the lids. Using a jar lifter, remove the sterilized jars from the canning pot, carefully pouring the water from each one back into the pot, and place them upright on a folded towel. Drain the water off the jar lids.

Ladle the hot preserves into the jars, leaving ¼ inch headspace at the top. Use a damp paper towel to wipe the rims of the jars, then put a flat lid and ring on each jar, adjusting the ring so that it's just finger-tight. Return the jars to the water in the canning pot, making sure the water covers the jars by at least 1 inch. Bring to a boil, and boil for 5 minutes to process. Remove the jars to a folded towel and do not disturb for 12 hours. After 1 hour, check that the lids have sealed by pressing down on the center of each; if it can be pushed down, it hasn't sealed, and the jar should be refrigerated immediately. Label the sealed jars and store.

Strawberry and Lavender Jam

MAKES ABOUT 4 HALF-PINT JARS

◇◇◇

DRIED OR FRESH, ENGLISH (*LAVANDULA ANGUSTIFOLIA*) OR FRENCH (*L. STOECHAS*) LAVENDER IS A POTENT HERB THAT CAN OVERWHELM DELICATE FRUIT. Just a few pinches of the blossoms will be enough to perfume this not-too-sweet strawberry jam with its piney, flowery scent.

3 pounds rinsed and hulled strawberries, diced (about 9 cups)

1½ cups sugar

3 tablespoons strained fresh lemon juice

1½ teaspoons dried lavender blossoms, or 1 tablespoon fresh

Prepare for water-bath canning: Sterilize the jars and keep them hot in the canning pot, put a small plate in the freezer, and put the flat lids in a heat-proof bowl. (See page 21 for details.)

Put the strawberries and sugar in a wide, 6- to 8-quart preserving pan. Bring to a simmer, stirring frequently, then continue to cook for 5 minutes. Pour into a colander set over a large bowl and stir the berries gently to drain off the juice. Return the juice to the pan and bring to a boil over high heat. Boil, stirring occasionally, until the syrup is reduced to about 1½ cups, about 20 minutes.

Return the strawberries and any accumulated juice to the pan, along with the lemon juice and lavender, and bring to a simmer. Simmer, stirring frequently, until a small dab of the jam spooned onto the chilled plate and returned to the freezer for a minute becomes somewhat firm (it will not gel), about 15 minutes. Skim off as much foam as you can, then remove from the heat and stir gently for a few seconds to distribute the fruit in the liquid.

Ladle boiling water from the canning pot into the bowl with the lids. Using a jar lifter, remove the sterilized jars from the canning pot, carefully pouring the water from each one back into the pot, and place them upright on a folded towel. Drain the water off the jar lids.

Ladle the hot jam into the jars, leaving ¼ inch headspace at the top. Use a damp paper towel to wipe the rims of the jars, then put a flat lid and ring on each jar, adjusting the ring so that it's just finger-tight. Return the jars to the water in the canning pot, making sure the water covers the jars by at least 1 inch. Bring to a boil, and boil for 5 minutes to process. Remove the jars to a folded towel and do not disturb for 12 hours. After 1 hour, check that the lids have sealed by pressing down on the center of each; if it can be pushed down, it hasn't sealed, and the jar should be refrigerated immediately. Label the sealed jars and store.

Strawberry Jam with Thai Herbs

MAKES ABOUT 4 HALF-PINT JARS

THIS IS A SWEET-TART PRESERVE, BUT THE MINERALY CILANTRO, FRAGRANT THAI BASIL, AND FRESH MINT GIVE IT A COMPLEXITY REMINISCENT OF A GOOD, WELL-BALANCED *YUM*, OR THAI SALAD. Strawberries pair so well with herbs, and indeed all sorts of crazy savory things—balsamic vinegar with strawberries being one surprisingly long-lived trend—that it didn't take much to come up with this extraordinary jam. Try this: Go out into the herb garden with a plate piled with halved berries and a little mound of sugar. (Or gather a bunch of leftover herbs from the refrigerator, or befriend a generous herb grower.) Dip a berry in the sugar, and pop it in your mouth with a few leaves of different herbs, tasting and tasting until you come up with a combination you like. It'll be a little different from the actual jam, of course, but you'll be able to tell if you'll like the finished result.

3 pounds rinsed and hulled strawberries, diced (about 9 cups)

1½ cups sugar

3 tablespoons strained fresh lemon juice

2 tablespoons minced fresh cilantro

1 tablespoon minced fresh Thai basil

1 tablespoon minced fresh mint

Prepare for water-bath canning: Sterilize the jars and keep them hot in the canning pot, put a small plate in the freezer, and put the flat lids in a heat-proof bowl. (See page 21 for details.)

Put the strawberries and sugar in a wide, 6- to 8-quart preserving pan. Bring to a simmer, stirring frequently, then continue to cook for 5 minutes. Pour into a colander set over a large bowl and stir the berries gently to drain off the juice. Return the juice to the pan and bring to a boil over high heat. Boil, stirring occasionally, until the syrup is reduced to about 1½ cups, about 20 minutes.

Return the strawberries and any accumulated juice to the pan, along with the lemon juice, and bring to a simmer. Simmer, stirring frequently, until a small dab of the jam spooned onto the chilled plate and returned to the freezer for a minute becomes somewhat firm (it will not gel), about 15 minutes. Skim off as much foam as you can, then remove from the heat and stir in the herbs.

Ladle boiling water from the canning pot into the bowl with the lids. Using a jar lifter, remove the sterilized jars from the canning pot, carefully pouring the water from each one back into the pot, and place them upright on a folded towel. Drain the water off the jar lids.

Ladle the hot jam into the jars, leaving ¼ inch headspace at the top. Use a damp paper towel to wipe the rims of the jars, then put a flat lid and ring on each jar, adjusting the ring so that it's just finger-tight. Return the jars to the water in the canning pot, making sure the water covers the jars by at least 1 inch. Bring to a boil, and boil for 5 minutes to process. Remove the jars to a folded towel and do not disturb for 12 hours. After 1 hour, check that the lids have sealed by pressing down on the center of each; if it can be pushed down, it hasn't sealed, and the jar should be refrigerated immediately. Label the sealed jars and store.

Chamomile-Scented Strawberry Syrup

MAKES ABOUT 3 HALF-PINT JARS

THIS RECIPE HAS JUST ENOUGH SUGAR TO BRING OUT THE STRAWBERRY FLAVOR AND THICKEN THE SYRUP A BIT, AND IT FEATURES THE HERBAL HINT OF CHAMOMILE. You could substitute dried mint or any other herb in a tea ball for the chamomile—this is a good recipe to experiment with. Try the syrup over pancakes and waffles, of course, but also as a drink: with seltzer, in cocktails, or diluted with water over ice, as a British kid would drink squash—the sweetened fruit-juice concentrate common in the U.K.

Put two half-pint jars in the boiling-water bath after you pull out the syrup jars, and make a quick Spiced Strawberry Butter (opposite) with the strawberry pulp in the sieve or jelly bag.

4 pounds rinsed and hulled strawberries, crushed
   (about 8 cups)
2 cups sugar
2 chamomile tea bags
¼ cup strained fresh lemon juice

Prepare for water-bath canning: Sterilize the jars and keep them hot in the canning pot, put a small plate in the freezer, and put the flat lids in a heat-proof bowl. (See page 21 for details.)

Put the strawberries in a wide, 6- to 8-quart preserving pan. Bring to a simmer, stirring frequently, then continue to cook for 5 minutes. Working in batches if necessary, pour into a very-fine-mesh sieve or jelly bag set over a large bowl and stir the berries gently to drain off all the juice. Rinse the preserving pan and return the juice to the pan. (Reserve the strawberry pulp for another use; see opposite.) Add the sugar, tea bags, and lemon juice and bring to a boil over high heat. Boil, stirring occasionally, until

a small dab of the syrup spooned onto the chilled plate and returned to the freezer for a minute becomes somewhat firm (it will not gel), about 30 minutes. Skim off as much foam as you can and remove the tea bag.

Ladle boiling water from the canning pot into the bowl with the lids. Using a jar lifter, remove the sterilized jars from the canning pot, carefully pouring the water from each one back into the pot, and place them upright on a folded towel. Drain the water off the jar lids.

Ladle the hot syrup into the jars, leaving ½ inch headspace at the top. Use a damp paper towel to wipe the rims of the jars, then put a flat lid and ring on each jar, adjusting the ring so that it's just finger-tight. Return the jars to the water in the canning pot, making sure the water covers the jars by at least 1 inch. Bring to a boil, and boil for 5 minutes to process. Remove the jars to a folded towel and do not disturb for 12 hours. After 1 hour, check that the lids have sealed by pressing down on the center of each; if it can be pushed down, it hasn't sealed, and the jar should be refrigerated immediately. Label the sealed jars and store.

Spiced Strawberry Butter

MAKES ABOUT 2 HALF-PINT JARS

SMOOTH, TANGY, AND WARM-SPICED STRAW-BERRY BUTTER IS A DELIGHTFUL FILLING BETWEEN LAYERS OF CAKE INSTEAD OF A SUGARY FROSTING. It's also great mixed into steamy oatmeal or spread on a peanut butter sandwich.

Strawberry pulp from making Chamomile-Scented
   Strawberry Syrup (opposite)
¾ cup sugar
2 tablespoons strained fresh lemon juice
½ teaspoon ground cinnamon
½ teaspoon ground ginger
¼ teaspoon ground cloves

Prepare for water-bath canning: Sterilize the jars and keep them hot in the canning pot, put a small plate in the freezer, and put the flat lids in a heat-proof bowl. (See page 21 for details.)

Puree the strawberry pulp in a food processor or blender. Put the pulp and all the remaining ingredients in a wide, 6- to 8-quart preserving pan and cook over medium or medium-low heat, stirring constantly to prevent sticking, until the mixture is very thick and a couple of shades darker, about 15 minutes.

Ladle boiling water from the canning pot into the bowl with the lids. Using a jar lifter, remove the sterilized jars from the canning pot, carefully pouring the water from each one back into the pot, and place them upright on a folded towel. Drain the water off the jar lids.

Ladle the hot strawberry butter into the jars, leaving ¼ inch headspace at the top. Use a chopstick to remove air bubbles around the inside of each jar. Use a damp paper towel to wipe the rims of the jars, then put a flat lid and ring on each jar, adjusting the ring so that it's just finger-tight. Return the jars to the water in the canning pot, making sure the water covers the jars by at least 1 inch. Bring to a boil, and boil for 5 minutes to process. Remove the jars to a folded towel and do not disturb for 12 hours. After 1 hour, check that the lids have sealed by pressing down on the center of each; if it can be pushed down, it hasn't sealed, and the jar should be refrigerated immediately. Label the sealed jars and store.

Strawberry Dumplings

SERVES 6

THOUGH I'M SURE MY MOM MADE THIS DESSERT ONLY WHEN STRAWBERRIES WERE AVAILABLE FRESH IN THE SPRING, IT HAS ALWAYS SEEMED LIKE A WINTER DESSERT TO ME, WITH THE TANGY ORANGE JUICE AND THE DUSTING OF NUTMEG ON THE PILLOWY DUMPLINGS. It turns out it's a wonderful way to use frozen whole strawberries. Leftovers are none too pretty (the strawberries lose their color and turn a bit gray), but they are tasty when warmed up.

1 pound hulled whole strawberries, frozen (opposite; not thawed) or fresh

1 cup fresh or good-quality orange juice

2 tablespoons cornstarch

1⅓ cups sugar

1 tablespoon unsalted butter

1½ cups all-purpose flour

1 tablespoon baking powder

½ teaspoon pure kosher salt

⅔ cup milk

2 tablespoons vegetable oil

Freshly grated nutmeg

Put the strawberries, orange juice, 1 cup water, the cornstarch, sugar, and butter in a deep, nonreactive skillet with a lid; the strawberries should cover the bottom of the skillet in a single layer. Stir gently to combine, then cover and place over medium heat. Bring to a boil and cook until the liquid is thickened, about 5 minutes.

Meanwhile, sift the flour, baking powder, and salt together into a medium bowl. Stir in the milk and oil until just combined. Using two large spoons, scoop the dough onto the boiling fruit mixture in about 6 portions. Grate nutmeg over the top of the dumplings. Wrap a clean kitchen towel around the inside of the lid and put it on the skillet, keeping the corners of the towel on top of the lid and away from the flame or burner (this will keep moisture from dripping from the inside of the lid down onto the dumplings), and cook over medium heat until the dumplings are puffed and cooked through, 12 to 15 minutes. Serve hot in bowls.

FREEZING STRAWBERRIES

You can, of course, simply slice strawberries, toss them with a little sugar (or none), put them in freezer bags, and throw them in the freezer—but that yields something more akin to cold jam than fresh strawberries. Surely there must be a more complicated way to freeze these guys.

I'm a fairly skeptical person, but I was intrigued by Alton Brown's method of using dry ice to quickly freeze delicate fruits, so that ice crystals don't have time to elongate as they form and puncture the fruit's cell walls—which is what makes home-frozen berries mushy when thawed. I did a side-by-side test: some berries frozen in dry ice, and some frozen in a regular (not deep-freeze) freezer on a baking sheet lined with waxed paper. When thawed at room temperature, the latter expelled several tablespoons of liquid and collapsed into a heap; the former were relatively dry and held their shape nicely. They were still a bit rubbery, and not something I'd use for, say, a fresh strawberry pie. The main advantage of the dry-ice method is speed: You can freeze a heck of a lot of strawberries quickly, and you don't have to make space for baking sheets in your freezer (always an issue for me, even since I acquired a chest freezer).

So, on your way home from berry-picking on a beautiful spring morning, car windows open, the heady smell of strawberries just beginning their quick decline into compost filling the air, stop at a grocery store. Buy a cheap Styrofoam cooler if you've forgotten to bring one, as I usually do—which is why I have about half a dozen of them kicking around the house—and look for the dry ice. Just about every grocery store has it, usually tucked away in a corner somewhere, in a cooler covered with warning labels. Scan the warnings, and buy a few blocks—this should set you back about three bucks. Put it in the cooler and motor on home.

Hull the berries, and rinse them briefly if they're dusty; pat them dry and refrigerate them for 2 to 4 hours. Use a hammer, a mallet, or gravity to crush the dry ice, still in the bags, to about the size of, oh, dice ice—that stuff they put in bad cocktails at bars where you know you should've just ordered beer in a can. Put heavy-duty kitchen gloves or fireproof gloves on, open the bags, and dump the dry ice into the cooler. Lay the whole strawberries over the ice and gently toss with your gloved hands to combine. Put the cooler lid on. In 30 minutes, the strawberries will be rock-hard. With gloves on, pick them out of the ice and seal them in quart- or gallon-size freezer bags—they'll clink satisfyingly as you drop them in—and put them in the freezer, where they'll keep for months. (Note that this is one case where sucking the air out of the bag with your mouth is not a good idea, as little bits of dry ice tend to get in with the berries. Dry ice is frozen CO_2, and as it reverts to its room-temperature state it becomes CO_2 *gas*, which is not something you want to breathe in deeply—trust me.)

Whole frozen strawberries can be tossed into smoothies (if you have a good blender, one that actually grinds up frozen things rather than just rounding them off, as mine does), or used as pretty ice cubes in a cold punch or a glass of lemonade, or, of course, used in the dumplings opposite.

Rhubarb and Orange Jam

MAKES ABOUT 6 HALF-PINT JARS

◇◇◇

MY FRIEND HEIDI BUTLER, FROM MICHIGAN, IS AN ENTHUSIASTIC RHUBARB EXPERIMENTER. She's lucky to live in a part of the country where, as I understand the local ordinances, every family is required by law to cultivate a patch of rhubarb in their backyard, and rhubarb clumps for planting are heavily subsidized by a benevolent state government. Sigh. Anyway, this past year I couldn't take it anymore, so I bit the bullet and spent a fortune on tons of it for my own enjoyment.

To my mind, tart rhubarb and tangy oranges are an even more natural pairing than the more common rhubarb and strawberries. Rhubarb has this earthy flavor—yes, it's tart, but also vegetal—that is brightened and animated by the addition of citrus.

Rhubarb preserves tend to fade and discolor over time; unless you want to add food coloring, you can either ignore the color change, as I do (the jam will remain lovely-tasting for at least a year), or use the jam within a few months.

2 navel oranges

¼ cup freshly squeezed lemon juice (reserve the squeezed hulls and seeds)

3 pounds rhubarb, trimmed of any green or soft areas, cut into ½-inch cubes (about 9 cups)

2 cups sugar

Prepare for water-bath canning: Sterilize the jars and keep them hot in the canning pot, put a small plate in the freezer, and put the flat lids in a heat-proof bowl. (See page 21 for details.)

Use a vegetable peeler to cut the zest from the oranges, then stack the slices and cut them into thin julienne strips. Segment the oranges (see page 257), working over a bowl to catch the juice and reserving the membranes. Put the membranes and any seeds, along with the reserved lemon hulls and seeds, in a cheesecloth bag and tie the bag closed.

Put the zest, orange, rhubarb, and sugar in a wide, 6- to 8-quart preserving pan.Cook over medium-high heat, stirring frequently, until the juices just cover the fruit, 10 to 15 minutes. Nestle the jelly bag in the fruit. Boil over high heat, stirring frequently, until a small dab of the jam spooned onto the chilled plate and returned to the freezer for a minute becomes somewhat firm (it will not gel), about 15 minutes. Skim off the foam, then remove from the heat and stir gently for a few seconds to distribute the fruit in the liquid.

Ladle boiling water from the canning pot into the bowl with the lids. Using a jar lifter, remove the sterilized jars from the canning pot, carefully pouring the water from each one back into the pot, and place them upright on a folded towel. Drain the water off the jar lids.

Ladle the hot jam into the jars, leaving ¼ inch headspace at the top. Use a damp paper towel to wipe the rims of the jars, then put a flat lid and ring on each jar, adjusting the ring so that it's just finger-tight. Return the jars to the water in the canning pot, making sure the water covers the jars by at least 1 inch. Bring to a boil, and boil for 5 minutes to process. Remove the jars to a folded towel and do not disturb for 12 hours. After 1 hour, check that the lids have sealed by pressing down on the center of each; if it can be pushed down, it hasn't sealed, and the jar should be refrigerated immediately. Label the sealed jars and store.

Rhubarb and Strawberry Jam

MAKES ABOUT 5 HALF-PINT JARS

STRAWBERRIES NOT ONLY SWEETEN THIS JAM BUT ALSO HELP IT KEEP ITS DEEP RED COLOR OVER THE MONTHS.

2 pounds rhubarb, trimmed of any green or soft areas, cut into ½-inch cubes (about 6 cups)
1 pound rinsed and hulled strawberries, diced (about 3 cups)
2 cups sugar
¼ cup freshly squeezed lemon juice

Prepare for water-bath canning: Sterilize the jars and keep them hot in the canning pot, put a small plate in the freezer, and put the flat lids in a heat-proof bowl. (See page 21 for details.)

Put the rhubarb, strawberries, sugar, and ½ cup water in a wide, 6- to 8-quart preserving pan. Cook over medium-high heat, stirring frequently, until the juices just cover the fruit, 10 to 15 minutes. Pour into a colander set over a large bowl and stir the fruit gently to drain off the juice. Return the juice to the pan and bring to a boil over high heat. Boil, stirring occasionally, until the syrup is reduced to about 1½ cups, about 20 minutes.

Return the fruit and any accumulated juice to the pan, along with the lemon juice, and bring to a simmer. Simmer, stirring frequently, until a small dab of the jam spooned onto the chilled plate and returned to the freezer for a minute becomes somewhat firm (it will not gel), about 15 minutes. Skim off as much foam as you can, then remove from the heat and stir gently for a few seconds to distribute the fruit in the liquid.

Ladle boiling water from the canning pot into the bowl with the lids. Using a jar lifter, remove the sterilized jars from the canning pot, carefully pouring the water from each one back into the pot, and place them upright on a folded towel. Drain the water off the jar lids.

Ladle the hot jam into the jars, leaving ¼ inch headspace at the top. Use a damp paper towel to wipe the rims of the jars, then put a flat lid and ring on each jar, adjusting the ring so that it's just finger-tight. Return the jars to the water in the canning pot, making sure the water covers the jars by at least 1 inch. Bring to a boil, and boil for 5 minutes to process. Remove the jars to a folded towel and do not disturb for 12 hours. After 1 hour, check that the lids have sealed by pressing down on the center of each; if it can be pushed down, it hasn't sealed, and the jar should be refrigerated immediately. Label the sealed jars and store.

FREEZING RHUBARB

If you're lucky enough to come by lots of rhubarb at a time, by all means make some space in the freezer for it. Wash it and trim off any traces of green leaves (the leaves are poisonous) and soft spots. Chop it into ½-inch slices, put them in resealable plastic bags, and freeze. If you stuff a quart-size bag as full of these slices as you can, you can pull out a bag one evening, let the fruit thaw and macerate overnight, and serve the beautiful freeform tarts on page 44 for dinner.

Cardamom Pinwheel Danishes

MAKES ABOUT 30

THIS IS AN OLD FREDLEY-FAMILY CLASSIC. It is just a perfect vehicle for any thickish jam, but especially for the Rhubarb and Strawberry Jam here. Don't worry if your pinwheels look a little wonky as you form the soft, stretchy dough; they'll rise and straighten themselves out a bit as they bake—and you can always drizzle pretty icing over the top.

For the danishes:
2 large eggs
1 tablespoon instant yeast
4 cups all-purpose flour, sifted
1 teaspoon pure kosher salt
2 tablespoons sugar
1½ teaspoons ground cardamom, or ground seeds of 10 cardamom pods
½ cup (1 stick) unsalted butter, plus 2 to 3 tablespoons softened butter
About ⅓ cup Rhubarb and Strawberry Jam (page 41)

For the icing (optional):
1¼ cups confectioners' sugar, sifted
2 tablespoons softened unsalted butter
1½ teaspoons pure vanilla extract
About 2 tablespoons warm water

¼ cup chopped nuts (such as toasted pecans or walnuts, or pistachios)

Make the danishes: In a medium bowl, beat the eggs, yeast, and ¾ cup warm water together until smooth. Set aside in the refrigerator for 15 minutes to cool.

In a large bowl, stir the flour, salt, sugar, and cardamom together, then cut in the ½ cup butter until the largest pieces of butter are about the size of peas.

Make a well in the center and scrape in the egg mixture. Gradually incorporate the flour mixture into the egg, then turn the dough out onto a floured work surface and knead until smooth and soft but not sticky, about 2 minutes. Clean the bowl, return the dough to the bowl, cover with plastic wrap, and let rise in a warm spot until doubled in volume, about 1½ hours.

Preheat the oven to 425°F. Line two baking sheets with parchment paper.

Divide the dough into quarters and roll one piece of dough out into a rectangle about 18 inches long and 3 inches wide. Cut into 6 or 8 rough squares. With a sharp knife or pastry wheel, cut a slit from each corner of each square toward the center, stopping about ½ inch from the center. Spread a bit of softened butter in the center of each square and spoon ½ teaspoon of the jam into the center of each. Bring every other point (four total) to the center of the pastry and pinch them together tightly over the jam. Using a spatula, carefully transfer the pastries to the baking sheets. Repeat with the remaining dough, butter, and jam. Bake for 8 to 10 minutes, until nicely browned. Let cool completely on wire racks.

If desired, make the icing: In a small bowl, whisk all the ingredients together, adding more water if necessary to make an icing that is just pourable. Drizzle it over the pastries (you won't need all of the icing).

Sprinkle the nuts over the pastries and serve.

Rustic Rhubarb Tarts

MAKES 4 GENEROUS SINGLE-SERVING TARTS

WHENEVER ONE OF OUR MOTHERS COMES TO VISIT US (OR, IF WE'RE BEING HONEST, COMES TO VISIT THALIA), WE TAKE HER TO A CHARMING LITTLE BAKERY-CAFÉ IN ATHENS, GEORGIA, CALLED BIG CITY BREAD. They have the most amazing rhubarb tarts on offer—but only sometimes, which is why I have been so determined to come up with my own version. Rhubarb has the unfortunate tendency to release buckets of water upon cooking, which makes baking it in piecrust a bit tricky. The method below yields a filling of tender (but not at all mushy) fruit in a thick, tart syrup that's deeply rhubarb-flavored because none of the juice is drained off—it's simply cooked down and drizzled over the tarts after they come out of the oven.

Serve these with a drift of whisked sour cream or plain thin yogurt sweetened with a bit of honey or agave nectar.

1½ pounds frozen rhubarb, cut into ½-inch slices
  (1 stuffed quart-size bag; see page 41)
1 cup granulated sugar
½ vanilla bean (optional)
½ teaspoon ground cinnamon (optional)
Juice of ½ lemon
3 tablespoons all-purpose flour
½ recipe (1 ball) Easy Pie Dough (page 211)
4 pats unsalted butter
2 tablespoons milk
1 tablespoon coarse turbinado sugar

Put the rhubarb in a colander and run cold water over it for a minute or so, gently breaking apart the pieces. Transfer to a large bowl and add the granulated sugar. If using, split the vanilla bean, scrape the seeds into the bowl, and nestle the pods in the rhubarb. Cover and refrigerate for at least 4 hours, or overnight. Remove the vanilla bean pods and set them aside for another use. Turn the rhubarb mixture out into a colander set over a small saucepan and stir gently to drain as much of the liquid off as possible. Return the rhubarb to the bowl and add the cinnamon, if using, the lemon juice, and the flour.

Preheat the oven to 400°F. Line a baking sheet with parchment paper.

Put the saucepan over high heat and boil until the syrup is reduced by half, 10 to 15 minutes. Set aside.

Meanwhile, divide the dough into 4 pieces and roll them out on a floured work surface ⅛ inch thick. Cut an 8-inch round from each. Divide the rhubarb mixture among the rounds, piling it high in the center. For each tart, fold the edges of the dough up over the filling toward the center, pleating it four or five times around the circumference so that it covers all but about 2 inches of the filling in the center of the tart, and making sure that any tears in the dough are pinched closed. Dot the exposed filling with butter, brush the edges of the dough with the milk, and sprinkle all over with the turbinado sugar.

Transfer the tarts to the prepared baking sheet. Bake for 40 to 50 minutes, until well browned and bubbly. Spoon some of the reduced syrup over the filling in each tart. Let cool for at least 30 minutes before serving.

Cherry Clafouti

SERVES 4

CLAFOUTI (SOMETIMES "CLAFOUTIS") IS A CLASSIC FRENCH DESSERT IN WHICH SWEET CHERRIES ARE BAKED IN AN EGGY, PUFFY, DUTCH BABY–LIKE BATTER. If you have some Bings in the freezer, throw a dinner party tonight, for goodness' sake—you're already halfway there!

This recipe is adapted from one in a sweet little British book called *Great Fruit Desserts* that I swiped from a publisher I worked for. It'll work with just about any fruit, but I prefer it with the classic sweet cherries. In old recipes, the cherries are used unpitted so that the almond flavor of the pits would permeate the dish, but I'm a lazier eater than baker, so I pit. Some bakers add a few drops of almond extract to approximate the flavor of the pits, but I'm not a fan of using almond extract in something that does not contain actual almonds, so I leave it out. You can omit the last sprinkling of sugar and sift some confectioners' sugar over the *clafouti* right as it comes out of the oven. Serve with dollops of gently whipped cream, plain yogurt or sour cream whisked together with a drizzle of honey and a few drops of vanilla extract, or crème fraîche.

¼ cup plus 2 tablespoons granulated sugar

3 cups frozen pitted sweet cherries (right), thawed and drained (they will collapse to about 1½ cups as they thaw; that's okay)

½ cup all-purpose flour

Pinch of pure kosher salt

3 large eggs

¼ cup Yogurt (page 287)

1 teaspoon pure vanilla extract

1 teaspoon grated orange zest

1 cup milk

1 tablespoon unsalted butter, at room temperature, plus more for the pie pan

Preheat the oven to 375°F. Butter a 10-inch pie pan and sprinkle it with 1 tablespoon of the sugar. Put the cherries in the pan, arranging them in a single layer.

Sift the flour, ¼ cup of the sugar, and the salt into a medium bowl. In a separate bowl, whisk together the eggs, yogurt, vanilla, and orange zest until very smooth, then whisk in the milk. Pour the egg mixture into the flour mixture and whisk to combine. Pour over the cherries, dot the top with the 1 tablespoon butter, and sprinkle with the remaining 1 tablespoon sugar. Bake until golden brown, 40 to 45 minutes. Scoop portions onto dessert plates and serve warm.

FREEZING CHERRIES

One time when I was living in New York, I went to Utah to visit my grandma and ended up bringing home about ten pounds of Bing cherries in my carry-on bag. After a couple days I began to get nervous, so I quickly pitted them with a paring knife ("quickly": ha!), stashed half of them in bags in the freezer, put the rest in a giant jar along with some peeled lychees I'd overbought in Chinatown, and filled the jar with vodka. For the next six months or so the frozen ones fueled my efforts to make the perfect cherry clafouti, and the liquored-up ones (yes, they lasted months in the fridge) served as excellent late-night post-dinner-party conversation continuers.

✳ Cherry Clafouti topped with melting whipped cream

SPRING VEGETABLES

Cocktail Onions

MAKES ABOUT 4 HALF-PINT JARS

‹›

THESE SIMPLY SPICED ONIONS ARE ESSENTIAL IN A GIBSON (A MARTINI GARNISHED WITH A SMALL PICKLED ONION). You could also drain a jar and toss the onions into a boeuf bourgignon or other rich beef stew. In the U.K., pearl onions pickled with malt vinegar (which you could use here as long as it's 5 percent acidity) are served as part of a ploughman's lunch, and with fish and chips.

You can use this recipe to make long-keeping refrigerator pickles: Simply skip the processing step, and put the jars of pickles in the refrigerator after filling them; they'll keep nicely for at least 4 months. Red pearl onions will turn the pickling liquid a beautiful light pink, though processed red onions will fade to white after a few months in the pantry.

2½ pounds pearl onions

½ cup plus 1 teaspoon pure kosher salt

1½ cups distilled white vinegar (5% acidity)

1 teaspoon mustard seeds

1 teaspoon dill seeds

Peel the onions: Bring a pot of water to a boil, drop in the onions, and leave for 1 minute; drain and transfer to a bowl of ice water. Cut off the root end and squeeze each onion from the opposite end to pop it out of the skin. In a medium bowl or sealable container, combine the ½ cup salt and 4 cups water and stir to dissolve the salt. Add the onions. Cover and refrigerate for 8 hours or overnight. Drain in a colander and rinse well.

Prepare for water-bath canning: Wash the jars and keep them hot in the canning pot, and put the flat lids in a heatproof bowl. (See page 21 for details.)

In a wide, 6- to 8-quart preserving pan, combine the vinegar, 1½ cups water, the mustard seeds, dill seeds, and 1 teaspoon salt. Bring to a boil, stirring to dissolve the salt. Add the onions and return to a boil. Remove from the heat.

Ladle boiling water from the canning pot into the bowl with the lids. Using a jar lifter, remove the hot jars from the canning pot, carefully pouring the water from each one back into the pot, and place them upright on a folded towel. Drain the water off the jar lids.

Ladle the hot onions and pickling liquid into the jars, leaving ¼ inch headspace at the top. Use a damp paper towel to wipe the rims of the jars, then put a flat lid and ring on each jar, adjusting the ring so that it's just finger-tight. Return the jars to the water in the canning pot, making sure the water covers the jars by at least 1 inch. Bring to a boil, and boil for 10 minutes to process. Remove the jars to a folded towel and do not disturb for 12 hours. After 1 hour, check that the lids have sealed by pressing down on the center of each; if it can be pushed down, it hasn't sealed, and the jar should be refrigerated immediately. Label the sealed jars and store.

TORRY KEBAB

Named after an area in Aberdeen, Scotland, that is apparently less than prosperous by U.K. standards, a "Torry kebab" consists of a cube of ham, a cube of Cheddar cheese, and a pickled onion on a cocktail pick or toothpick. It's pretty intense, as snacks go (even low-carb ones), and should probably be consumed only when you have a cold beer to pair with it.

Baby Artichokes with Lemon and Olive Oil

MAKES ABOUT 4 PINTS

THIS RECIPE IS ADAPTED FROM ONE IN EUGENIA BONE'S EXCELLENT *WELL-PRESERVED.* These artichokes and the Roasted Red Peppers on page 149 are the only recipes in this volume that use lemon juice as a key preserving agent, so if you want to be absolutely safe, use bottled rather than fresh so that the artichokes achieve the proper level of acidity. Also, because oil is used in the pickling liquid, be sure to wipe the rims of the hot jars very well before you put the flat lids on—any stray oil can prevent a seal from forming.

Use these artichokes as part of an antipasto plate, chopped and mixed with cheese for a pastry or tart filling, or in a risotto. One thing I learned a while back when testing a recipe for vegan paella, in a book by Tal Ronnen, is that preserved artichokes can successfully take the place of seafood—without, of course, losing their own character: Toast a sheet of nori (the seaweed used for sushi) by holding it with tongs and waving it over a gas flame, then grind it to a powder. Warm artichokes in a pan over low heat and dust them with some of the nori powder. Already toothsome and briny, with the addition of the seaweed they do closely resemble seafood.

6 pounds baby globe artichokes

1 cup bottled or strained fresh lemon juice, plus
   2 tablespoons for the trimmed artichokes

2 cups white wine vinegar (6% acidity)

1 cup extra-virgin olive oil

2 cloves garlic, sliced

2 teaspoons pure kosher salt

Using a sharp serrated knife, cut off the top ¾ inch of each artichoke, then pull off the tough green outer leaves until you reach the pale yellow center. Use a paring knife to smooth the base of the artichoke a bit and peel the stem. As you trim each artichoke, put it in a large bowl of water with the 2 tablespoons lemon juice.

Prepare for water-bath canning: Wash the jars and keep them hot in the canning pot, and put the flat lids in a heatproof bowl. (See page 21 for details.)

In a wide, 6- to 8-quart preserving pan, combine the 1 cup lemon juice, vinegar, oil, garlic, and salt. Bring to a boil, then drain the artichokes and add them to the pan. Boil for 10 minutes.

Ladle boiling water from the canning pot into the bowl with the lids. Using a jar lifter, remove the hot jars from the canning pot, carefully pouring the water from each one back into the pot, and place them upright on a folded towel. Drain the water off the jar lids.

Use a slotted spoon to transfer the hot artichokes to the jars and ladle in the liquid, leaving ½ inch headspace at the top. Use a chopstick to remove air bubbles around the inside of each jar (be diligent about removing the bubbles here). Use a damp paper towel to wipe the rims of the jars well, then put a flat lid and ring on each jar, adjusting the ring so that it's just finger-tight. Return the jars to the water in the canning pot, making sure the water covers the jars by at least 1 inch. Bring to a boil, and boil for 25 minutes to process. Remove the jars to a folded towel and do not disturb for 12 hours. After 1 hour, check that the lids have sealed by pressing down on the center of each; if it can be pushed down, it hasn't sealed, and the jar should be refrigerated immediately. Label the sealed jars and store.

✳ CLOCKWISE FROM TOP: Pickled Asparagus, Cocktail Onions
(page 49), Pickled Romano Beans with Indian Spices (page 136)

Pickled Asparagus

MAKES ABOUT 2 PINT JARS

◇◇◇

BLANCH ANY TENDER TRIMMINGS FROM THE BOTTOM OF THE STALKS AND FREEZE THEM IN FREEZER BAGS. Or, as an alternative, cook the trimmings in boiling water until tender, then puree and freeze.

1 pound thick asparagus tips cut 4 inches long (from about 3 bunches)
2 cups rice vinegar (4% acidity)
1½ teaspoons pure kosher salt
1½ teaspoons sugar
2 teaspoons pickling spice (see page 126)
2 cloves garlic, peeled

Prepare for water-bath canning: Wash the jars and keep them hot in the canning pot, and put the flat lids in a heatproof bowl. (See page 21 for details.)

In a wide saucepan, bring 2 inches water to a boil, then add the asparagus; bring back to a boil, then immediately drain and transfer to a bowl of ice water to cool. Drain well.

In a nonreactive pot, combine the vinegar, 1 cup water, the salt, and sugar. Bring to a boil.

Ladle boiling water from the canning pot into the bowl with the lids. Using a jar lifter, remove the hot jars from the canning pot, carefully pouring the water from each one back into the pot, and place them upright on a folded towel. Drain the water off the jar lids.

Divide the asparagus, pickling spice, and garlic cloves between the hot jars. Ladle the hot vinegar mixture into the jars, leaving ½ inch headspace at the top. Use a chopstick to remove air bubbles around the inside of each jar. Use a damp paper towel to wipe the rims of the jars, then put a flat lid and ring on each jar, adjusting the ring so that it's just finger-tight. Return the jars to the water in the canning pot, making sure the water covers the jars by at least 1 inch. Bring to a boil, and boil for 10 minutes to process. Remove the jars to a folded towel and do not disturb for 12 hours. After 1 hour, check that the lids have sealed by pressing down on the center of each; if it can be pushed down, it hasn't sealed, and the jar should be refrigerated immediately. Label the sealed jars and store.

Asparagus Flans

SERVES 6

◇◇

IF YOU'RE LUCKY ENOUGH TO COME INTO A LOT OF ASPARAGUS IN APRIL OR MAY, OR IF YOU FIND IT CHEAP AT THE FARMERS' MARKET, BE SURE TO SAVE SOME FOR LATER. It freezes remarkably well, and I'm not sure why you don't see bags of frozen asparagus in the freezer section of the grocery stores alongside the green beans. These flans, made with frozen asparagus puree (see below), are particularly good served with a tomato chutney or tomato preserve.

1 tablespoon softened butter for the cups
4 large eggs
¾ cup milk
¼ cup freshly grated Parmesan cheese (1 ounce)
¾ teaspoon pure kosher salt
Pinch of freshly ground black pepper
2 cups frozen asparagus puree (see below; from about
  2 pounds asparagus), thawed

Preheat the oven to 350°F and put a kettle of water on to boil. Line the bottom of a 9-by-13-inch baking pan with a clean folded dish towel. Generously butter 6 small (⅔-cup) custard cups, line the bottoms with parchment or waxed paper, and butter the paper. Set the cups in the baking pan.

In a large bowl, lightly whisk the eggs, then whisk in the milk, cheese, salt, pepper, and asparagus puree. Divide the mixture among the prepared cups. Put the baking pan with the cups in the oven and pour boiling water into the pan to come halfway up the sides of the cups. Bake for 35 to 40 minutes, until a knife inserted in the center of one flan comes out clean. Remove the cups to a wire rack to cool for a few minutes, then run a knife around the edge of each one and turn it out onto a serving plate. Serve the flans warm.

FREEZING ASPARAGUS

Frozen pureed asparagus can be popped out of its container into a saucepan with a little stock or water and warmed gently over medium heat; add salt and pepper, maybe a little crème fraîche and chopped fresh basil, and a squeeze of lemon juice, and you've got a beautiful simple soup.

Frozen asparagus puree: Snap off the tough bottoms of the spears. Chop, cook in a pot of boiling water until quite tender (about 3 minutes), drain, and puree in a food processor. If you want an extra-smooth puree (flans with an asparagus puree base work bet-

ter when every little fiber has been removed), push the puree through a sieve with a spatula and discard the stringy bits. Transfer to airtight containers, leaving 1 inch of headspace to allow for expansion, let cool to room temperature, put the lids on, and freeze.

Frozen asparagus spears: Blanch in boiling water (I do this in a steep-sided sauté pan) for 1 minute, then remove with tongs to a bowl of ice water to stop the cooking. Drain and pat dry with a clean kitchen towel. Line up the spears in freezer bags, suck out the air in the bags as well as you can, seal, and freeze.

Pickled Beets

MAKES ABOUT 4 PINT JARS

◇◇

MOST PICKLED BEETS ARE SO ACHINGLY SWEET I TEND TO FORGET I'M EATING BEETS, OR PICKLES. All you need is a touch of honey to mellow out the vinegar a bit.

3 pounds beets, tops removed, scrubbed
4 cups cider vinegar (5% acidity)
¼ cup mild honey
2 teaspoons pure kosher salt
2 cinnamon sticks
1 teaspoon whole allspice
½ teaspoon whole black peppercorns

Cook the beets in boiling water to cover until tender, 20 to 30 minutes. Drain and transfer to a bowl of ice water to cool. Rub off the skins, trim, quarter, and cut into ¼-inch-thick slices. Set aside.

Prepare for water-bath canning: Wash the jars and keep them hot in the canning pot, and put the flat lids in a heatproof bowl. (See page 21 for details.)

In a wide, 6- to 8-quart preserving pan, combine the vinegar, 1½ cups water, the honey, salt, cinnamon, allspice, and peppercorns. Bring to a boil over high heat, then immediately add the beets; bring just to a simmer.

Ladle boiling water from the canning pot into the bowl with the lids. Using a jar lifter, remove the hot jars from the canning pot, carefully pouring the water from each one back into the pot, and place them upright on a folded towel. Drain the water off the jar lids.

Working quickly, using tongs or a slotted spoon, transfer the hot beets (and some of the spices)

to the hot jars. Ladle or pour in the hot vinegar mixture, leaving ½ inch headspace at the top. Use a chopstick to remove air bubbles around the inside of each jar. Use a damp paper towel to wipe the rims of the jars, then put a flat lid and ring on each jar, adjusting the ring so that it's just finger-tight. Return the jars to the water in the canning pot, making sure the water covers the jars by at least 1 inch. Bring to a boil, and boil for 30 minutes to process. Remove the jars to a folded towel and do not disturb for 12 hours. After 1 hour, check that the lids have sealed by pressing down on the center of each; if it can be pushed down, it hasn't sealed, and the jar should be refrigerated immediately. Label the sealed jars and store.

PICKLED BEET AND PESTO SANDWICHES

1 cup roughly chopped fresh cilantro
¼ cup pepitas (hulled pumpkin seeds), toasted
¼ cup finely grated Parmesan cheese
Pinch of salt
3 to 4 tablespoons extra-virgin olive oil
4 square-ish ciabatta rolls, split and toasted
1 pint Pickled Beets (above)
6 ounces feta cheese, sliced

Put the cilantro, pepitas, Parmesan cheese, and salt in a mini food processor and pulse to finely chop. Add the oil, a tablespoon at a time, processing to make a smooth paste. Spread pesto on the cut rolls, top with the beets and feta cheese, and close to serve sandwich style.

Šaltibarščiai (Chilled Beet Soup)

SERVES 4

OR, AS MY FRIEND REGAN CALLED IT AFTER USING SOME OF MY PICKLES TO MAKE THIS VERSION OF HER FRIEND VICTORIA'S ŠALTIBARŠČIAI, "PICKLED BEET APOTHEOSIS." Victoria's recipe for the Lithuanian soup uses buttermilk and sour cream instead of yogurt, and regular canned beets (not pickled), and she apparently adds diced cucumber and minced hard-cooked egg, neither of which I've found to be essential. What is pretty much ideal, however, is a dense black bread, buttered and salted, to nibble on between spoonfuls.

1 large scallion, finely chopped
1 large sprig dill, chopped
Pure kosher salt
1 cup plain yogurt
¾ cup vegetable stock or water
½ pint Pickled Beets (page 55), with a little of the pickling liquid

Put the scallion, dill, and ½ teaspoon salt in a large serving bowl. Mash and stir with a fork until the scallion is wilted. Stir in the yogurt and stock.

Finely dice the beets and stir them into the yogurt mixture. Add a splash of the pickling liquid, if desired, taste, and season with more salt if necessary. Cover and chill for at least 1 hour in the refrigerator. Serve very cold.

Do Chua (Vietnamese Carrot and Daikon)

MAKES ABOUT 1 PINT

DO CHUA (LITERALLY "PICKLED THINGS") IS PROBABLY THE MOST COMMON QUICK PICKLE ON THE VIETNAMESE TABLE. You'll see it used as a dipping sauce (where just a few of the vegetables will be floating in a small bowl of brine), piled on plates as a side dish (the pickle is fairly mild and can be enjoyed as you would a vegetable dish), and especially in *bahn mi* sandwiches (*bahn mi* means simply "bread"), one of the most brilliant examples of fusion cuisine ever. Piled on a split roll of special baguette (made with wheat and rice flours), which is usually slathered with mayonnaise, are various combinations of sliced grilled or roasted pork, pâté, tofu, ham, chicken, and crumbled meatballs, topped with julienned cucumbers, sliced hot chiles, *do chua*, and loads of fresh cilantro.

I prefer *do chua* whose daikon and carrot are very thinly sliced so it's easier to eat in a sandwich, but you can also cut them into thicker matchsticks; if you do slice them thicker, let them sit in the salt for about 1 hour, until you can bend a piece almost into a circle without it snapping. Radishes that are fresh, firm, and crisp are best for this, but I've used older limp ones with great success as well.

1 pound daikon (about 2 small)

1 small carrot

2 teaspoons pure kosher salt

2 tablespoons sugar

½ cup distilled white vinegar (5% acidity)

Peel the daikon and carrot and cut them into very thin julienne strips: The easiest way to do this is to shave off thin slices with a vegetable peeler, then stack the slices and cut them into thin strips. Put the daikon and carrot in a bowl and toss with the salt. Let sit for 30 minutes, or until the vegetables are very limp and have released a lot of water, then drain in a sieve and squeeze out as much of the water as possible. Taste; if too salty, rinse and squeeze dry again. Stuff the vegetables into a pint-size glass jar or other container.

In a measuring cup or bowl, combine the sugar, vinegar, and ½ cup warm water and stir until the sugar is dissolved. Pour over the vegetables in the jar and refrigerate for at least 2 hours before serving. The pickle will keep in the refrigerator for about 1 month.

"Asia Tacos" with Crisped Braised Pork

SERVES 4 TO 6

I AM A TACO FANATIC—A CONNOISSEUR, EVEN—AND I HAVE TO SAY THAT THESE, BIZARRE AS THEY MAY SEEM, ARE QUITE POSSIBLY THE BEST I'VE EVER EATEN. I'd been reading a lot about the Kogi Korean BBQ taco trucks that have been all the rage in L.A. I'd also been reading about the Asia Dog hot dog carts roaming Brooklyn and lower Manhattan. It all sounded pretty good to me: street food in general, tacos and hot dogs in particular, Korean-Viet-Thai stuff, warm corn tortillas. So anyway, this recipe is a mash-up of, well, everything that's right about *food*, and if you can't get your griddle out to the sidewalk to serve them up hot and fresh to random passersby, you should definitely at least call some friends over. Put a twelve-pack on ice, cut up a watermelon, and call it a party. Everything can be prepared a few days in advance (braise the pork and keep it in the refrigerator, refrigerate the cilantro sauce, wrap the tortillas in plastic wrap and refrigerate them), so all you have to do at the last minute is warm up the tortillas and crisp the pork.

For the pork:

1½ cups beef or chicken broth, or water

1 tablespoon soy sauce

Juice of 1 lime

1 cube ginger-garlic paste (page 70), or 2 teaspoons minced ginger and 1 teaspoon minced garlic

2½ pounds bone-in country-style pork ribs, trimmed

For the cilantro sauce:

1 cup roughly chopped fresh cilantro, including stems

1 hot green chile, stemmed and chopped

Juice of 1 lime

1 teaspoon sugar

½ teaspoon pure kosher salt, or to taste

¼ cup olive oil

For the tacos:

12 fresh corn tortillas (see page 152)

1 pint Do Chua (page 57), drained

1 Asian pear, thinly sliced

2 tablespoons sesame seeds, toasted

Make the pork: Preheat the oven to 325°F. In a flame-proof roasting pan, combine the broth, soy sauce, lime juice, and ginger-garlic paste and bring to a boil over high heat. Remove from the heat and arrange the pork in the pan, turning to coat it with the liquid. Cover the pan with aluminum foil. Transfer to the oven and cook until the pork is very tender and can be easily pulled from the bones, 2 to 3 hours. Let cool, then pull the meat from the bones in bite-size chunks, discarding the bones and any large pieces of fat. Discard the broth, or save it for another use. Set the meat aside.

Make the cilantro sauce: Combine all the ingredients in a food processor and puree until smooth.

Make the tacos: Heat a heavy skillet or griddle over medium-high heat, then add 1 or 2 tortillas and cook for about 1 minute on each side, until heated through, transferring to a plate and covering them with plastic wrap as they cook.

When all the tortillas have been heated, return the pan to high heat, add the pork, and cook, turning it frequently with a spatula, until nicely browned and crisp on the outside, about 5 minutes. Fill the tortillas with the pork, top with *do chua* and pear, drizzle with the cilantro sauce, and sprinkle the sesame seeds on top. Serve immediately.

✳ CLOCKWISE FROM TOP: Cocktail Onions (page 49), Quick Lift (Middle Eastern Pickled Turnips) (page 234), Kohlrabi and Radish Refrigerator Pickle

Kohlrabi and Radish Refrigerator Pickle

MAKES 1 QUART

THIS SIMPLE PICKLE CAN BE SERVED LIKE A *TSUKEMONO* IN A LITTLE BOWL AT THE END OF A HOMEY JAPANESE-STYLE MEAL. Or enjoy it as a midmorning snack, as part of a bento box, or as a tangy counterpoint to an eggy fried rice dish—heck, it's even good as a topping for burgers and in quesadillas.

1 medium kohlrabi (about 1 pound)
6 radishes (about 6 ounces)
1½ cups rice vinegar (4% acidity)
½ cup mirin
¾ teaspoon pure kosher salt
2 large pinches hot red pepper flakes

Use a sharp knife to peel the kohlrabi and remove any woody areas. Cut it in half, then into ⅛-inch-thick slabs. Stack the slabs, cut them into ⅛-inch julienne strips, and put them in a large bowl. Trim the radishes and cut them into julienne strips, and add them to the kohlrabi.

In a small saucepan, bring the remaining ingredients to a boil over high heat, stirring to dissolve the salt. Pour the liquid over the vegetables and toss to combine. Let cool to room temperature, then chill in the refrigerator. If you'd like, transfer the pickle to a clean quart jar with a lid. Serve cold. The pickle will keep in the refrigerator for at least 3 weeks.

North Indian Carrot Pickle

MAKES 2 PINT JARS

THIS POWERFUL, SPICY REFRIGERATOR PICKLE IS GREAT WITH RICE, LENTILS, PLAIN YOGURT, OR ANY DAL.

1 pound carrots, scrubbed and patted dry
1½ tablespoons crushed red pepper flakes
1 tablespoon mustard seeds, coarsely crushed
1 tablespoon pure kosher salt
½ teaspoon turmeric
½ cup vegetable oil
¼ teaspoon asafetida (optional; see page 248)
⅓ cup strained fresh lemon juice

Wash 2 pint jars well, then dry them thoroughly inside and out. Wash and dry the lids. Cut the carrots into ¼- to ½-inch-thick sticks 4 inches long (to fit in pint jars). Pat dry and put in a dry medium-sized bowl. Add the red pepper flakes, mustard seeds, salt, and turmeric; toss to combine. Set aside.

In a medium sauté pan, heat the oil over high heat for 30 seconds, then sprinkle in the asafetida, if using. Add the carrots and spices. Cook, stirring constantly but carefully with a clean, dry spoon, for 1 minute. Add the lemon juice and cook, stirring, for 1 minute more. Remove from the heat.

Using dry tongs, transfer the carrots to the jars, then divide the liquid and spices between the jars. Let cool to room temperature, then put the lids on and refrigerate for 4 days before serving. The pickle will keep for at least 6 weeks; be sure to use only dry utensils to scoop out the pickle as you use it, as it will spoil if any water comes in contact with it.

Spicy Carrot Pickles

MAKES 4 PINT JARS

◇◇

I'VE BEEN READING AND HEARING ABOUT THE SPICY CARROTS SERVED WITH CHEESY SANDWICHES AT TARTINE BAKERY & CAFE IN SAN FRANCISCO AND APPRECIATING THEM FROM AFAR. Like my mom, who made the most amazing squab b'stillas back in the '70s, long before she tried the real thing in Morocco (only to learn that they don't even use squab there anymore), I have no problem copying something I've never tasted. I honestly don't know if the carrots I've come up with—which are very, very good—are even remotely similar to Tartine's, but maybe someday I'll find out.

Use the best carrots you can find, preferably small ½-inch-diameter true baby carrots, which can be left whole.

2 pounds carrots, trimmed and scrubbed

5½ cups cider vinegar (5% acidity)

1 tablespoon pure kosher salt

3 tablespoons sugar

3 cinnamon sticks

3 bay leaves

8 dried hot chiles, stemmed

4 cloves garlic, sliced

4 sprigs thyme

1 to 2 teaspoons crushed red pepper flakes, to taste

½ teaspoon whole black peppercorns

½ small white onion, thinly sliced lengthwise

Peel the carrots, if desired, and cut larger carrots into sticks no more than ½ inch thick. Cut into 4-inch lengths to fit upright in pint jars. Set aside in a bowl of ice water.

Prepare for water-bath canning: Wash the jars and keep them hot in the canning pot, and put the flat lids in a heatproof bowl. (See page 21 for details.)

In a wide, 6- to 8-quart preserving pan, combine the vinegar, 1 cup water, the salt, sugar, cinnamon sticks, and bay leaves. Bring to a boil, then simmer for 5 minutes. Add the carrots and cook until just crisp-tender, 8 to 10 minutes.

Ladle boiling water from the canning pot into the bowl with the lids. Using a jar lifter, remove the hot jars from the canning pot, carefully pouring the water from each one back into the pot, and place them upright on a folded towel. Drain the water off the jar lids.

Working quickly, divide the chiles, garlic, thyme, red pepper flakes, and peppercorns among the jars. Using tongs or a slotted spoon, transfer the hot carrots to the jars (do not pack them too tightly) and fill in empty spaces loosely with slivers of onion. Ladle the hot pickling liquid into the jars, leaving ½ inch headspace at the top. Use a chopstick to remove air bubbles around the inside of each jar. Use a damp paper towel to wipe the rims of the jars, then put a flat lid and ring on each jar, adjusting the ring so that it's just finger-tight. Return the jars to the water in the canning pot, making sure the water covers the jars by at least 1 inch. Bring to a boil, and boil for 15 minutes to process. Remove the jars to a folded towel and do not disturb for 12 hours. After 1 hour, check that the lids have sealed by pressing down on the center of each; if it can be pushed down, it hasn't sealed, and the jar should be refrigerated immediately. Label the sealed jars and store.

Grilled Fontina Sandwiches with Truffle Oil
SERVES 2

PERHAPS THE BEST THING TO DO WITH CARROT PICKLES BESIDES EATING THEM STRAIGHT FROM THE JAR IS TO PUT THEM ON A PLATE NEXT TO A HOT SANDWICH OOZING CHEESE. You could also, of course, slice the pickles and put them right in the sandwich.

4 slices good sourdough bread
2 tablespoons truffle oil (see Note)
1 cup grated fontina cheese (about 3 ounces)
Salt and freshly ground black pepper
Freshly grated nutmeg
2 to 4 Spicy Carrot Pickles (opposite)

Heat a heavy skillet over medium heat. Generously brush one side of each slice of bread with oil and place two slices, oiled side down, in the skillet.

Divide the cheese between the slices in the pan, sprinkle lightly with salt and pepper and nutmeg, and top with the other two bread slices, oiled side up. Cook until the bottom is well browned and the cheese is starting to melt, 1 to 2 minutes, then press down on the sandwiches with a spatula, flip, and brown the other side. Cut each sandwich in half and serve with the carrot pickles on the side.

Note: Truffle oil adds a layer of deep flavor to the sandwich, though almost none of the truffle oils readily available on the market ever came in contact with a mushroom (the aroma is synthesized). If the oil you're using came in a tiny jar, was very expensive, and is intensely aromatic, use just ½ teaspoon or so and make up the rest with plain olive oil so it doesn't overpower the cheese.

* TOP: North Indian Carrot Pickle (page 61)
BOTTOM: Pickled Fennel with Orange and Mint

Pickled Fennel with Orange and Mint

MAKES ABOUT 3 PINT JARS

◇◇

SCATTER PICKLED FENNEL OVER CARPACCIO OR A WHOLE ROASTED FISH, OR TOSS IT WITH BITTER GREENS AND A VINAIGRETTE MADE FROM SOME OF THE PICKLING LIQUID WHISKED WITH OLIVE OIL. This also makes a fine (and crisp) refrigerator pickle without processing: Pour the hot vinegar mixture over the fennel mixture, let cool to room temperature, then cover and put in the refrigerator, where it will keep for at least 1 month.

2 medium bulbs fennel (about 2 pounds), stalks
    trimmed off
3½ teaspoons pure kosher salt
Zest of 1 navel orange, cut into (or removed in) thin
    strips
3 cups white wine vinegar (6% acidity)
2 tablespoons mild honey
2 teaspoons fennel seeds
4 sprigs fresh mint

Cut the fennel bulbs into quarters lengthwise and cut out the core. Cut the fennel crosswise into ⅛-inch-thick slices and toss them in a large bowl with 2 teaspoons of the salt; let sit for 1 hour, then rinse in cold water and drain. Toss the fennel with the orange zest and set aside.

Prepare for water-bath canning: Wash the jars and keep them hot in the canning pot, and put the flat lids in a heatproof bowl. (See page 21 for details.)

In a nonreactive pot, combine the vinegar, 1½ cups water, the remaining 1½ teaspoons salt, and the honey. Bring just to a boil.

Ladle boiling water from the canning pot into the bowl with the lids. Using a jar lifter, remove the hot jars from the canning pot, carefully pouring the water from each one back into the pot, and place them upright on a folded towel. Drain the water off the jar lids.

Divide the fennel mixture, fennel seeds, and mint among the hot jars. Ladle the hot vinegar mixture into the jars, leaving ½ inch headspace at the top. Use a chopstick to remove air bubbles around the inside of each jar. Use a damp paper towel to wipe the rims of the jars, then put a flat lid and ring on each jar, adjusting the ring so that it's just finger-tight. Return the jars to the water in the canning pot, making sure the water covers the jars by at least 1 inch. Bring to a boil, and boil for 15 minutes to process. Remove the jars to a folded towel and do not disturb for 12 hours. After 1 hour, check that the lids have sealed by pressing down on the center of each; if it can be pushed down, it hasn't sealed, and the jar should be refrigerated immediately. Label the sealed jars and store.

Pickled Young Spring Garlic

MAKES 1 PINT

◇◇◇

SPRING GARLIC IS BECOMING MORE COMMON AT FARMERS' MARKETS AROUND THE COUNTRY, AND IT IS WELL WORTH TRYING. The bulbs at this point in the season are still very small and look like lumpy scallions. They're great fresh, sliced and used in egg dishes or brothy soups, for example. This easy pickle, in which two soaks in rice vinegar help to mellow the bite of fresh garlic, is of Korean origin and would be most at home on a table full of small plates of *banchan*, or side dishes.

About 16 heads young spring garlic
About 1¾ cups rice vinegar (4% acidity)
2 tablespoons sugar or Korean corn malt syrup
2 tablespoons soy sauce

Trim the roots from the garlic. Cut the tops off the garlic, leaving only the bottom 4 inches and peeling off one or two outer layers. Stand the garlic in a clean wide-mouth pint jar and cover with vinegar. Put the lid on and refrigerate for 1 week.

In a nonreactive saucepan, combine ½ cup vinegar, ¾ cup water, the sugar, and soy sauce and bring to a boil. Remove from the heat and let cool to room temperature.

Pour the vinegar off the garlic and replace it with the boiled vinegar mixture. Cover the jar and refrigerate for 1 to 2 weeks before using. The pickle will keep for several months in the refrigerator.

GROW YOUR OWN GARLIC

If sources for spring garlic are few and far between where you live, you can easily cultivate your own crop. In the fall or early spring, find a couple heads of fresh, firm garlic. (Asian markets are some of the best places to procure good garlic, probably because of their high turnover, but you can also buy fancy varieties from seed companies.) Separate the cloves, leaving the peel on, put them in a bowl or jar, and cover with water. Add a few pinches of baking soda and, if you have it, a dash of liquid seaweed (I just snip in some kombu, though I don't know if it makes much difference in preventing disease), and let the cloves soak for a few hours or overnight. Plant them about 6 inches deep, 6 inches apart, with the flat root sides down, and cover with a thick layer of mulch. If you plant in the fall, they will sprout and then stop growing until spring, when they will shoot up. When they're ½ to 1 inch in diameter, pull them up and pickle them, or let them keep growing until about a third to a half of the leaves are brown and the bulbs are large but still tight.

Preserved Ginger

MAKES ABOUT 4 HALF-PINT JARS

THERE ARE MUCH EASIER WAYS TO PRESERVE GINGER IF YOU COME INTO A LOT OF IT (SEE PAGE 70), BUT THIS METHOD IS WELL WORTH THE EFFORT. Adapted from an old edition of *The Joy of Cooking*, the recipe is designed for long-term storage of relatively thick slices or cubes, and it is perfect for making a large batch, as described here. The repeated boiling and soaking ensures that the sugar completely and evenly saturates the ginger, which is what preserves it.

To peel the ginger, scrape it with a spoon held with the concave side toward the ginger—this results in much less waste than a vegetable peeler or paring knife, as the spoon can easily negotiate all the little bumps and crannies.

A tiny spoonful of ginger preserves, in their thick, spicy syrup, would be nice with a plain, nutty cake like the Rustic Almond Cake on page 277, or on a coarse multigrain bread with good butter.

1½ pounds fresh ginger, peeled and cut into ¼-inch
   cubes or ¼-inch-thick round slices (about 4 cups)
3 cups sugar
1 lemon, thinly sliced, seeds removed
1 cup light corn syrup

Put the ginger in a medium saucepan with 6 cups cold water. Bring to a boil over medium-high heat, then cover and lower the heat to maintain a simmer; cook for about 20 minutes, until just tender. Add 1 cup of the sugar and bring to a boil, stirring. Remove from the heat, cover, and let sit at room temperature for 4 hours or overnight.

Bring to a boil a second time, then lower the heat and simmer for 15 minutes. Add the lemon and corn syrup and simmer for 15 more minutes. Remove from the heat, cover, and let sit for 4 hours.

Bring to a boil a third time, stirring frequently, and stir in 1 cup of the sugar. Simmer for 30 minutes, stirring frequently. Stir in the remaining 1 cup sugar, bring just to a boil, then remove from the heat, cover, and let sit for 4 hours.

Prepare for water-bath canning: Wash the jars and keep them hot in the canning pot, and put the flat lids in a heatproof bowl. (See page 21 for details.)

Bring the ginger to a boil and cook for about 35 minutes, until the ginger is translucent and the syrup is very thick.

Ladle boiling water from the canning pot into the bowl with the lids. Using a jar lifter, remove the hot jars from the canning pot, carefully pouring the water from each one back into the pot, and place them upright on a folded towel. Drain the water off the jar lids.

Ladle the ginger and syrup into the jars, leaving ¼ inch headspace at the top. Use a damp paper towel to wipe the rims of the jars, then put a flat lid and ring on each jar, adjusting the ring so that it's just finger-tight. Return the jars to the water in the canning pot, making sure the water covers the jars by at least 1 inch. Bring to a boil, and boil for 10 minutes to process. Remove the jars to a folded towel and do not disturb for 12 hours. After 1 hour, check that the lids have sealed by pressing down on the center of each; if it can be pushed down, it hasn't sealed, and the jar should be refrigerated immediately. Label the sealed jars and store.

The Best Gingerbread, with Grapefruit Sauce

MAKES 1 (9-INCH) SQUARE CAKE; SERVES 6

THIS CAKE IS PERFECTLY DELIGHTFUL WITH GINGER IN JUST ONE FORM. It becomes really special, though, when you can taste not only the sharp bite of ground dried ginger but also chewy nuggets of the milder candied ginger.

For the cake:
2½ cups all-purpose flour
1½ teaspoons baking soda
2 teaspoons dry mustard powder
1 teaspoon ground ginger
½ teaspoon ground cinnamon
½ teaspoon ground cloves
½ cup (1 stick) unsalted butter, at room temperature
⅓ cup sugar
1 large egg, at room temperature
1 cup molasses
1 (4-ounce) jar Preserved Ginger (page 67), finely chopped, with syrup; or ½ cup minced crystallized ginger (page 70)
1 cup hot water

For the sauce:
4 small or 3 large grapefruits
⅓ cup sugar
2 tablespoons cornstarch
Pinch of pure kosher salt
2 tablespoons unsalted butter

Make the cake: Preheat the oven to 350°F. Generously butter a 9-inch square baking pan.

Sift the flour, baking soda, mustard powder, ground ginger, cinnamon, and cloves together into a medium bowl.

Using an electric mixer, in a large bowl, cream the butter and sugar until light and fluffy, then add the egg and molasses and beat until very light in color, 5 to 8 minutes. If using preserved ginger, beat it in now. Add the flour mixture a third at a time, alternating with the hot water, and beat until thoroughly incorporated. If using crystallized ginger, stir it in now. Scrape the batter into the prepared pan. Bake for 30 to 35 minutes, until a toothpick inserted in the center comes out clean. Remove to a wire rack to cool to warm or room temperature.

Make the sauce: Use a sharp knife to peel and segment the grapefruit (see page 257), working over a bowl to catch the juice and segments and squeezing the membranes to extract the juice; discard the membranes. Drain the segments, reserving 1 cup of the juice. Set aside.

In a medium saucepan, combine the sugar, cornstarch, and salt, then stir in 1 cup water and the reserved juice. Bring to a boil over low heat, stirring constantly, then lower the heat and simmer for 1 minute. Remove from the heat and stir in the butter. Before serving, rewarm the sauce over low heat and gently stir in the grapefruit sections.

Cut the cake into squares and serve with the sauce.

Sushi Ginger

MAKES ABOUT 4 HALF-PINT JARS

YOUNG GINGER—IDENTIFIABLE BY ITS REDDISH-PINK TIPS—IS AVAILABLE IN LATE SPRING AND EARLY SUMMER IN ASIAN MARKETS. It's the traditional ginger pickled for sushi, and it turns a pale pink as it floats in the rice vinegar—though not the hot pink of commercial bottled sushi ginger, which is usually tinted with dye. (Some storage, or older, ginger will blush in vinegar, but it's not a sure thing.)

If you'd like to make a smaller batch and keep the ginger in the refrigerator, put the blanched ginger in a preheated clean glass jar (any size), cover with the boiling vinegar mixture, then let cool to room temperature before putting the lid on. It will keep for months in the refrigerator.

1 pound very fresh ginger, preferably young
2 cups rice vinegar (4% acidity)
⅔ cup sugar
Pinch of pure kosher salt

Prepare for water-bath canning: Sterilize the jars and keep them hot in the canning pot, and put the flat lids in a heatproof bowl. (See page 21 for details.)

Using a spoon, peel the ginger. With a sharp knife, slice it lengthwise, cutting parallel to the fibers, as thinly as possible. Bring a large saucepan of water to a boil and add the ginger; blanch for 1 minute (30 seconds for young ginger), then drain in a colander.

In a nonreactive saucepan, bring the vinegar, sugar, and salt just to a boil, stirring to dissolve the sugar and salt.

Ladle boiling water from the canning pot into the bowl with the lids. Using a jar lifter, remove the sterilized jars from the canning pot, carefully pouring the water from each one back into the pot, and place them upright on a folded towel. Drain the water off the jar lids.

Put the blanched ginger in the jars, leaving 1 inch headspace at the top. Ladle the hot vinegar mixture into the jars, leaving ½ inch headspace. Use a chopstick to remove air bubbles around the inside of each jar. Use a damp paper towel to wipe the rims of the jars, then put a flat lid and ring on each jar, adjusting the ring so that it's just finger-tight. Return the jars to the water in the canning pot, making sure the water covers the jars by at least 1 inch. Bring to a boil, and boil for 5 minutes to process. Remove the jars to a folded towel and do not disturb for 12 hours. After 1 hour, check that the lids have sealed by pressing down on the center of each; if it can be pushed down, it hasn't sealed, and the jar should be refrigerated immediately. Label the sealed jars and store.

KEEPING GINGER

Fresh ginger stores pretty well for a few weeks in the refrigerator, but during the fall and winter it becomes too expensive to buy in my usual grocery stores, so I stock up whenever I happen to be at an Asian market.

Refrigerated ginger in dry sherry: This is as simple as it sounds. Peel the ginger, cut it into rounds, put them in a clean glass jar, cover with dry sherry that's past its prime (somehow I always have some in the door of the fridge; I suppose I must be over my dry sherry phase), and put a lid on. It'll keep for months in the fridge. Just lift slices out of the sherry with a fork and use them as you would use fresh ginger. The sherry flavor doesn't come through enough to have any effect on the finished dish.

Frozen ginger-garlic paste: Peel and chop a bunch of ginger—and some garlic cloves, if you'd like—and put it in a mini food processor with a little water. Puree until smooth, then spoon the paste into ice-cube trays, freeze, and transfer the cubes to a freezer bag. Many Indian and Asian dishes start with a puree of fresh ginger and water, sometimes with garlic, and it's nice to be able to pull an ice-cube-sized hunk or two out of the freezer and avoid gunking up the food processor at every meal. (And as my friend the cookbook author and editor Leda Scheintaub observes, knife-minced ginger-and-garlic just isn't the same as the pureed paste.) If the recipe asks you to cook the paste in the pan with oil or ghee before adding any other liquid, it's best to thaw the cube first so it doesn't stick and brown too quickly.

Frozen ginger juice: Puree the ginger as above, adding enough water to make a thin paste. Dump the paste into a fine-mesh sieve set over a bowl with a pouring spout. Drain, pressing as much juice out as possible, then pour the juice into ice-cube trays and freeze. Ginger juice, or "extract," is a common ingredient in Asian meat marinades. One dish I particularly like is thinly sliced beef marinated in ginger juice, soy sauce, oyster sauce, Shaoxing cooking wine, black pepper, and a few drops of sesame oil, then stir-fried in vegetable oil with a package of preserved sour mustard cabbage that's been soaked in cold water for 30 minutes, then rinsed and sliced (this can be found in plastic bags in the refrigerated produce section of Asian grocery stores). A couple cubes of ginger juice also add a warming spiciness to a winter punch.

Crystallized ginger: To make crystallized ginger instead of canning it in jars, remove it from the syrup at the end of the 35-minute boiling as described on page 67—reserve the syrup for another use (glazing a lemon cake, for example, or stirring into rum-based drinks)—and spread the ginger out on a wire rack set over a baking sheet to dry overnight. It should be just a bit sticky; if it needs more drying time, put it in the oven at the lowest setting for an hour and a half or so. Toss with sugar to coat completely, then store in an airtight container in a cool, dark spot; it'll keep for at least 2 months. In a pinch, you can quickly make a small batch of crystallized ginger, though it likely won't last as long as it does using the method above: Peel and thinly slice ginger into rounds to make about 1 cup. Put in a small saucepan, cover with water, bring to a boil and boil for 5 minutes. Drain and repeat boiling twice more. Drain and set aside. In the saucepan, combine ½ cup water and 1 cup sugar; bring to a boil and boil for 5 minutes. Add the blanched ginger and cook until tender and translucent, 5 to 7 minutes. Let cool in the syrup, then remove the ginger and put it on a wire rack to dry. When just sticky, toss with sugar, if desired.

Quinoa Salad with Sushi Ginger Dressing

SERVES 4

QUINOA, WHICH IS NOT A GRAIN BUT THE SMALL SEED OF A PLANT NATIVE TO THE ANDES, IS NOW ALSO GROWN AT HIGH ALTITUDES IN THE UNITED STATES AND SO IS BECOMING WIDELY AVAILABLE HERE. Check the bulk bins at natural-foods stores or larger grocery stores. It is considered a "complete" protein, meaning that it contains all eight essential amino acids, and it is very high in fiber.

Black, brown, red, or pale white quinoa varieties are pretty much interchangeable. Be sure to rinse the quinoa well in cold water before cooking it; this removes saponins that can give it a strange soapy taste.

Here, nutty, toothsome quinoa is fluffed up and tossed with colorful vegetables and a tangy ginger vinaigrette. It makes a satisfying lunch on its own or with a few leaves of spinach or other greens, or a small piece of pan-seared or grilled meat or fish.

1 cup quinoa

Pure kosher salt

¼ cup pickling liquid from Sushi Ginger (page 69)

3 tablespoons olive oil

1 teaspoon Dijon-style mustard

Freshly ground black pepper

4 small tomatoes, diced

1 cucumber, peeled if desired, seeded, and diced

2 scallions, thinly sliced

3 tablespoons chopped fresh herbs such as cilantro, mint, and basil

2 tablespoons minced Sushi Ginger (page 69)

Put the quinoa in a sieve and rinse very well under cold running water. Put in a small saucepan with 1½ cups water and a generous pinch of salt. Bring to a boil, then cover and lower the heat to medium-low. Cook until tender, 15 to 17 minutes. Drain in the sieve and rinse with cold water to cool. Drain well.

In a medium bowl, whisk together the pickling liquid, oil, mustard, and salt and pepper to taste. Add the quinoa and remaining ingredients and toss to combine. Let stand for at least 30 minutes before serving to allow the dressing to permeate the quinoa. Taste and season with salt again if necessary, and serve at room temperature or chilled.

Pickled Sugar Snap Peas with Mint

MAKES 2 PINT JARS OR 1 QUART JAR

◇◇

IT'S POSSIBLE TO CAN PICKLED SUGAR SNAP PEAS IN A BOILING-WATER BATH, BUT WHILE THE FLAVOR IS DELIGHTFUL, THEY LOSE THEIR CHARACTERISTIC CRUNCH. It's not worth it. After all, the point of a sugar snap pea is the snap, right? But with these crisp refrigerator pickles you can extend the season by 3 or 4 weeks.

1½ cups white wine vinegar (6% acidity)
1 tablespoon pure kosher salt
1½ tablespoons mild honey
2 dried hot chiles such as arbol, broken in half
2 small shallots, thinly sliced
4 sprigs fresh mint
1 pound sugar snap peas, stems removed

Submerge the jars (or 1 quart jar, if you don't plan to share the pickles) in a pot of hot water.

In a wide, 6- to 8-quart preserving pan, combine the vinegar, 1½ cups water, the salt, and honey and bring to a boil over high heat.

Remove the warmed jars from the water and set them upright on a towel. Divide the chiles, shallots, and mint between the hot jars, then fill the jars with the peas. Ladle or pour in the hot vinegar mixture. Let cool to room temperature, then put the lids on and refrigerate; the peas will keep for several weeks.

• •

Radish Pickles

MAKES ABOUT 2 PINT JARS

◇◇

TRY THESE ON A THICK SLICE OF DARK BREAD WITH SOFT BUTTER.

2 pounds red radishes, tops and roots removed, scrubbed
¼ cup plus ¼ teaspoon pure kosher salt
1½ cups distilled white vinegar (5% acidity)
1 tablespoon sugar
1 teaspoon black peppercorns
1 teaspoon fennel seeds
1 teaspoon mustard seeds

Cut the radishes into ⅛-inch-thick rounds. In a medium bowl or sealable container, combine the ¼ cup salt with 2½ cups water and stir to dissolve the salt. Add the radishes. Cover and refrigerate for 8 hours or overnight. Drain in a colander and rinse.

Prepare for water-bath canning: Wash the jars and keep them hot in the canning pot, and put the flat lids in a heatproof bowl. (See page 21 for details.)

In a wide, 6- to 8-quart preserving pan, combine the vinegar, 1½ cups water, the sugar, ¼ teaspoon salt, and the spices. Bring to a boil, stirring to dissolve the salt and sugar. Add the radishes and return to a boil. Remove from the heat.

Ladle boiling water from the canning pot into the bowl with the lids. Using a jar lifter, remove the hot jars from the canning pot, carefully pouring the water from each one back into the pot, and place them upright on a folded towel. Drain the water off the jar lids.

Working quickly, fill the hot jars loosely with the hot radishes and vinegar mixture, leaving ½ inch headspace at the top. Use a chopstick to remove air bubbles around the inside of each jar. Use a damp paper towel to wipe the rims of the jars, then put a flat lid and ring on each jar, adjusting the ring so that it's just finger-tight. Return the jars to the water in the canning pot, making sure the water covers the jars by at least 1 inch. Bring to a boil, and boil for 10 minutes to process. Remove the jars to a folded towel and do not disturb for 12 hours. After 1 hour, check that the lids have sealed by pressing down on the center of each; if it can be pushed down, it hasn't sealed, and the jar should be refrigerated immediately. Label the sealed jars and store.

Tamarind Paste

MAKES ABOUT 2 ICE-CUBE TRAYS FULL

I FIND STORE-BOUGHT TAMARIND PASTE TO BE SOMEWHAT LACKING IN VIBRANCY AND MUCH PREFER THE STUFF I PAINSTAKINGLY SOFTEN, KNEAD, AND STRAIN MYSELF. Admittedly, this may be a case of something tasting better simply because it took great effort to prepare. At any rate, if you come across fresh tamarind pods—cheap in the springtime at Asian and Latin American markets—it's worth taking an hour or so to stock up the aromatics section of your freezer, as having tart, earthy tamarind concentrate on hand means that easy dishes like the one on page 74 are only minutes away. The next time you cook Indian food, thaw a cube of tamarind paste and swirl it into a small bowl of plain yogurt to serve as a tangy condiment. Or make a simple *chat*: Drain a can of chickpeas, fold in some tamarind paste, diced cooked potato, diced red onion, and fresh cilantro, and season with salt to taste. Garnish the *chat* with a sprinkle of crunchy fried mung beans, puffy *boondi* (see Sources, page 291), or even Corn Chex, and drizzle with thinned yogurt. Or use tamarind paste in pad thai, curries, barbecue sauces, or meaty stews with dried fruit.

1 pound fresh tamarind pods

Remove the shells from the tamarind and put the pulp and seeds in a large bowl. Add 2½ cups warm water and let soak for about 1 hour, until very soft. Rub the pulpy mess with your hands and pick out and discard the hard inner seeds—you're basically peeling the seeds, and it's okay if the outer shell of the seed is left in the mixture. Working in batches, put the mixture in a sieve set over a bowl and use a metal spoon to push the pulp through; discard the fibrous stuff left in the sieve. Spoon the smooth tamarind paste into ice-cube trays and freeze until solid, then transfer the cubes to freezer bags and store in the freezer for up to 6 months.

Shrimp with Tamarind and Chile Sauce

SERVES 4

THIS ADAPTATION OF A NYONYA (MALAYSIAN CHINESE) CRAB DISH USUALLY MADE WITH KETCHUP IS WONDERFUL SERVED ALONGSIDE NASI GORENG WITH ACHAR (PAGE 132). It's one of those special dishes that are even more special because they can be made with ingredients you might already have on hand. I often have a bag of individually quick-frozen shrimp in the freezer, and the freezer door is home to a wide variety of easy-to-use flavorings and aromatics: cubes of tamarind, of course, as well as frozen chopped chiles and cubes of ginger-garlic paste (which you can use here instead of chopping fresh; see page 70).

6 cubes Tamarind Paste (page 73), thawed
¼ cup brown sugar
2 tablespoons brandy
1 medium red onion, chopped
2 to 3 hot red chiles, seeded and chopped
1 inch fresh ginger, peeled and chopped
2 cloves garlic, chopped
1 tablespoon vegetable oil
1 pound extra-large shrimp, peeled and deveined
Fresh cilantro leaves or sliced scallions

In a small bowl, combine the tamarind paste, brown sugar, brandy, and 1 cup water. Set aside.

Put the onion, chiles, ginger, and garlic in a mini food processor and pulse to finely chop but not puree.

In a large sauté pan over medium-high heat, heat the oil. Add the onion and chile mixture and cook, stirring constantly, until fragrant and beginning to brown, about 2 minutes. Add the tamarind paste mixture and stir well. Bring to a boil, then lower the heat and simmer until the sauce has reduced by about half and is fairly thick, about 3 minutes. Add the shrimp and cook until pink and opaque, about 2 minutes. Transfer to a serving bowl, scatter the cilantro over the shrimp, and serve immediately.

Thai Green Curry Paste

MAKES ABOUT 28 (2-TABLESPOON) CUBES

WHEN I COME INTO A LOT OF GALANGAL (RELATED TO GINGER BUT WITH A VERY DIFFERENT FLAVOR), I TRY TO REMEMBER TO ALSO PICK UP A BAGFUL OF CHILES. That way I can stock up the freezer door, otherwise known as the Door of Aromatics, with curry paste—something that's a pain in the neck to make fresh each time I want a curry, which is at least every couple weeks. I also keep little freezer bags of trimmed and roughly chopped lemongrass and whole kaffir lime leaves in the Door. Yes, you can buy Thai curry paste in any decent grocery store, but homemade is so much better. Use good Thai fish sauce, which has much more flavor than those made in other countries.

¼ cup coriander seeds

2 tablespoons cumin seeds

1 teaspoon whole black peppercorns

1 pound hot green chiles, stemmed and chopped

½ cup peeled and finely chopped fresh galangal

2 cups roughly chopped fresh cilantro, with stems

6 cloves garlic, chopped

6 stalks lemongrass, bottom 2 inches only, finely minced

10 kaffir lime leaves, tough center ribs removed, leaves minced

¼ cup fish sauce, preferably Thai

In a heavy skillet over medium heat, toast the coriander, cumin, and peppercorns, then transfer to a plate to cool. Grind in a spice mill.

Put the spices and all the remaining ingredients with ¾ cup water in a food processor and process to a fine paste. Transfer to ice-cube trays and freeze until solid. Pop the cubes out and put them in a freezer bag. The paste will keep in the freezer for at least 6 months.

Basic Chicken Curry

SERVES 4

1½ pounds boneless, skinless chicken breasts, or a mixture of breasts and thighs

1 tablespoon vegetable oil

1 onion, thinly sliced

3 cubes Thai Green Curry Paste (opposite), thawed

2 (13.5-ounce) cans unsweetened coconut milk, preferably Thai

½ red bell pepper, julienned

2 kaffir lime leaves

1 (8-ounce) can sliced bamboo shoots, drained

2 tablespoons fish sauce, preferably Thai

4 sprigs fresh Thai basil

2 sprigs fresh mint

Hot cooked jasmine rice

Trim any excess fat from the chicken and cut the meat into ½-inch-thick slices or cubes.

In a large sauté pan over medium-high heat, heat the oil. Add the chicken and cook, stirring frequently, until no longer pink on the outside, about 3 minutes. Add the onion and cook, stirring, until it is just starting to brown, about 5 minutes. Stir in the curry paste and cook for 30 seconds, then add the coconut milk, bell pepper, kaffir lime leaves, bamboo shoots, and fish sauce. Bring to a simmer and cook for about 3 minutes, until the pepper and bamboo shoots are tender. Tear up the basil and mint and scatter them over the curry. Serve hot, with rice on the side.

Summer

Just as my mom forced my brother and me to do every summer, I take my daughter, Thalia, wild blackberry picking. There's a big patch of brambles just up the hill from our house (I imagine that wherever we live I'll be able to find a wild berry patch of some sort). We get started early in the morning to sneak in and out before the heat overtakes us and renders us—well, me—completely incapable of any physical activity that doesn't involve water hoses, but the patch is situated on top of a hill and we can never realistically get there before it's in full sun. We wear long sleeves, long pants, tall boots, scarves around our hair, and gloves (though the gloves come off soon enough; they always seem like a good idea but just end up getting in the way).

The blackberries are well protected by fire ants in their two-foot-high hills, and by poison ivy, which Thalia learned to recognize at an early age. She's only three and a half now, so we share a bucket. I leave the low-hanging blackberries at the side of the road for her, and occasionally I leave her there while I traipse into the middle of the bramble by myself (when she was a baby, I'd take her with me). She waits patiently, telling me to "be careful of ants, and don't get stuck," and I pick as fast as I can, checking my picking hand every few seconds to try to brush off the ants before they can sting. We come home exhausted, in my case with arms and hands covered with scratches and ant bites and, if I was greedy or careless, a bit of poison ivy as well, but usually with enough blackberries for a batch of jam, or at least a pie or frozen yogurt. We head straight for the kiddie pool and leave the cooking for later.

I always thought of myself as exceptionally determined when it came to picking wild berries—Derek routinely reminds me that it's actually okay to *buy* fruit, in a *store*—but then my mom described how she would go berrying with her grandma, mom, and sister in western Pennsylvania, and I realized that generation by generation the berry picking is getting easier:

> Grandma wore World War I army boots—and when I was big enough to wear them, I did. They were leather, knee high, good for protecting against snakes and briars. So that we wouldn't spill the berries, and had two hands for picking, our buckets were tied

around our waists. The little blue graniteware bucket that you have. Also, sometimes we'd take old-fashioned lunch pails—cylindrical, with a bail.

Behind Grandma Bovard's house there were mostly black raspberries (my favorite), blackberries, and a few red raspberries. After Grandpap Barron no longer kept pigs (he died), the old pigpen grew up in brambles. We moved into that house, and in a few years we discovered the biggest, juiciest blackberries anybody had ever seen!

In summer, Mum and Grandma couldn't use all the berries, so Grandpa's cousins would come and pick. Grandma made blackberry jelly, but the Boosels made jam. I got the impression that they couldn't be bothered with dripping jelly. It was easier to make jam, but Grandma considered that a bit crude, to leave the seeds in. After the cousins were done berry picking, Mum would have lemonade ready. Even Dad's cousins from Claytonia would come.

Blueberries grew in a field up the road, and that was hard work—down on the ground, pulling the berries off above a wide pan. Kathleen and I tired of that easily, and mostly played on the maple saplings. You could hang on a branch and stand on a branch and bounce up and down until the branch broke. The advantage was that it was shady under the trees. Once or twice, Mrs. Campbell took Mum to pick blueberries on a hill beside the railroad track. Snakes were so bad there that Mum made me wait at the bottom of the hill in the heat. Not fun, but that's what you do for berries.

Nowadays my mom hunts for wild Saskatoon berries on the mountain behind her house in far northeastern Washington state. She cans them and sends them to me for pies. It's easy picking: All she has to deal with, other than the mountain, are mosquitoes.

SUMMER FRUITS

Apricot and Vanilla-Bean Preserves

MAKES ABOUT 5 HALF-PINT JARS

FRESH APRICOTS EATEN OUT OF HAND—AT LEAST ONES SOLD IN THIS COUNTRY—ARE ALMOST ALWAYS A LITTLE DISAPPOINTING. This is true even of ones you pick yourself and let ripen on the counter for a few days, until they're just soft to the touch. (I was told by growers in Washington state that apricots are never picked ripe, as they're too fragile to travel.) While I wouldn't say that fruit in general can be *improved* by preserving, even supermarket apricots, in a preserve like this one, become perfectly delicious: The vanilla beans and wine play up the distinctive flavor of apricots without overpowering it, and adding sugar compensates for a lack of sweetness in the fresh fruit.

3 pounds ripe apricots, halved and pitted (no need to peel)
½ cup rosé or white wine, or 3 tablespoons fresh lemon juice
1½ cups sugar
2 vanilla beans, split lengthwise

Prepare for water-bath canning: Sterilize the jars and keep them hot in the canning pot, put a small plate in the freezer, and put the flat lids in a heat-proof bowl. (See page 21 for details.)

Cut the apricots into ¼-inch slices. Put the apricots, wine, sugar, and vanilla beans in a wide, 6- to 8-quart preserving pan. Bring to a simmer, stirring frequently, then continue to cook until the juices are just deep enough to cover the apricots, about 5 minutes. Pour into a colander set over a large bowl and stir the apricots gently to drain off the juice. Return the juice to the pan and bring to a boil over high heat. Boil, stirring occasionally, until the syrup is reduced by about half, 5 to 10 minutes.

Return the apricots and vanilla beans and any accumulated juice to the pan and bring to a simmer. Simmer, stirring frequently, until a small dab of the jam spooned onto the chilled plate and returned to the freezer for a minute becomes somewhat firm (it will not gel), 10 to 15 minutes. Remove from the heat and stir gently for a few seconds to distribute the fruit in the liquid.

Ladle boiling water from the canning pot into the bowl with the lids. Using a jar lifter, remove the sterilized jars from the canning pot, carefully pouring the water from each one back into the pot, and place them upright on a folded towel. Drain the water off the jar lids.

Remove the vanilla-bean pods and ladle the hot jam into the jars, leaving ¼ inch headspace at the top. Slide a piece of vanilla-bean pod into each jar so that it's visible from the outside. Use a damp paper towel to wipe the rims of the jars, then put a flat lid and ring on each jar, adjusting the ring so that it's just finger-tight. Return the jars to the water in the canning pot, making sure the water covers the jars by at least 1 inch. Bring to a boil, and boil for 5 minutes to process. Remove the jars to a folded towel and do not disturb for 12 hours. After 1 hour, check that the lids have sealed by pressing down on the center of each; if it can be pushed down, it hasn't sealed, and the jar should be refrigerated immediately. Label the sealed jars and store.

Apricot Halves with Honey and Ginger

MAKES ABOUT 4 PINT JARS

◇◇

SERVE THESE WITH A PANNA COTTA OR FLAN,
IN SMALL BOWLS WITH A CRISP COOKIE ON
THE SIDE. Or use them in place of the peaches in
Toffee-Topped Vanilla Peaches (page 109).

4 pounds small ripe apricots, halved and pitted (no
    need to peel)
½ cup strained fresh lemon juice
Zest of 1 lemon, removed in large strips with a
    vegetable peeler
¾ cup sugar
½ cup mild honey
4 teaspoons chopped fresh ginger or crystallized
    ginger (page 70)

Prepare for water-bath canning: Wash the jars and
keep them hot in the canning pot, and put the flat
lids in a heatproof bowl. (See page 21 for details.)

Sprinkle the apricots with a little of the lemon juice
and set aside.

In a large pot, combine the remaining lemon juice,
the lemon zest, sugar, honey, and 4 cups water.
Bring to a boil, stirring to dissolve the sugar.

Ladle boiling water from the canning pot into the
bowl with the lids. Using a jar lifter, remove the hot
jars from the canning pot, carefully pouring the
water from each one back into the pot, and place
them upright on a folded towel. Drain the water off
the jar lids.

Pack the apricot halves into the hot jars, leaving 1
inch headspace at the top, and divide the ginger
among the jars. Ladle in the boiling syrup, dividing
the zest equally among the jars. Use a chopstick to
remove air bubbles around the inside of each jar.
Use a damp paper towel to wipe the rims of the jars,
then put a flat lid and ring on each jar, adjusting the
ring so that it's just finger-tight. Return the jars to
the water in the canning pot, making sure the water
covers the jars by at least 1 inch. Bring to a boil, and
boil for 15 minutes to process. Remove the jars to a
folded towel and do not disturb for 12 hours. After
1 hour, check that the lids have sealed by pressing down on the center of each; if it can be pushed
down, it hasn't sealed, and the jar should be refrigerated immediately. Label the sealed jars and store.

FREEZING PEACHES, NECTARINES, APRICOTS, AND PLUMS

For peaches, nectarines, and apricots, which
tend to discolor, fill a large bowl with water and
stir in about 1 teaspoon ascorbic acid mix (such
as Fruit Fresh), or 1 tablespoon lemon juice or
vinegar. Rinse the fruit, peel peaches if desired
(see page 108), then halve, pit, and slice the fruit,
dropping them into the acidulated water as you
slice. Drain well, and toss with a bit of sugar—I use
about 1 tablespoon per quart of fruit. The sugar
helps the fruit maintain its shape and flavor over
the months in the freezer. Pack in freezer bags
and lay them flat to freeze. Thaw and add sugar
and a thickener such as instant tapioca, flour, or
cornstarch to use in cobblers, crisps, and pies, or
just spoon the fruit over something creamy.

Blackberry Jam with Lemon Zest

MAKES ABOUT 5 HALF-PINT JARS

◇◇

1 pound Granny Smith apples (about 3 small)

3 pounds blackberries (about 8 cups), rinsed

2 cups sugar

3 tablespoons strained fresh lemon juice

Grated zest of 2 small lemons

Prepare for water-bath canning: Sterilize the jars and keep them hot in the canning pot, put a small plate in the freezer, and put the flat lids in a heat-proof bowl. (See page 21 for details.)

Quarter and core the apples, reserving the cores and seeds. Put as many of the apple trimmings in a jelly bag or 4 layers of cheesecloth as will fit, and tie the bag closed.

Put the blackberries and sugar in a wide, 6- to 8-quart preserving pan. Bring to a simmer, stirring frequently, then continue to cook until the juices are just deep enough to cover the blackberries, about 5 minutes. Pour into a colander set over a large bowl and stir the berries gently to drain off the juice. Return the juice to the pan, along with the apples and the bag with the trimmings. Bring to a boil over high heat and cook, stirring occasionally, until the syrup is reduced and thick and registers about 220°F on a candy thermometer, 15 to 20 minutes.

Return the blackberries and any accumulated juice, along with the lemon juice and zest, to the pan and bring to a simmer. Simmer, stirring frequently, until a small dab of the jam spooned onto the chilled plate and returned to the freezer for a minute wrinkles when you nudge it, about 10 minutes. Remove from the heat and stir gently for a few seconds to distribute the fruit in the liquid. Remove the bag and the apples. (Reserve the apples for another use; see page 94.)

Ladle boiling water from the canning pot into the bowl with the lids. Using a jar lifter, remove the sterilized jars from the canning pot, carefully pouring the water from each one back into the pot, and place them upright on a folded towel. Drain the water off the jar lids.

Ladle the hot jam into the jars, leaving ¼ inch headspace at the top. Use a damp paper towel to wipe the rims of the jars, then put a flat lid and ring on each jar, adjusting the ring so that it's just finger-tight. Return the jars to the water in the canning pot, making sure the water covers the jars by at least 1 inch. Bring to a boil, and boil for 5 minutes to process. Remove the jars to a folded towel and do not disturb for 12 hours. After 1 hour, check that the lids have sealed by pressing down on the center of each; if it can be pushed down, it hasn't sealed, and the jar should be refrigerated immediately. Label the sealed jars and store.

Old-Fashioned Blackberry Jelly

MAKES ABOUT 5 HALF-PINT JARS

ONE OF THE MOST COMPELLING REASONS TO PICK YOUR OWN BLACKBERRIES IS THAT YOU CAN SNAG A FEW TART, JUST-UNDERRIPE BERRIES FOR MAKING JELLY WITHOUT ADDED COMMERCIAL PECTIN. Store-bought or even prepicked produce is likely to be all ripe, sweet, and not as good for jelly making. The jelly's even better made with wild berries, whose seeds add a touch of bitterness to the juice that I think pleasantly offsets the sweetness.

4 pounds blackberries, preferably wild, some of them tart and not quite ripe, gently rinsed
About 3 cups sugar
3 tablespoons strained fresh lemon juice

Put the blackberries in a wide, 6- to 8-quart preserving pan and crush them with your hands. Add ½ cup water and bring to a boil; boil until the berries are tender and have released their juices, about 5 minutes.

Set a large, very-fine-mesh sieve (or jelly bag) over a deep bowl or pot. Pour the blackberries into the sieve and let drain for 30 minutes, stirring occasionally but not pressing down too hard on the solids; discard the solids. Measure the juice; you should have about 4 cups.

Prepare for water-bath canning: Sterilize the jars and keep them hot in the canning pot, put a small plate in the freezer, and put the flat lids in a heat-proof bowl. (See page 21 for details.)

Rinse the preserving pan and pour in the blackberry juice. Add ¾ cup sugar for each cup of juice, then add the lemon juice. Bring to a boil over high heat and cook, stirring occasionally, until the mixture registers about 220°F on a candy thermometer or a small dab of it spooned onto the chilled plate and returned to the freezer for a minute wrinkles when you nudge it, about 20 minutes.

Ladle boiling water from the canning pot into the bowl with the lids. Using a jar lifter, remove the sterilized jars from the canning pot, carefully pouring the water from each one back into the pot, and place them upright on a folded towel. Drain the water off the jar lids.

Ladle the hot jelly into the jars, leaving ¼ inch headspace at the top. Use a damp paper towel to wipe the rims of the jars, then put a flat lid and ring on each jar, adjusting the ring so that it's just finger-tight. Return the jars to the water in the canning pot, making sure the water covers the jars by at least 1 inch. Bring to a boil, and boil for 5 minutes to process. Remove the jars to a folded towel and do not disturb for 12 hours. After 1 hour, check that the lids have sealed by pressing down on the center of each; if it can be pushed down, it hasn't sealed, and the jar should be refrigerated immediately. Label the sealed jars and store.

Blackberry Frozen Yogurt

MAKES ABOUT 3 QUARTS

◇◇◇

THE BASIC FROZEN YOGURT TECHNIQUE DETAILED HERE CAN BE ADAPTED TO JUST ABOUT ANY FRUIT. (Obviously some fruit will need to be diced before it's cooked, and some won't need any straining to remove seeds.) My mom made it every July with black raspberries, and because it keeps so well—at least 6 months in the freezer—I always make plenty of it to enjoy any time I miss fresh berries. The egg whites add body and help keep the frozen yogurt soft enough to scoop out straight from the freezer—or with just a little time at room temperature. The whites are not cooked, however, so if your immune system is compromised, you should simply omit them and the cream of tartar and salt, and reduce the sugar to 2 cups.

Consider starting this project the night before with a bit of homemade yogurt making—you'll need quite a lot of yogurt for this recipe, and making your own is much more economical than buying it.

4 cups blackberries

2¼ cups sugar

3 large eggs, separated

4 teaspoons fresh lemon juice

4 teaspoons pure vanilla extract

¼ teaspoon salt

¼ teaspoon cream of tartar

2 quarts Yogurt (page 287)

Put the blackberries and 2 cups of the sugar in a small saucepan; bring to a boil and cook, stirring, until the sugar is dissolved and the berries are broken down a bit.

In a large bowl, beat the egg yolks. Set a sieve over the bowl, add about half the blackberry mixture, and use a spatula to push the mixture through and remove some of the seeds. (If you'd prefer no seeds, strain the other half of the blackberry mixture; I tend to like the texture they provide.) Stir in the remaining blackberry mixture, the lemon juice, and vanilla. Set the bowl in another bowl of ice water and let cool to room temperature, stirring frequently. Chill in the refrigerator for at least 4 hours.

Beat the egg whites, salt, and cream of tartar until soft peaks form. Add the remaining ¼ cup sugar and continue beating until stiff peaks form.

In a large bowl, whisk the yogurt, then fold in the blackberry mixture, then fold the yogurt mixture into the egg whites.

Freeze in an ice cream maker until it's the consistency of runny soft-serve ice cream, then transfer to the freezer until completely frozen.

✳ OPPOSITE: Blackberry Frozen Yogurt
ABOVE: Old-Fashioned Blackberry

Blueberry and Apple Jam

MAKES ABOUT 5 HALF-PINT JARS

◇◇

1 pound Granny Smith apples (about 3 small)

2 pounds blueberries, rinsed

1½ cups sugar

3 tablespoons fresh lemon juice

Grated zest of 1 lemon

Prepare for water-bath canning: Sterilize the jars and keep them hot in the canning pot, put a small plate in the freezer, and put the flat lids in a heat-proof bowl. (See page 21 for details.)

Peel, core, and dice the apples, reserving the peels, cores, and seeds. Put as many of the apple trimmings in a jelly bag or 4 layers of cheesecloth as will fit, and tie the bag closed.

Put the blueberries and sugar in a wide, 6- to 8-quart preserving pan. Bring to a simmer, stirring frequently, then continue to cook until the juices are just deep enough to cover the blueberries, about 5 minutes. Pour into a colander set over a large bowl and stir the berries gently to drain off the juice. Return the juice to the pan, along with the apples and the bag with the trimmings, and bring to a boil over high heat. Boil, stirring occasionally, until the syrup is reduced and thick and registers about 220°F on a candy thermometer, 15 to 20 minutes.

Return the blueberries and any accumulated juice, along with the lemon juice and zest, to the pan and bring to a simmer. Simmer, stirring frequently, until a small dab of the jam spooned onto the chilled plate and returned to the freezer for a minute wrinkles when you nudge it, 5 to 8 minutes. Remove from the heat and stir gently for a few seconds to distribute the fruit in the liquid.

Ladle boiling water from the canning pot into the bowl with the lids. Using a jar lifter, remove the sterilized jars from the canning pot, carefully pouring the water from each one back into the pot, and place them upright on a folded towel. Drain the water off the jar lids.

Ladle the hot jam into the jars, leaving ¼ inch headspace at the top. Use a damp paper towel to wipe the rims of the jars, then put a flat lid and ring on each jar, adjusting the ring so that it's just finger-tight. Return the jars to the water in the canning pot, making sure the water covers the jars by at least 1 inch. Bring to a boil, and boil for 5 minutes to process. Remove the jars to a folded towel and do not disturb for 12 hours. After 1 hour, check that the lids have sealed by pressing down on the center of each; if it can be pushed down, it hasn't sealed, and the jar should be refrigerated immediately. Label the sealed jars and store.

FREEZING BLUEBERRIES

In the name of research, I froze a bunch of blueberries with dry ice, as Alton Brown does with strawberries, but I started to feel dizzy as I stood there picking the little BBs out of the dry ice one by one, the ones in the bag thawing as I put more on top of them, so I can't recommend doing this yourself. Just eat the darn blueberries when you have them, or make them into ice cream, or toss the berries (unwashed) straight into freezer bags and rinse them when you use them.

Blueberry and Meyer Lemon Marmalade

MAKES ABOUT 5 HALF-PINT JARS

MEYER LEMONS MAKE EXCELLENT MARMA-LADES (SEE THE MEYER LEMON AND ROSE PETAL MARMALADE ON PAGE 250 FOR A PURE ONE): The rind is milder and more floral than that of regular lemons, and the flesh and juice are super tart. Blueberries are low in natural pectin, so blueberry preserves benefit from the addition of whole citrus—the fragrant but not overpowering Meyer lemon is an ideal match.

1 pound Meyer lemons (about 4), well scrubbed
2 pounds blueberries, rinsed
2 tablespoons fresh lemon juice (Meyer or regular)
1½ cups sugar

Prepare for water-bath canning: Sterilize the jars and keep them hot in the canning pot, put a small plate in the freezer, and put the flat lids in a heat-proof bowl. (See page 21 for details.)

Cut the top and bottom off each Meyer lemon and cut the lemon into segments (see page 257), leaving the peel on and reserving the membranes and seeds. Cut the lemon segments crosswise into ¼-inch chunks. Put the lemon membranes and seeds in a jelly bag or 4 layers of cheesecloth and tie the bag closed. Set the lemons and bag aside.

Put the blueberries, lemon juice, and sugar in a wide, 6- to 8-quart preserving pan. Bring to a simmer, stirring frequently, then continue to cook until the juices are just deep enough to cover the blueberries, about 5 minutes. Pour into a colander set over a large bowl and stir the berries gently to drain off the juice. Return the juice to the pan and bring to a boil over high heat. Add the lemons and the bag with the lemon trimmings. Boil, stirring

occasionally, until the syrup is reduced and thick and registers about 220°F on a candy thermometer, 15 to 20 minutes.

Return the blueberries and any accumulated juice to the pan and bring to a simmer. Simmer, stirring frequently, until a small dab of the jam spooned onto the chilled plate and returned to the freezer for a minute wrinkles when you nudge it, 5 to 8 minutes. Squeeze as much of the juice as possible from the bag into the jam in the pan, then discard the membranes and seeds. Remove from the heat and stir gently for a few seconds to distribute the fruit in the liquid.

Ladle boiling water from the canning pot into the bowl with the lids. Using a jar lifter, remove the sterilized jars from the canning pot, carefully pouring the water from each one back into the pot, and place them upright on a folded towel. Drain the water off the jar lids.

Ladle the hot marmalade into the jars, leaving ¼ inch headspace at the top. Use a damp paper towel to wipe the rims of the jars, then put a flat lid and ring on each jar, adjusting the ring so that it's just finger-tight. Return the jars to the water in the canning pot, making sure the water covers the jars by at least 1 inch. Bring to a boil, and boil for 5 minutes to process. Remove the jars to a folded towel and do not disturb for 12 hours. After 1 hour, check that the lids have sealed by pressing down on the center of each; if it can be pushed down, it hasn't sealed, and the jar should be refrigerated immediately. Label the sealed jars and store.

Brandied Sweet Cherries with Red Wine

MAKES ABOUT 6 HALF-PINT JARS

SO EASY AND REWARDING! You don't even have to process these; just store them in the refrigerator, where they'll keep for at least a couple months (you might want to halve the quantities, though, for the sake of refrigerator shelf space). They are a great excuse for making Sidecars (page 99) or Manhattans, or Roast Cornish Hens (page 92)—that is, if you can resist swiping them from the jar.

2 cups brandy

1 cup red wine

1 cup sugar

Zest of 1 orange, removed in large strips with a
    vegetable peeler

3 pounds sweet cherries, pitted (see page 99)

Prepare for water-bath canning: Sterilize the jars and keep them hot in the canning pot, put a small plate in the freezer, and put the flat lids in a heat-proof bowl. (See page 21 for details.)

In a wide, 6- to 8-quart preserving pan, combine the brandy, wine, sugar, and orange zest. Bring to a boil, stirring to dissolve the sugar. Boil for 5 minutes, then add the cherries, return to a boil, and lower the heat and simmer, stirring occasionally, until the cherries are tender but still hold their shape, about 5 minutes. Remove from the heat.

Ladle boiling water from the canning pot into the bowl with the lids. Using a jar lifter, remove the sterilized jars from the canning pot, carefully pouring the water from each one back into the pot, and place them upright on a folded towel. Drain the water off the jar lids.

Ladle the hot cherries and syrup into the jars, leaving ¼ inch headspace at the top. Use a damp paper towel to wipe the rims of the jars, then put a flat lid and ring on each jar, adjusting the ring so that it's just finger-tight. Return the jars to the water in the canning pot, making sure the water covers the jars by at least 1 inch. Bring to a boil, and boil for 5 minutes to process. Remove the jars to a folded towel and do not disturb for 12 hours. After 1 hour, check that the lids have sealed by pressing down on the center of each; if it can be pushed down, it hasn't sealed, and the jar should be refrigerated immediately. Label the sealed jars and store.

Holiday Cherries

MAKES ABOUT 5 HALF-PINT JARS

THIS IS ADAPTED FROM A RECIPE FOR SPICED CHERRIES IN CATHERINE PLAGEMANN'S WONDERFUL *FINE PRESERVING*, WHICH WAS PUBLISHED IN 1967 AND REISSUED IN THE '80S IN AN EDITION ANNOTATED BY M.F.K. FISHER. Fisher had strong opinions about many of the preserves in the book ("Banana jam sounds not only awful but impossible"). It probably speaks highly of this cherry preserve that Fisher felt no need to comment on it.

Preserves made with dark sweet cherries (such as Bing) are delicious, but they pale somewhat in comparison to those made with sour (or "pie") cherries—which sadly fall into the category of fruit crops Americans won't support with their dollars, probably because tart fruits don't tend to provide immediate satisfaction when eaten raw (quince and red currants are in this neglected group). That's why I love these vinegared cherries so much: The tart-sweet syrup somehow brings out the intense cherry flavor that can be missing in the standard Bing. They get better with age and so, with their sweet spices, are perfect to pop open during the holidays (perhaps a time, too, when the relatively high sugar content of these preserves won't be minded so much). Plagemann suggests arranging the whole cherries over custard in a tart and topping the entire thing with whipped cream, and that sounds neat to me, too.

1 cup cider vinegar (5% acidity)

3 cups sugar

½ teaspoon ground cinnamon

½ teaspoon ground cloves

¼ teaspoon ground allspice

Small pinch of ground cayenne

2 pounds sweet cherries, pitted (see page 99; about
   5 cups)

Prepare for water-bath canning: Sterilize the jars and keep them hot in the canning pot, put a small plate in the freezer, and put the flat lids in a heat-proof bowl. (See page 21 for details.)

In a wide, 6- to 8-quart preserving pan, combine the vinegar, sugar, and spices. Bring to a boil, stirring to dissolve the sugar. Add the cherries, return to a boil, then lower the heat and simmer, stirring occasionally, until a small dab of the syrup spooned onto the chilled plate and returned to the freezer for a minute becomes somewhat thick, about 10 minutes. Remove from the heat and stir gently for a few seconds to distribute the fruit in the liquid.

Ladle boiling water from the canning pot into the bowl with the lids. Using a jar lifter, remove the sterilized jars from the canning pot, carefully pouring the water from each one back into the pot, and place them upright on a folded towel. Drain the water off the jar lids.

Ladle the hot cherries and syrup into the jars, leaving ¼ inch headspace at the top. Use a damp paper towel to wipe the rims of the jars, then put a flat lid and ring on each jar, adjusting the ring so that it's just finger-tight. Return the jars to the water in the canning pot, making sure the water covers the jars by at least 1 inch. Bring to a boil, and boil for 5 minutes to process. Remove the jars to a folded towel and do not disturb for 12 hours. After 1 hour, check that the lids have sealed by pressing down on the center of each; if it can be pushed down, it hasn't sealed, and the jar should be refrigerated immediately. Label the sealed jars and store.

Roast Cornish Hens with Brandied Cherries

SERVES 2

CORNISH HENS, WHICH ARE ACTUALLY NOTHING MORE THAN SMALL CHICKENS, ARE NOT ONLY TASTY (THE BREAST MEAT STAYS MOIST WITH ROASTING AT HIGH HEAT, AND THE DARK MEAT IS LESS FATTY THAN THAT OF NORMAL-SIZED CHICKENS); THEY'RE ALSO INCREDIBLY CONVENIENT. Usually available frozen, they're quick to thaw: Put them, still in their packaging, in a bowl of cold water set in the sink and let cold water from the faucet just barely drip into the bowl to keep the water moving; small ones should be thawed and ready to go in about 45 minutes.

2 small (1¼-pound) Cornish hens
Pure kosher salt and freshly ground black pepper
½ cup beef or chicken stock
½ pint Brandied Sweet Cherries with Red Wine
   (page 90)
1 tablespoon cold unsalted butter

Preheat the oven to 500°F.

"Spatchcock" the hens: Use a heavy knife or poultry shears to cut along either side of the backbone and remove it. Lay the hens out flat on a cutting board, breast side up, and press down in the center with your palm to crack the breastbone and flatten the hens. Pat dry with paper towels and season generously on both sides with salt and pepper.

Put a large, oven-safe skillet or sauté pan over medium-high heat for 2 minutes. Add the hens, breast side down, and cook for about 5 minutes, until nicely browned on the bottom, pressing down on them with a spatula occasionally so that more surface area is browned. Turn the hens over, then transfer the skillet to the oven. Roast until the juices are clear (not pink) when the thigh is pricked with a small knife and you can easily wiggle a drumstick in its socket, 20 to 25 minutes. Carefully remove the hens to a cutting board and let rest for 5 minutes.

While the hens are resting, return the skillet to medium heat. Add the stock, stirring to scrape up any browned bits on the bottom of the skillet. Cook for 1 minute. Drain the cherries, reserving 2 tablespoons of the syrup, and add the cherries and syrup to the skillet. Cook until the sauce has reduced by about half, about 2 minutes. Swirl in the butter until melted, then taste and season with salt and pepper if necessary. Serve the hens with the cherries and sauce spooned over the top.

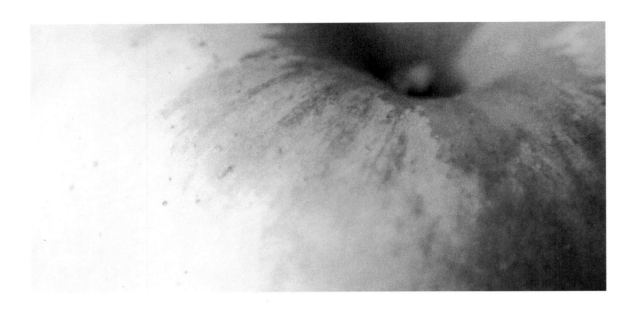

THE QUARTERED APPLES

In several of the jam recipes here, you're asked to cook quartered, unpeeled green apples with a lower-pectin fruit and then remove the apples when their work—pectin contribution—is finished. I've done several wonderful things with these syrup-infused apples. They never go to waste.

Most obviously, you can just squeeze the pulp from the peel, discard the peel, and return the pulp to the jam. In most cases it won't alter the flavor or appearance of the jam much at all. In some jams with a more delicate flavor, however, such as peach, it's best to pull the apples out so they don't compete with the main fruit.

Squeeze out the pulp, mash it up, and fold it into unsweetened whipped cream, like a simplified "fool" (page 118), or make a slightly fancier dessert like a trifle, layering the mashed apples with whipped cream or yogurt and crushed crisp cookies, amaretti, or even plain old graham crackers.

If you have space in the canning pot for one more jar, mash the pulp, heat it in a small saucepan just until it bubbles (adding a bit of water or juice from the jam if necessary to keep it from sticking), and spoon it into a sterilized jar, leaving ¼ inch headspace. Wipe the rim, put the lid on, and process it for 5 minutes when you process the other jars of jam. It makes a nice spread on its own.

Freeze it and use it in spice cake batters; see the Afternoon Applesauce Spice Cake on page 182 for a recipe using plain unsweetened green apple pulp—reduce the sugar a bit if you use apples from jam making.

Cherry Jam

MAKES ABOUT 6 HALF-PINT JARS

◇◇◇

YOU CAN USE EITHER SWEET (BING) OR SOUR CHERRIES FOR THIS JAM. If you use sweet cherries, consider using only 1½ cups sugar (though this will result in a slightly looser consistency), and adding the lemon zest to make up for the lack of tartness in the cherries. If you prefer a fairly thick jam, go ahead and leave the apple pulp in—it won't appreciably diminish the cherry flavor here; just use tongs to pick out the peels when they start to separate from the softened apples, and then smush the pulp up a bit to incorporate it into the cherries. If you're feeling weird and decadent, swirl a few ounces of chopped dark chocolate into the jam at the last minute.

1 pound Granny Smith apples (about 4 small)

4 pounds sweet or sour cherries (about 10 cups), rinsed and pitted (see page 99)

1½ to 2 cups sugar

3 tablespoons strained fresh lemon juice

Grated zest of 1 lemon (optional)

Prepare for water-bath canning: Sterilize the jars and keep them hot in the canning pot, put a small plate in the freezer, and put the flat lids in a heatproof bowl. (See page 21 for details.)

Quarter and core the apples, reserving the cores and seeds. Put as many of the apple trimmings in a jelly bag or 4 layers of cheesecloth as will fit, and tie the bag closed.

Put the cherries and sugar in a wide, 6- to 8-quart preserving pan. Bring to a simmer, stirring gently to keep from breaking the cherries apart, then continue to cook until the juices are just deep enough to cover the cherries, about 5 minutes. Pour into

a colander set over a large bowl and let the juice drain. Return the juice to the pan, along with the apples and the bag with the trimmings. Bring to a boil over high heat and cook, stirring occasionally, until the syrup is reduced and thick, 10 to 15 minutes.

Return the cherries and any accumulated juice, along with the lemon juice and zest, to the pan and bring to a simmer. Simmer, stirring frequently, until a small dab of the jam spooned onto the chilled plate and returned to the freezer for a minute wrinkles when you nudge it, about 10 minutes. Remove from the heat. Remove the bag and the apples. (Reserve the apples for another use; see opposite.)

Ladle boiling water from the canning pot into the bowl with the lids. Using a jar lifter, remove the sterilized jars from the canning pot, carefully pouring the water from each one back into the pot, and place them upright on a folded towel. Drain the water off the jar lids.

Ladle the jam into the jars, leaving ¼ inch headspace at the top. Use a damp paper towel to wipe the rims of the jars, then put a flat lid and ring on each jar, adjusting the ring so that it's just fingertight. Return the jars to the water in the canning pot, making sure the water covers the jars by at least 1 inch. Bring to a boil, and boil for 5 minutes to process. Remove the jars to a folded towel and do not disturb for 12 hours. After 1 hour, check that the lids have sealed by pressing down on the center of each; if it can be pushed down, it hasn't sealed, and the jar should be refrigerated immediately. Label the sealed jars and store.

Cherry Macaroon Tarts

MAKES 12 MUFFIN-SIZE TARTS

A TRADITIONAL ENGLISH BAKEWELL TART CONSISTS OF A SWEET SHORT CRUST SPREAD WITH A THIN LAYER OF JAM AND CROWNED BY A SPONGY EGG-BUTTER-ALMOND TOPPING. The macaroon topping in this somewhat simplified version is based on a mincemeat tart recipe in an old British cookbook of my mom's. You can use any jam you have on hand, but cherries work especially well here. And instead of the jam, of course, chunky, dark mincemeat would be delicious, as would a smooth layer of tangy lemon curd.

For the pastry shells:

2 cups all-purpose flour

½ cup sugar

¼ teaspoon pure kosher salt

¾ cup (1½ sticks) cold unsalted butter, cut into bits

2 large egg yolks

Grated zest of 1 lemon (optional)

For the filling:

2 large egg whites

Pinch of salt

6 tablespoons sugar

3 ounces finely ground almonds (¾ cup)

⅛ teaspoon almond extract

1 pint Cherry Jam (page 95)

Sliced or coarsely chopped almonds

Preheat the oven to 375°F. Butter a 12-cup dark (or nonstick) standard-size muffin pan.

Make the pastry shells: In a large bowl, combine the flour, sugar, and salt. Using your fingertips, two knives held together, or a pastry cutter, cut in the butter until the largest pieces are the size of peas. Lightly beat the egg yolks in a small bowl, then drizzle them into the flour mixture, tossing with your hands or a spatula to combine. Gather the dough into a ball. If it's very soft, wrap in plastic and chill in the refrigerator until firm.

Roll out the dough to about ⅛ inch thick. Cut out 12 (3¼- to 3½-inch) rounds (a tuna can works well) and fit them into the prepared muffin cups. Put in the freezer to chill while you make the filling.

Make the filling: In a medium bowl, beat the egg whites together with the salt until firm peaks form. Gradually add the sugar, beating until glossy, firm peaks form and the sugar is dissolved. Gently fold in the ground almonds and almond extract.

Put about 1 tablespoon of the jam in each pastry shell, then spoon in the egg white mixture, filling each shell to the top and spreading it so it covers the jam. Sprinkle each with a few sliced almonds. Bake on the center rack of the oven for 25 to 30 minutes, or until the edges of the crust and topping are just starting to turn golden brown. Let cool in the pan on a wire rack, then tip out the tarts and serve.

Sour Cherry Preserves

MAKES ABOUT 7 HALF-PINT JARS (IF MACERATED OVERNIGHT; 6 IF NOT)

◇◇◇

IF I COULD HAVE ONLY ONE FRUIT PRESERVE FOR THE REST OF MY LIFE, THIS WOULD BE IT. Tart, tender cherries in slightly sweet, not-too-thick syrup—I can't imagine anything better dripping off creamy peaks of hard-frozen ice cream, or puddled next to a plain cake, or as the most important part of a Black Forest Cake. Just about any cocktail—a Manhattan, for example, or a Sidecar (page 99)—would be better with a few preserved sour cherries sunk in the bottom. Or try spreading Lemon Curd (page 245) in tartlet shells and spoon the cherries and some of their syrup over it.

You don't have to let the cherries macerate in the syrup overnight, but it does result in much rounder, plumper, prettier fruit.

4 pounds sour cherries (about 10 cups), rinsed and
    pitted (see page 99)
2 cups sugar
1 pound Granny Smith apples (about 3 small)
3 tablespoons strained fresh lemon juice

Prepare for water-bath canning: Sterilize the jars and keep them hot in the canning pot, put a small plate in the freezer, and put the flat lids in a heat-proof bowl. (See page 21 for details.)

Put the cherries and sugar in a wide, 6- to 8-quart preserving pan. Bring to a simmer, stirring gently to keep from breaking the cherries apart, and cook just until the juices are deep enough to cover the cherries. Remove from the heat, let cool to room temperature, cover, and let soak overnight.

Quarter and core the apples, reserving the cores and seeds. Put as many of the apple trimmings in a jelly bag or 4 layers of cheesecloth as will fit, and tie the bag closed.

Pour the cherries into a colander set over a large bowl and let the juice drain. Return the juice to the pan, along with the apples and the bag with the trimmings. Bring to a boil over high heat and cook, stirring occasionally, until the syrup is reduced and thick, 10 to 15 minutes.

Return the cherries and any accumulated juice, along with the lemon juice, to the pan and bring to a simmer. Simmer, stirring frequently, until the cherries are just tender, about 5 minutes. Remove from the heat. Remove the bag and the apples. (Reserve the apples for another use; see page 94.)

Ladle boiling water from the canning pot into the bowl with the lids. Using a jar lifter, remove the sterilized jars from the canning pot, carefully pouring the water from each one back into the pot, and place them upright on a folded towel. Drain the water off the jar lids.

Use a slotted spoon to put the cherries in the jars, leaving ½ inch headspace at the top. Ladle in the syrup, leaving ¼ inch headspace. Use a chopstick to remove air bubbles around the inside of each jar. Use a damp paper towel to wipe the rims of the jars, then put a flat lid and ring on each jar, adjusting the ring so that it's just finger-tight. Return the jars to the water in the canning pot, making sure the water covers the jars by at least 1 inch. Bring to a boil, and boil for 5 minutes to process. Remove the jars to a folded towel and do not disturb for 12 hours. After 1 hour, check that the lids have sealed by pressing down on the center of each; if it can be pushed down, it hasn't sealed, and the jar should be refrigerated immediately. Label the sealed jars and store.

The Perfect Sidecar

MAKES 2 COCKTAILS

THE SIDECAR IS ONE OF MY FAVORITE COCK-TAILS—TART AND JUST A LITTLE SWEET, IT'S WARMING IN WINTERTIME AND REFRESHING IN THE SUMMER. You can replace the Cointreau, a lovely liqueur made from bitter oranges, with another orange liqueur such as (not-blue) curaçao or even triple sec . . . but then it wouldn't be quite perfect. Fresh lemon juice is a must; bottled leaves an unpleasant aftertaste. And as always with cocktails that are shaken over ice, *use lots and lots of good-sized ice cubes, and shake well,* for at least 5 seconds past the point at which condensation forms on the outside of the shaker. This will both thoroughly chill the drink and whip up a fine froth that will float to the top of the finished drink all pretty and festive-like.

Vanilla sugar, preferably superfine
3 tablespoons freshly squeezed lemon juice (reserve a piece of the squeezed lemon)
2 tablespoons Cointreau
¼ cup brandy
2 Brandied Sweet Cherries (page 90) or Sour Cherry Preserves (page 97)

Chill 2 small stemmed cocktail glasses in the freezer. Spread the vanilla sugar on a small plate. Rub the rim of each glass with the reserved piece of lemon and dip it in the sugar.

Fill a cocktail shaker with ice and add the lemon juice, Cointreau, and brandy. Shake well, then immediately strain into the prepared glasses. Drop in the cherries and serve immediately.

CHERRY PITTING: YOU HAVE OPTIONS

At U-pick cherry orchards, my dad likes to ask the proprietors which row the pitless cherries are in (har). But until that travesty hits the grocery stores alongside seedless—and bland—watermelons, pit we must. For jam, or for any application in which the cherries can (or should) be chopped or broken down into pieces, a mechanical cherry pitter is perfectly acceptable. The Oxo cherry-and-olive pitter is pretty effective and easy to use. For preserves, in which you want the cherries to retain their shape as much as possible, however, the best tool is one that leaves only one hole in the fruit, and that would be a large regular paperclip. Unfold it so that there's a bight, or bend, at each end. Hold the large bend in your dominant hand, the cherry in your other hand, and insert the small bend into the top of the cherry. Gently lever and pull the pit out. This method works best with fresh, tender sour cherries (after you have a quarter pound of cherries under your belt it'll become second nature, and will likely be faster than the Oxo); it works somewhat less well with very firm sweet cherries that have been refrigerated.

Mango Jam with Lime

MAKES ABOUT 8 HALF-PINT JARS

◇◇

THE ACIDITY OF RIPE MANGOES VARIES CON-
SIDERABLY, AND SOME MAY NOT BE QUITE
ACID ENOUGH FOR SAFE BOILING-WATER-
BATH PROCESSING. The pairing with lime here
would be appropriately tasty even if it weren't
necessary. Mangoes are also low in pectin, so I've
enlisted a few green apples for a bit of thickening.

About 8 pounds ripe mangoes (about 5 large)
1 pound Granny Smith apples (about 3 small)
2 cups sugar
⅓ cup strained fresh lime juice
3 tablespoons strained fresh lemon juice

Peel and pit the mangoes and thinly slice them.
Quarter and core the apples, reserving the cores
and seeds. Put the apple trimmings in a jelly bag or
4 layers of cheesecloth, and tie the bag closed. Set
aside.

Prepare for water-bath canning: Sterilize the jars
and keep them hot in the canning pot, put a small
plate in the freezer, and put the flat lids in a heat-
proof bowl. (See page 21 for details.)

Put the mangoes, apple quarters, the bag with the
trimmings, and the remaining ingredients in a wide,
6- to 8-quart preserving pan. Bring to a simmer,
stirring frequently, then continue to cook until a
small dab of the jam spooned onto the chilled plate
and returned to the freezer for a minute becomes
somewhat firm (it will not gel), about 20 minutes.
Remove the bag and the apples. (Reserve the apples
for another use; see page 94).

Ladle boiling water from the canning pot into the
bowl with the lids. Using a jar lifter, remove the
sterilized jars from the canning pot, carefully pouring the water from each one back into the pot, and
place them upright on a folded towel. Drain the
water off the jar lids.

Ladle the hot jam into the jars, leaving ¼ inch
headspace at the top. Use a damp paper towel to
wipe the rims of the jars, then put a flat lid and
ring on each jar, adjusting the ring so that it's just
finger-tight. Return the jars to the water in the canning pot, making sure the water covers the jars by
at least 1 inch. Bring to a boil, and boil for 5 minutes
to process. Remove the jars to a folded towel and do
not disturb for 12 hours. After 1 hour, check that the
lids have sealed by pressing down on the center of
each; if it can be pushed down, it hasn't sealed, and
the jar should be refrigerated immediately. Label
the sealed jars and store.

Mango and Peach Habanero Hot Sauce

MAKES ABOUT 10 FOUR-OUNCE JARS, OR 5 HALF-PINT JARS

◇◇◇

HABANERO AND SCOTCH BONNET CHILES ARE BOTH VARIETIES OF THE SPECIES *CAPSICUM CHINENSE*, THE ONLY DIFFERENCE BEING POD SHAPE. They're some of the hottest peppers in the world, with a Scoville heat rating of something like 66 billion, but they're also some of the most flavorful.

This hot sauce is hot, yes, but you won't have to put a lot of *X*s on the jar labels: The complementary fruit, salt, and acid tame the heat enough to allow all those flavors to have their way with your palate. Taste as you go, and add more salt or honey if you'd like. If you'd prefer a thinner sauce, add more lime juice or vinegar; don't, however, use less, and don't add more chiles, or you could compromise the pH level and safety of the canned sauce.

If you want to put this sauce in a bunch of tiny four-ounce sample-size jars (a little goes a long way, and this is an excellent candidate for gift giving), simply load as many full jars into your canning pot as will fit, process them for 10 minutes, then remove them, carefully lower the remaining jars into the hot water, return the remaining sauce to a simmer, then fill the hot jars and process as before.

12 orange or red habanero or Scotch bonnet chiles
1 pound, 6 ounces mangoes, chopped (about 3 cups)
6 ounces peaches, diced (about 1 cup)
¾ cup fresh lime juice, or more to taste (but not less)
½ cup cider vinegar (5% acidity)
4 teaspoons pure kosher salt
1 tablespoon honey

Prepare for water-bath canning: Wash the jars and keep them hot in the canning pot, and put the flat lids in a heatproof bowl. (See page 21 for details.)

Wearing kitchen gloves and being very careful to keep chile juice off your skin and, especially, out of your eyes, cut the chiles in half, remove the seeds and stems, and coarsely chop. Put them in a wide, 6- to 8-quart preserving pan with the remaining ingredients and bring to a simmer. Cook, stirring frequently to prevent sticking, until the chiles are soft, about 10 minutes. Working in batches, and covering the blender with a towel, puree the mixture until very smooth, then return it to the pan. Bring just to a simmer, keeping the pan partly covered, as the sauce has a tendency to pop up out of the pan as it simmers.

Ladle boiling water from the canning pot into the bowl with the lids. Using a jar lifter, remove the hot jars from the canning pot, carefully pouring the water from each one back into the pot, and place them upright on a folded towel. Drain the water off the jar lids.

Ladle the hot mixture into the jars, leaving ¼ inch headspace at the top. Use a damp paper towel to wipe the rims of the jars, then put a flat lid and ring on each jar, adjusting the ring so that it's just finger-tight. Return the jars to the water in the canning pot, making sure the water covers the jars by at least 1 inch. Bring to a boil, and boil four-ounce and half-pint jars for 10 minutes to process. Remove the jars to a folded towel and do not disturb for 12 hours. After 1 hour, check that the lids have sealed by pressing down on the center of each; if it can be pushed down, it hasn't sealed, and the jar should be refrigerated immediately. Label the sealed jars and store.

Jerk Chicken

SERVES 4 TO 6

SLOSH SOME CHICKEN PIECES AROUND IN THIS FRUITY, HOT, AND AROMATIC MARINADE FOR AN EASY RENDITION OF JAMAICAN JERK BARBECUE. Serve with coconut-milk-infused rice and red beans, maybe with a pile of Pickled Greens with Chiles (page 231) on the side.

1 (4-ounce) jar Mango and Peach Habanero Hot Sauce (opposite)

2 tablespoons whole allspice, ground in a spice mill

⅓ cup chopped, fresh thyme

½ onion, chopped; or 3 scallions, chopped

1 tablespoon brown sugar

1 teaspoon pure kosher salt

2 (3-pound) chickens, cut into 8 serving pieces each, or about 4 pounds chicken pieces

In a mini food processor, combine all the ingredients except the chicken and process to a paste. Put the chicken in a gallon-size resealable plastic bag and scrape in the jerk paste. Close the bag and toss it around to coat the chicken with the paste. Let marinate in the refrigerator for at least 4 hours, or up to overnight.

Preheat the oven to 350°F. Alternatively, prepare a charcoal fire with plenty of charcoal piled to one side of the grill.

Lightly oil a large baking dish and arrange the chicken pieces in it skin side up. Roast until well browned and the juices from a thigh piece run clear when pierced with a knife, about 45 minutes. If grilling, when the coals are white, put the chicken on the grate about 6 inches above the coals. Cover the grill and cook, turning occasionally and moving the pieces to hotter or cooler areas as necessary to avoid flare-ups and to prevent burning.

Serve with plain white rice or rice and peas.

DRIED GROUND HABANERO CHILES

You don't often see habanero chile powder, but the stuff is brilliant, and it retains its potency for years—I know, because for years I hoarded and doled out pinches of the little container of ground habanero my mom gave me when I moved away from home (no desk set for me) as if it were platinum-plated saffron. If you happen to have a glut of fresh chiles, string them up using a needle and thread and hang them in a warm, dry spot for a couple weeks. (Alternatively, cut them in half and dry them in a dehydrator.) When they're completely dry and brittle, pulverize them in a spice grinder, then transfer to an airtight container and keep in a dark, cool cupboard. I like to add a few shakes to cold tomato juice and Bloody Marys, and you could also pound some chopped scallions, fresh thyme, ground allspice, rum, brown sugar, and some ground habanero together with a mortar and pestle for another variation on jerk paste rub.

Green Mango Chutney with Whole Spices

MAKES ABOUT 11 HALF-PINT JARS, OR 4 PINT JARS

◇◇◇

THIS RECIPE IS ADAPTED FROM ONE IN NEELAM BATRA'S *1,000 INDIAN RECIPES*, AN EXCELLENT BOOK THAT'S JUST LOADED WITH INTERESTING CHUTNEY AND PICKLE RECIPES. Use only hard, tart unripe green mangoes that are being sold specifically as green mangoes—some varieties stay green even when they're ripe.

The chutney suffers not a bit from being processed in two batches if your canning pot isn't large enough to hold all eleven jars at once (whose is?). Just return the chutney to a boil before ladling it into the second batch of jars and processing.

6 pounds firm, unripe green mangoes (about 6)

2 tablespoons fennel seeds

1 tablespoon green cardamom pods, lightly crushed

1 tablespoon whole black peppercorns

4 teaspoons crushed fenugreek seeds

2 teaspoons *kalonji* seeds

2 teaspoons whole cloves

1 teaspoon ground cinnamon

4½ cups sugar

4 teaspoons pure kosher salt

2 small hot green chiles such as serrano, minced

1 cup distilled white vinegar (5% acidity)

Using a vegetable peeler, peel the mangoes. Cut each side off the pit, halve each slab lengthwise, and cut into ¼-inch-thick slices. Cut as much of the remaining flesh off the pit as you can. Set aside.

Prepare for water-bath canning: Sterilize the jars and keep them hot in the canning pot, and put the flat lids in a heatproof bowl. (See page 21 for details.)

In a wide, 6- to 8-quart preserving pan over medium-high heat, toast the fennel, cardamom, peppercorns, fenugreek, *kalonji*, and cloves for 1 minute. Add ½ cup water, the cinnamon, sugar, salt, chiles, and mangoes and stir to combine. Bring to a boil, stirring constantly, then lower the heat and simmer briskly for about 10 minutes, skimming the foam from the surface and stirring occasionally, until the mango slices are evenly translucent.

Add the vinegar, return to a brisk simmer, and cook, stirring occasionally, for 20 to 25 minutes longer, until the liquid has thickened somewhat and the mangoes are falling apart.

Ladle boiling water from the canning pot into the bowl with the lids. Using a jar lifter, remove the sterilized jars from the canning pot, carefully pouring the water from each one back into the pot, and place them upright on a folded towel. Drain the water off the jar lids.

Ladle the hot chutney into the jars, leaving ¼ inch headspace at the top. Use a chopstick to remove air bubbles around the inside of each jar. Use a damp paper towel to wipe the rims of the jars, then put a flat lid and ring on each jar, adjusting the ring so that it's just finger-tight. Return the jars to the water in the canning pot, making sure the water covers the jars by at least 1 inch. Bring to a boil, and boil half-pint jars for 5 minutes or pint jars for 10 minutes to process. Remove the jars to a folded towel and do not disturb for 12 hours. After 1 hour, check that the lids have sealed by pressing down on the center of each; if it can be pushed down, it hasn't sealed, and the jar should be refrigerated immediately. Label the sealed jars and store.

Nectarine Jam

MAKES ABOUT 6 HALF-PINT JARS

◇◇

UNTIL ONE DAY THIS PAST SUMMER, I'D COM-PLETELY FORGOTTEN ABOUT NECTARINES. Sort of shoved between the peaches and plums, they just didn't exist to me in any meaningful way. On a lark (yes, it's a wild life I lead, it's true), I bought two of them at the local grocery store. That evening after supper, I found myself cutting them up, putting them in bowls, and pouring milk over them for Thalia—just as my mom had done probably once a week for our dessert when my brother and I were kids. It happens that the specimens I'd bought were stellar examples of the nectarine form, and Thalia sweetly declared nectarines and milk to be "the best bedtime snack [she'd] ever had," and for me they were a revelation. I called my mom about them, and she said, "Of course they're good. They're like peaches, but easier."

The nectarine is actually a type of peach with a smooth skin. Nectarines also tend to be sweeter than fuzzy peaches. The smooth and tender skin, and the fact that nectarines are usually quite firm even when very ripe and flavorful, make them ideal for use in preserves: You don't have to peel them, and the juice they give off has time to cook down and thicken while the fruit becomes tender in the pot. I like to add one or two split vanilla beans right at the beginning. When you're filling the jars, slip a piece of vanilla bean in too.

Perhaps the prettiest preserve I've ever made was a combination of orange and white nectarines suspended in their pink-hued syrup.

4 pounds orange or white nectarines, pitted and
    chopped (about 10 cups)
1½ cups sugar
3 tablespoons strained fresh lemon juice

Prepare for water-bath canning: Sterilize the jars and keep them hot in the canning pot, put a small plate in the freezer, and put the flat lids in a heat-proof bowl. (See page 21 for details.)

Put the nectarines, sugar, and lemon juice in a wide, 6- to 8-quart preserving pan. Bring to a simmer, stirring frequently, and cook until the nectarines are very tender and somewhat translucent but still hold their shape, and a small dab of the jam spooned onto the cold plate and set in the freezer for a minute becomes somewhat firm (it will not gel), about 25 minutes. Remove from the heat and stir gently for a few seconds to distribute the fruit in the liquid.

Ladle boiling water from the canning pot into the bowl with the lids. Using a jar lifter, remove the sterilized jars from the canning pot, carefully pouring the water from each one back into the pot, and place them upright on a folded towel. Drain the water off the jar lids.

Ladle the hot jam into the jars, leaving ¼ inch headspace at the top. Use a damp paper towel to wipe the rims of the jars, then put a flat lid and ring on each jar, adjusting the ring so that it's just finger-tight. Return the jars to the water in the canning pot, making sure the water covers the jars by at least 1 inch. Bring to a boil, and boil for 5 minutes to process. Remove the jars to a folded towel and do not disturb for 12 hours. After 1 hour, check that the lids have sealed by pressing down on the center of each; if it can be pushed down, it hasn't sealed, and the jar should be refrigerated immediately. Label the sealed jars and store.

Peaches in Vanilla Syrup

MAKES ABOUT 10 PINT JARS OR 4 QUART JARS

◇◇◇

USE LATE-SEASON FREESTONE PEACHES FOR THIS RECIPE. If you have to, buy one, go out to the car, and cut it open to make sure the pit comes out easily before springing for 8 pounds' worth, because 8 pounds is a lot to pit if they're clingstone.

1 teaspoon ascorbic acid mix (such as Fruit Fresh), or
    1 tablespoon lemon juice or vinegar
8 pounds peaches
4 cups sugar
2 vanilla beans, split, each piece cut in half

Fill a large bowl or pot with cold water and stir in the ascorbic acid mix. Blanch and peel the peaches (see sidebar), putting them in the acidulated water as you peel. Halve and pit the peaches. Slice or quarter them. Return to the acidulated water.

Prepare for water-bath canning: Wash the jars and keep them hot in the canning pot, and put the flat lids in a heatproof bowl. (See page 21 for details.)

In a large saucepan, combine the sugar and 2 quarts water and bring the syrup to a boil.

Ladle boiling water from the canning pot into the bowl with the lids. Using a jar lifter, remove the hot jars from the canning pot, carefully pouring the water from each one back into the pot, and place them upright on a folded towel. Drain the water off the jar lids.

Drain the peaches and pack them tightly into the jars, leaving 1 inch headspace at the top. Ladle the hot syrup into the jars, leaving ½ inch headspace. Slip 1 or 2 pieces of vanilla bean into each jar. Use a chopstick to remove air bubbles around the inside of each jar. Use a damp paper towel to wipe the rims of the jars, then drain the water off the jar lids and put a flat lid and ring on each jar, adjusting the ring so that it's just finger-tight. Return the jars to the water in the canning pot, making sure the water covers the jars by at least ½ inch. Bring to a boil, and boil pints for 20 minutes or quarts for 25 minutes. Remove the jars to a folded towel and do not disturb for 12 hours. After 1 hour, check that the lids have sealed by pressing down on the center of each; if it can be pushed down, it hasn't sealed, and the jar should be refrigerated immediately. Label the sealed jars and store.

PEELING PEACHES

Bring a large pot of water to a boil, and fill a large bowl with ice water. Gently drop 3 or 4 peaches into the water, then fish them out with a slotted spoon after 30 seconds to 1 minute and put them in the ice water to cool. Slip off the peels. Easy, right? Right. Except that some peaches resist peeling like a toddler resists bedtime. I've read that peaches ripened on the tree rather than after picking are easier to peel, but of course unless you pick them yourself it's hard to know where they ripened. And in my experience, even tree-ripened peaches don't always come through like peeling champions. Sometimes rubbing the peel with dry paper towels can remove it, but sometimes the paring knife is the only solution.

Toffee-Topped Vanilla Peaches

SERVES 4

IN A WEIRD OLD BRITISH COOKBOOK FROM MY MOM'S COLLECTION I SAW A RECIPE FOR "TOFFEE" PEACHES THAT LOOKED TOO EASY TO BE GOOD. I wondered how peaches covered with whipped cream and coarse sugar and broiled could possibly impress. And why the ridiculous "toffee" descriptor? How could this be like toffee? I probably don't have to tell you that this adaptation of the recipe may be one of the most delightful dishes you cook from this book. The vanilla bean–specked peaches and pillowy whipped cream mingle where they meet, and the sugar melts into the very top of the cream and caramelizes at the edges ever so slightly into something that's neither cream nor sugar but better than either. You can use room-temperature peaches straight from the jar, or you can do all the preparation in advance and chill the custard cups in the refrigerator for several hours before broiling, making this an excellent dinner-party dessert. Also, you could certainly put the whole thing in one larger baking dish and just scoop out individual servings.

1 quart Peaches in Vanilla Syrup (opposite)
¾ cup heavy cream
3 teaspoons coarse turbinado or Demerara sugar

Preheat the broiler to high and set a rack 4 inches from the heating element. Put 4 broiler-safe custard cups or ramekins on a baking sheet.

Drain the peaches and divide them among the custard cups. Set aside.

Whip the cream until firm peaks form, then dollop it over the peaches in the cups. Sprinkle each cup with ¾ teaspoon of the sugar. Broil, watching closely so the sugar doesn't burn, until the sugar is bubbly and golden brown around the edges, about 3 minutes. Carefully transfer the cups to napkin-lined plates and serve immediately.

> ### PITTING STONE FRUIT
>
> Cut the fruit in half through the crease, grasp one hemisphere in the palm of each hand, and twist your hands, hard, in opposite directions. One half will pull away from the pit. If the second half doesn't come off the pit easily, use a spoon (a serrated grapefruit spoon works well) to dig the pit out. Some people then scrape the reddish-brown flesh off the area that was in contact with the pit, but I never bother.

Classic Peach Jam

MAKES ABOUT 5 HALF-PINT JARS

◇⨯⨯⨯⨯⨯⨯⨯⨯⨯⨯⨯⨯⨯⨯⨯⨯⨯⨯⨯⨯⨯⨯⨯⨯⨯⨯⨯⨯⨯⨯⨯⨯◇

CLASSIC EXCEPT FOR THE MUCH LOWER SUGAR CONTENT, THAT IS—AND THE APPLES. Put this naturally sweet, golden-pink preserve on good, old-fashioned Southern-style biscuits, and you may never find cause to make another jam.

12 ounces Granny Smith apples (about 2 large)
4 pounds peaches, peeled, pitted (see pages 108 and 109), and diced (about 6 cups)
2 cups sugar
3 tablespoons strained fresh lemon juice

Prepare for water-bath canning: Sterilize the jars and keep them hot in the canning pot, put a small plate in the freezer, and put the flat lids in a heat-proof bowl. (See page 21 for details.)

Cut the apples into quarters and core them. Tie the cores and seeds in a cheesecloth bag and set aside.

Put the peaches and sugar in a wide, 6- to 8-quart preserving pan. Bring to a simmer, stirring frequently, and cook until the juices just cover the peaches. Pour into a colander set over a large bowl and stir the peaches gently to drain off the juice. Return the juice to the pan, along with the apples and cheesecloth bag, and bring to a boil over high heat. Boil, stirring occasionally, until the syrup is thick and reduced, about 15 minutes.

Return the peaches and any accumulated juice to the pan, along with the lemon juice, and bring to a simmer. Simmer, stirring frequently, until the peaches are very tender and a small dab of the jam spooned onto the chilled plate and returned to the freezer for a minute becomes somewhat firm (it will not gel), about 15 minutes. Remove from the heat and stir gently for a few seconds to distribute the fruit in the liquid. Remove the bag and the apples. (Reserve the apples for another use; see page 94.)

Ladle boiling water from the canning pot into the bowl with the lids. Using a jar lifter, remove the sterilized jars from the canning pot, carefully pouring the water from each one back into the pot, and place them upright on a folded towel. Drain the water off the jar lids.

Ladle the hot jam into the jars, leaving ¼ inch headspace at the top. Use a damp paper towel to wipe the rims of the jars, then put a flat lid and ring on each jar, adjusting the ring so that it's just finger-tight. Return the jars to the water in the canning pot, making sure the water covers the jars by at least 1 inch. Bring to a boil, and boil for 5 minutes to process. Remove the jars to a folded towel and do not disturb for 12 hours. After 1 hour, check that the lids have sealed by pressing down on the center of each; if it can be pushed down, it hasn't sealed, and the jar should be refrigerated immediately. Label the sealed jars and store.

Peach Jam with Lemon Thyme and Almonds

MAKES ABOUT 5 HALF-PINT JARS

◇◇

WITH A BIT OF TOASTY CRUNCH AND A SUBTLE HERBAL FRAGRANCE, THIS JAM IS EXCEEDINGLY ELEGANT. It would not be out of place on a cheese plate or alongside a dollop of crème fraîche and a delicate shortbread cookie.

½ cup slivered almonds

12 ounces Granny Smith apples (about 2 large)

4 pounds peaches, peeled, pitted (see pages 108 and 109), and diced (about 6 cups)

1½ cups sugar

3 tablespoons strained fresh lemon juice

2 teaspoons fresh lemon thyme leaves

Prepare for water-bath canning: Sterilize the jars and keep them hot in the canning pot, put a small plate in the freezer, and put the flat lids in a heat-proof bowl. (See page 21 for details.)

In a small skillet over medium-high heat, toast the almonds, stirring constantly, until golden brown and fragrant, about 3 minutes. Remove to a plate and set aside.

Cut the apples into quarters and core them. Tie the cores and seeds in a cheesecloth bag and set aside.

Put the peaches and sugar in a wide, 6- to 8-quart preserving pan. Bring to a simmer, stirring frequently, and cook until the juices just cover the peaches. Pour into a colander set over a large bowl and stir the peaches gently to drain off the juice. Return the juice to the pan, along with the apples and cheesecloth bag, and bring to a boil over high heat. Boil, stirring occasionally, until the syrup is thick and reduced, about 15 minutes.

Return the peaches and any accumulated juice to the pan, along with the lemon juice, almonds, and thyme, and bring to a simmer. Simmer, stirring frequently, until the peaches are very tender and a small dab of the jam spooned onto the chilled plate and returned to the freezer for a minute becomes somewhat firm (it will not gel), about 15 minutes. Remove from the heat and stir gently for a few seconds to distribute the fruit in the liquid. Remove the bag and the apples. (Reserve the apples for another use; see page 94.)

Ladle boiling water from the canning pot into the bowl with the lids. Using a jar lifter, remove the sterilized jars from the canning pot, carefully pouring the water from each one back into the pot, and place them upright on a folded towel. Drain the water off the jar lids.

Ladle the hot jam into the jars, leaving ¼ inch headspace at the top. Use a damp paper towel to wipe the rims of the jars, then put a flat lid and ring on each jar, adjusting the ring so that it's just finger-tight. Return the jars to the water in the canning pot, making sure the water covers the jars by at least 1 inch. Bring to a boil, and boil for 5 minutes to process. Remove the jars to a folded towel and do not disturb for 12 hours. After 1 hour, check that the lids have sealed by pressing down on the center of each; if it can be pushed down, it hasn't sealed, and the jar should be refrigerated immediately. Label the sealed jars and store.

Peach and Cilantro Salsa

MAKES ABOUT 5 PINT JARS

◇◇

SWEET PEACHES AND TART LIME, SPICY SER-RANOS AND FRAGRANT CILANTRO: This salsa is great not only with tortilla chips and tacos and such but also with grilled pork loin or fish.

5 pounds ripe peaches, peeled, pitted (see pages 108 and 109), and diced (about 9 cups)

½ cup fresh lime juice

6 ounces sweet onion, diced (about 1 cup)

3 ounces red bell pepper, diced (about ½ cup)

2 tablespoons minced seeded serrano chiles

4 to 6 tablespoons sugar, to taste

4 teaspoons pure kosher salt

¼ cup cider vinegar (5% acidity)

1 teaspoon crushed red pepper flakes

½ cup chopped fresh cilantro

2 tablespoons chopped fresh mint

Prepare for water-bath canning: Wash the jars and keep them hot in the canning pot, and put the flat lids in a heatproof bowl. (See page 21 for details.)

Put all the ingredients except the cilantro and mint in a wide, 6- to 8-quart preserving pan. Bring to a boil over high heat, then lower the heat and simmer, stirring occasionally, until the onion is tender and the peaches are soft and easy to smush against the side of the pot with the spoon, about 30 minutes. Stir in the cilantro and mint.

Ladle boiling water from the canning pot into the bowl with the lids. Using a jar lifter, remove the hot jars from the canning pot, carefully pouring the water from each one back into the pot, and place them upright on a folded towel. Drain the water off the jar lids.

Ladle the hot salsa into the jars, leaving ¼ inch headspace at the top. Use a damp paper towel to wipe the rims of the jars, then put a flat lid and ring on each jar, adjusting the ring so that it's just finger-tight. Return the jars to the water in the canning pot, making sure the water covers the jars by at least 1 inch. Bring to a boil, and boil for 10 minutes to process. Remove the jars to a folded towel and do not disturb for 12 hours. After 1 hour, check that the lids have sealed by pressing down on the center of each; if it can be pushed down, it hasn't sealed, and the jar should be refrigerated immediately. Label the sealed jars and store.

Pineapple Jam with Chinese Five-Spice

MAKES ABOUT 3 HALF-PINT JARS

THIS IS ONE SWEET JAM (AND MANY OTHER RECIPES FOR PINEAPPLE PRESERVES USE EVEN MORE SUGAR THAN THIS!), BUT PINEAPPLE ITSELF IS INTENSELY SO, AND THIS IS ONE INSTANCE WHERE I ACTUALLY PREFER AN ALMOST CARAMELIZED FLAVOR. The savory five-spice tones down the brightness a bit, and the jam becomes a deep caramel color as it reduces. Besides the obvious uses (on banana splits, for example, or in a pork marinade cut with some cider vinegar and cayenne), having a jar of it on hand brings you at least an hour closer to Malaysian Chinese New Year Pineapple Tarts (page 114).

You can puree all of the pineapple if you prefer a smoother, pastelike spread, or if you plan to use it all in tarts; I like the texture of half puree, half slices.

1 (5-pound) pineapple, washed, peel and eyes
    removed (see Note), quartered, and cored
2 cups sugar
3 tablespoons strained fresh lemon juice
¾ teaspoon Chinese five-spice powder (cinnamon,
    cloves, star anise, fennel, and Szechuan pepper-
    corns)

Cut the pineapple quarters lengthwise into 4 strips, then thinly slice; you should have about 8 cups. In a food processor, puree about half of it until finely ground.

Prepare for water-bath canning: Sterilize the jars and keep them hot in the canning pot, put a small plate in the freezer, and put the flat lids in a heat-proof bowl. (See page 21 for details.)

Put all of the pineapple, the sugar, lemon juice, and five-spice powder in a wide, 6- to 8-quart preserving pan and bring to a boil over high heat. Cook, stirring frequently, until the jam is thick and caramel colored and a dab of it spooned onto the chilled plate and returned to the freezer for a minute becomes somewhat firm (it will not gel), about 45 minutes. Skim off as much foam as you can, then remove from the heat and stir gently for a few seconds to distribute the fruit in the liquid.

Ladle boiling water from the canning pot into the bowl with the lids. Using a jar lifter, remove the sterilized jars from the canning pot, carefully pouring the water from each one back into the pot, and place them upright on a folded towel. Drain the water off the jar lids.

Ladle the hot jam into the jars, leaving ¼ inch headspace at the top. Use a chopstick to remove air bubbles around the inside of each jar. Use a damp paper towel to wipe the rims of the jars, then put a flat lid and ring on each jar, adjusting the ring so that it's just finger-tight. Return the jars to the water in the canning pot, making sure the water covers the jars by at least 1 inch. Bring to a boil, and boil for 5 minutes to process. Remove the jars to a folded towel and do not disturb for 12 hours. After 1 hour, check that the lids have sealed by pressing down on the center of each; if it can be pushed down, it hasn't sealed, and the jar should be refrigerated immediately. Label the sealed jars and store.

Note: To remove the eyes with as little waste and fuss as possible, use a chef's knife to cut them out in shallow diagonal strips that spiral around the pineapple from top to bottom.

Malaysian Chinese New Year Pineapple Tarts

MAKES ABOUT 30 TARTS

◇◇

THIS VERSION OF THE TRADITIONAL CELE-
BRATORY PASTRIES CONSISTS OF BUTTERY-
TENDER COOKIE DOUGH SURROUNDING
INTENSE PINEAPPLE JAM IN SHORT LOG
SHAPES. If forming the logs (just one of several
common shapes for the tarts) proves too fussy, you
could form them into tricorner hammantaschen-
type cookies instead by pulling three sides of the
circle up over the filling and sealing into a triangle
shape. Have them with tea in the afternoon, or serve
them as part of a Chinese New Year feast.

2½ cups all-purpose flour
3 tablespoons confectioners' sugar
2 tablespoons cornstarch
¼ teaspoon salt
1 cup (2 sticks) unsalted butter, at room temperature
3 large egg yolks
1 pint Pineapple Jam with Chinese Five-Spice (page
    113), pureed in a food processor

In a medium bowl, whisk together the flour, confectioners' sugar, cornstarch, and salt. Set aside.

In a large bowl, using an electric mixer, cream the
butter until smooth. Add 2 of the egg yolks and
beat to combine. Gradually add the flour mixture,
stirring until it is incorporated; the dough will look
like coarse bread crumbs, but if it's very dry add a
tablespoon or two of cold water. Gather the dough
into a ball, cover with plastic wrap, and chill in the
refrigerator for 30 minutes.

Preheat the oven to 350°F. Line two baking sheets
with parchment paper.

Working with half of the dough at a time, roll the
dough out between sheets of waxed paper ⅛ inch
thick; cut out 3-inch circles (a standard-mouth
canning jar ring makes a good cutter). Put 1 scant
teaspoon of the jam in the center of each circle,
then fold up the edges of the dough to completely
enclose the jam in a log shape, pinching the seam
together tightly. (The logs will look a bit like
quenelles, or little kayaks.) Repeat with the remaining dough and jam, placing the filled tarts seam
side down on the baking sheets at least 1 inch apart.
Use a sharp knife to score the tops, being careful
not to cut all the way through the dough. Beat the
remaining egg yolk together with 1 teaspoon water
and brush it over the tops of the tarts. Bake for 20
to 25 minutes, until golden brown. Remove to wire
racks to cool completely before serving.

Pineapple and Peach Jam with Mint

MAKES ABOUT 4 HALF-PINT JARS

◇◇

1 (3½-pound) pineapple, washed, peel and eyes
    removed (see page 113), quartered, and cored

1½ pounds peaches, peeled, pitted (see pages 108 and
    109), and thinly sliced (about 2½ cups)

1½ cups sugar

3 tablespoons strained fresh lemon juice

1 tablespoon minced fresh mint

Prepare for water-bath canning: Sterilize the jars
and keep them hot in the canning pot, put a small
plate in the freezer, and put the flat lids in a heat-
proof bowl. (See page 21 for details.)

Cut the pineapple quarters lengthwise into 4 strips,
then thinly slice; you should have about 4 cups.

Put the pineapple, peaches, and sugar in a wide,
6- to 8-quart preserving pan. Bring to a simmer, stirring frequently, and cook until the juices just cover
the fruit. Pour into a colander set over a large bowl
and stir the fruit gently to drain off the juice. Return
the juice to the pan and bring to a boil over high
heat. Boil, stirring occasionally, until the syrup is
thick and reduced, about 10 minutes.

Return the fruit and any accumulated juice to the
pan, along with the lemon juice, and bring to a
simmer. Simmer, stirring frequently, until the fruit
is very tender and a small dab of the jam spooned
onto the chilled plate and returned to the freezer for
a minute becomes somewhat firm (it will not gel),
about 15 minutes. Remove from the heat and stir in
the mint.

Ladle boiling water from the canning pot into the
bowl with the lids. Using a jar lifter, remove the
sterilized jars from the canning pot, carefully pouring the water from each one back into the pot, and
place them upright on a folded towel. Drain the
water off the jar lids.

Ladle the hot jam into the jars, leaving ¼ inch
headspace at the top. Use a damp paper towel to
wipe the rims of the jars, then put a flat lid and
ring on each jar, adjusting the ring so that it's just
finger-tight. Return the jars to the water in the canning pot, making sure the water covers the jars by
at least 1 inch. Bring to a boil, and boil for 5 minutes
to process. Remove the jars to a folded towel and do
not disturb for 12 hours. After 1 hour, check that the
lids have sealed by pressing down on the center of
each; if it can be pushed down, it hasn't sealed, and
the jar should be refrigerated immediately. Label
the sealed jars and store.

Cardamom Plum Jam

MAKES ABOUT 5 HALF-PINT JARS

◇◇

THIS IS ONE OF MY FAVORITE JAMS OF ALL TIME: UNCOMPLICATED, FAIRLY TART, AND AROMATIC. Black plums with dark red flesh make a deep ruby jam, but even yellow-fleshed black plums will take on a rosy tint.

4 pounds ripe black plums, pitted and diced
2 cups sugar
3 tablespoons strained fresh lime juice
1 tablespoon freshly ground cardamom seeds (or a little more if using preground)

Prepare for water-bath canning: Sterilize the jars and keep them hot in the canning pot, put a small plate in the freezer, and put the flat lids in a heat-proof bowl. (See page 21 for details.)

Put the plums and sugar in a wide, 6- to 8-quart preserving pan. Bring to a simmer, stirring frequently, then continue to cook for 5 minutes. Pour into a colander set over a large bowl and stir the plums gently to drain off the juice. Return the juice to the pan and bring to a boil over high heat. Boil, stirring occasionally, until the syrup is reduced and thick, about 10 minutes.

Return the plums and any accumulated juice to the pan, along with the lime juice and cardamom, and bring to a simmer. Simmer, stirring frequently, until a small dab of the jam spooned onto the cold plate and set in the freezer for a minute becomes somewhat firm (it will not gel), about 15 minutes. Remove from the heat.

Ladle boiling water from the canning pot into the bowl with the lids. Using a jar lifter, remove the sterilized jars from the canning pot, carefully pouring the water from each one back into the pot, and place them upright on a folded towel. Drain the water off the jar lids.

Ladle the hot jam into the jars, leaving ¼ inch headspace at the top. Use a damp paper towel to wipe the rims of the jars, then put a flat lid and ring on each jar, adjusting the ring so that it's just finger-tight. Return the jars to the water in the canning pot, making sure the water covers the jars by at least 1 inch. Bring to a boil, and boil for 5 minutes to process. Remove the jars to a folded towel and do not disturb for 12 hours. After 1 hour, check that the lids have sealed by pressing down on the center of each; if it can be pushed down, it hasn't sealed, and the jar should be refrigerated immediately. Label the sealed jars and store.

FRUIT-JUICE STAIN REMOVAL

Black plums and sweet cherries stain clothes and dish towels like very few things do, and especially if your kitchen helper is a three-year-old, you'll probably have a few items of laundry charmingly decorated with mauve to blood-red splotches at the end of a morning of jam making. Here's how to get the stains out: Lay the stained clothes out flat in the bathtub, and bring a kettle of water to a boil. Quickly bring the kettle to the tub and, holding it as high as possible (standing on a chair next to the tub if you have to), pour the close-to-boiling water directly onto the stains. They should disappear. Repeat if necessary, then wash the clothes or towels in a washing machine or by hand.

Blood Plum and Apple Jam with Rosewater

MAKES ABOUT 5 HALF-PINT JARS

◇◇◇

TINY, DEEP CRIMSON BLOOD PLUMS HAVE A VERY DELICATE FLAVOR THAT PAIRS NICELY WITH FRAGRANT ROSEWATER. The apples add just enough pectin to make a thickish spread, and themselves thicken the juices a bit.

3 pounds small blood plums, pitted and diced (about 6 cups)

10 ounces Granny Smith apples (about 2 small)

1½ cups sugar

3 tablespoons strained fresh lemon juice

1 tablespoon rosewater

Prepare for water-bath canning: Sterilize the jars and keep them hot in the canning pot, put a small plate in the freezer, and put the flat lids in a heat-proof bowl. (See page 21 for details.)

Peel, core, and dice the apples, reserving the peels, cores, and seeds. Put as many of the apple trimmings in a jelly bag or 4 layers of cheesecloth as will fit, and tie the bag closed.

Put the plums and sugar in a wide, 6- to 8-quart preserving pan. Bring to a simmer, stirring frequently, then continue to cook until the juices are just deep enough to cover the plums, about 5 minutes. Pour into a colander set over a large bowl and stir the plums gently to drain off the juice. Return the juice to the pan, along with the apples and the bag with the trimmings, and bring to a boil over high heat. Boil, stirring occasionally, until the syrup is reduced and thick, 10 to 15 minutes.

Return the plums and any accumulated juice, along with the lemon juice, to the pan and bring to a simmer. Simmer, stirring frequently, until a small dab of the jam spooned onto the chilled plate and returned to the freezer for a minute becomes somewhat firm (it will not gel) and the apples are very soft, about 15 minutes. Remove from the heat, stir in the rosewater, and stir gently for a few seconds to distribute the fruit in the liquid.

Ladle boiling water from the canning pot into the bowl with the lids. Using a jar lifter, remove the sterilized jars from the canning pot, carefully pouring the water from each one back into the pot, and place them upright on a folded towel. Drain the water off the jar lids.

Ladle the hot jam into the jars, leaving ¼ inch headspace at the top. Use a damp paper towel to wipe the rims of the jars, then put a flat lid and ring on each jar, adjusting the ring so that it's just finger-tight. Return the jars to the water in the canning pot, making sure the water covers the jars by at least 1 inch. Bring to a boil, and boil for 5 minutes to process. Remove the jars to a folded towel and do not disturb for 12 hours. After 1 hour, check that the lids have sealed by pressing down on the center of each; if it can be pushed down, it hasn't sealed, and the jar should be refrigerated immediately. Label the sealed jars and store.

Blood Plum and Rosewater Fool

SERVES 6

JAM IS WONDERFUL JUST BARELY FOLDED INTO STABILIZED WHIPPED CREAM AND CHILLED IN SMALL DESSERT GLASSES—A CLASSIC DESSERT CALLED A "FOOL." Scatter some fresh untreated rose petals on top, if you have them.

1½ cups cold heavy cream
1 teaspoon unflavored gelatin powder
1 teaspoon rosewater
1 half-pint jar Blood Plum and Apple Jam with
   Rosewater (page 117)

Put 2 tablespoons of the cream in a tiny saucepan and sprinkle in the gelatin. Let soak for 10 minutes, then place over very low heat and cook, tilting the pan, until the gelatin is just dissolved.

Whip the remaining cream and rosewater together until soft peaks form, then gradually whisk in the gelatin mixture. Whip until firm peaks form. Put the jam in a large bowl and stir in one third of the whipped cream. Gently and quickly fold in the remaining cream, cover the bowl, and chill for 1 hour. Serve in small bowls or glasses.

MY PIE AND COBBLER FILLINGS

Pie is not at all time consuming to make start to finish, but having the fruit filling pretty much already made means that all you have to do is fix some Easy Pie Dough (page 211). Cobbler is even easier: Just mix up the topping in one bowl while you heat the filling in a baking dish in the oven.

Official recipes for canned pie fillings consist of sliced fruit in a syrup thickened with something called Clear-Jel, which is cornstarch that has been specially engineered to remain stable when heated during processing—other starches break down and lose their thickening power in the canning pot. I'm sure these pie fillings are just fine, but when putting up stone fruit or muscadines or Concord grapes to be used in pies (or cobblers), I prefer to more closely replicate what one does when making a pie from scratch, so that the juices being thickened are the fruit's own rather than plain water plus lots of modified cornstarch. I simply add the thickener—instant tapioca, a little flour, or regular cornstarch—when I open the quart jar of fruit to make the pie. If it makes life easier for you, attach a little packet containing 4 tablespoons instant tapioca or all-purpose flour, or about 3 tablespoons cornstarch, to each jar so it's all ready to go when you want to bake.

If you have space in your freezer, of course, you can just slice the fruit, put about 4 generous cups into a quart-size freezer bag, add 1 tablespoon lemon juice, ¾ to 1 cup sugar, and some spices, toss a bit to combine, and freeze the bags flat. When you want to make pie, thaw the fruit in the bag, then stir in the thickener of your choice and dump it into the pie shell (or baking dish for cobbler).

Plums for Pies and Cobblers

MAKES 3 QUARTS, ENOUGH FOR 3 (9-INCH) PIES

YES, YOU CAN ALWAYS FIND PLUMS AT THE SUPERMARKET, NO MATTER THE TIME OF YEAR, AND IT DOESN'T TAKE MUCH EFFORT TO PIT AND SLICE THEM FRESH FOR PIE. But as they're one of those fruits that definitely, absolutely tastes better in season than in the wintertime, I think they're well worth preserving when they're cheap and plentiful and good.

Taste the plums to see how much sugar you'll need, but be aware that plums can seem much more tart after cooking than they do raw, and also that sugar will help thicken the juices.

6 pounds plums, pitted and cut into eighths (about 12 generous cups)

3 tablespoons strained fresh lemon juice

About 3 cups sugar, or to taste

1½ teaspoons ground cinnamon

2 generous pinches ground cloves

Put the plums, lemon juice, and 2 cups of the sugar in a large bowl. Toss gently to combine. Let stand at room temperature for about 1 hour, until the plum juices are almost deep enough to cover the plums. Working in batches if necessary, drain the plums in a colander set over a nonreactive pot. Return the plums to the bowl and toss with the remaining 1 cup sugar (or more to taste), the cinnamon, and cloves.

Prepare for water-bath canning: Wash the jars and keep them hot in the canning pot, and put the flat lids in a heatproof bowl. (See page 21 for details.)

Bring the plum syrup to a boil.

Ladle boiling water from the canning pot into the bowl with the lids. Using a jar lifter, remove the hot jars from the canning pot, carefully pouring the water from each one back into the pot, and place them upright on a folded towel. Drain the water off the jar lids.

Pack the plums into the jars, leaving 1½ inches headspace at the top. Ladle the hot syrup into the jars, leaving ½ inch headspace. Use a chopstick to remove air bubbles around the inside of each jar. Use a damp paper towel to wipe the rims of the jars, then drain the water off the jar lids and put a flat lid and ring on each jar, adjusting the ring so that it's just finger-tight. Return the jars to the water in the canning pot, making sure the water covers the jars by at least 1 inch. Bring to a boil, and boil for 25 minutes to process. Remove the jars to a folded towel and do not disturb for 12 hours. After 1 hour, check that the lids have sealed by pressing down on the center of each; if it can be pushed down, it hasn't sealed, and the jar should be refrigerated immediately. Label the sealed jars and store.

Chinese Plum Sauce

MAKES ABOUT 8 HALF-PINT JARS

◇◇◇

1 cinnamon stick

2 pieces star anise

½ teaspoon whole black peppercorns

½ teaspoon fennel seeds

4 pounds black plums, pitted and coarsely chopped (about 8 cups)

1 medium onion, chopped

4 cloves garlic, chopped

¼ cup chopped peeled fresh ginger

½ cup rice vinegar (4% acidity)

3 tablespoons dark soy sauce, or more to taste

1¼ cups packed brown sugar, or more to taste

½ cup pitted prunes

½ teaspoon crushed red pepper flakes

Prepare for water-bath canning: Sterilize the jars and keep them hot in the canning pot, and put the flat lids in a heatproof bowl. (See page 21 for details.)

Put the cinnamon, star anise, peppercorns, and fennel seeds in a spice bag or several layers of cheesecloth and tie shut.

Put the bag and all the remaining ingredients in a wide, 6- to 8-quart preserving pan and bring to a boil. Lower the heat and simmer, stirring occasionally, until the onion is very soft, about 30 minutes. Remove the spice bag. Working in batches, puree the sauce in a blender, covering the lid with a towel to keep the hot liquid from erupting, and return it to the pan. Bring to a simmer and cook, stirring frequently, until thickened slightly and a shade darker in color, about 10 minutes. Taste and add more soy sauce or brown sugar as necessary. The sauce should be quite sweet and salty.

Ladle boiling water from the canning pot into the bowl with the lids. Using a jar lifter, remove the sterilized jars from the canning pot, carefully pouring the water from each one back into the pot, and place them upright on a folded towel. Drain the water off the jar lids.

Ladle the hot sauce into the jars, leaving ¼ inch headspace at the top. Use a damp paper towel to wipe the rims of the jars, then put a flat lid and ring on each jar, adjusting the ring so that it's just finger-tight. Return the jars to the water in the canning pot, making sure the water covers the jars by at least 1 inch. Bring to a boil, and boil for 5 minutes to process. Remove the jars to a folded towel and do not disturb for 12 hours. After 1 hour, check that the lids have sealed by pressing down on the center of each; if it can be pushed down, it hasn't sealed, and the jar should be refrigerated immediately. Label the sealed jars and store.

Mu Shu Pork with Plum Sauce

SERVES 4 TO 6

CAVEAT: THIS IS A TOTALLY INAUTHENTIC VERSION OF MU SHU PORK, WHICH IS SUPPOSED TO INCLUDE LOTUS BUDS. No matter. This dish, loaded with crunchy cabbage, silky shredded egg, and meaty mushrooms (yes, you could leave out the pork for a vegetarian version), in a glistening, dark, sweet-sour-salty plum sauce, is immensely satisfying. The pancakes are unbelievably simple to make, but if you're pressed for time, just serve the dish with steamed white rice.

For the Mandarin pancakes:
2 cups all-purpose flour
1 cup boiling water
2 tablespoons sesame oil

For the filling:
3 tablespoons dark soy sauce
3 tablespoons Shaoxing (Chinese cooking wine) or dry sherry
1 pint Chinese Plum Sauce (opposite)
Vegetable oil
3 large eggs, lightly beaten
8 ounces extra-thin boneless pork chops, cut into ⅛-inch-thick slices
½ cup (about ½ ounce) dried wood ear mushrooms (a.k.a. black fungus), soaked in hot water for 30 minutes, then drained and thinly sliced
1 small head Napa cabbage, cored and thinly sliced
6 scallions, trimmed and cut into 1-inch lengths
1 (8-ounce) can sliced bamboo shoots, drained and cut into thin matchsticks

Make the Mandarin pancakes: Put the flour in a medium bowl and pour in the boiling water. Stir to combine, then knead the dough in the bowl for a couple minutes until it's smooth and not too sticky.

Shape the dough into a log about 16 inches long and wrap it in plastic wrap. Set aside for 30 minutes.

Unwrap the dough and cut the log into 16 rounds. On a lightly floured surface, using the palm of your hand, flatten the rounds into 3- to 4-inch circles. Brush half of the circles with sesame oil, cover with the remaining circles, and roll out the double circles to about 6 inches in diameter. Heat a heavy skillet over medium-high heat, then add one of the double pancakes and cook until lightly browned, about 1 minute on each side. Peel the two pancakes apart and wrap in a large piece of aluminum foil to keep warm. Repeat with the remaining pancakes to make a total of 16.

Make the filling: In a small bowl, stir together the soy sauce, Shaoxing, and ½ cup plum sauce. Set the sauce aside.

In a large sauté pan, heat 2 tablespoons oil over high heat until it shimmers, then add the eggs. After about 30 seconds, use a spatula to flip the omelet over and cook just until the bottom is set. Remove to a cutting board and thinly slice.

Return the pan to medium heat. Add 1 tablespoon oil to the pan and add the pork; cook, stirring frequently, until no longer pink, about 1 minute. Add the mushrooms, cabbage, scallions, and bamboo shoots and cook, turning constantly with tongs or a spatula, until the cabbage is wilted and tender, about 3 minutes. Add the sauce and the eggs and cook for 30 seconds to 1 minute, tossing to combine, until heated through. Serve the pancakes, filling, and the remaining plum sauce for spreading on the pancakes before filling them.

Raspberry Jam with Mint and Lavender

MAKES ABOUT 5 HALF-PINT JARS

◇◇◇

FRESH RASPBERRIES, THE DELICATE AND FRAGILE BANE OF ANY CROSS-COUNTRY FRUIT SHIPPER'S EXISTENCE, ARE IN MANY PARTS OF THE COUNTRY ALMOST TOO DEAR TO MAKE INTO A PRESERVE AND PUT INTO JARS. But raspberry preserves are so delightful—especially when, as here, just a little bit of sugar is used so that the distinctive flavor of the berries shines though—that it might be worth a fair bit of expense. This past summer, despairing over the Southeast's lack of decent berries due to various pests and droughts, I went so far as to travel—by air, *with a toddler*—to my folks' place in northeastern Washington state, where in summertime raspberries are plentiful and of amazingly good quality. My parents were kind enough to ship a few jars of this particular jam back home to Georgia for me. It's that good.

1 pound Granny Smith apples (about 4 small)

3 pounds raspberries, rinsed if necessary (about 10 cups)

2 cups sugar

3 tablespoons strained fresh lemon juice

Grated zest of 2 small lemons

1 tablespoon chopped fresh mint

2 tablespoons fresh lavender blossoms, or 2 teaspoons dried

Prepare for water-bath canning: Sterilize the jars and keep them hot in the canning pot, put a small plate in the freezer, and put the flat lids in a heat-proof bowl. (See page 21 for details.)

Quarter and core the apples, reserving the cores and seeds. Put as many of the apple trimmings in a jelly bag or 4 layers of cheesecloth as will fit, and tie the bag closed.

Put the raspberries and sugar in a wide, 6- to 8-quart preserving pan. Bring to a simmer, stirring frequently. (If you'd like fewer seeds, spoon half of the berries into a sieve held over the pan and push the juice and pulp through, discarding the seeds.) Add the apples and the bag with the trimmings, and the lemon juice and zest. Bring to a boil over high heat and cook, stirring frequently to prevent it from sticking, until a small dab of the jam spooned onto the chilled plate and returned to the freezer for a minute becomes somewhat firm (it will not gel), 15 to 20 minutes. Stir in the mint and lavender and cook for 1 minute. Remove from the heat and stir gently for a few seconds to distribute the fruit in the liquid. Remove the bag and the apples. (Reserve the apples for another use; see page 94.)

Ladle boiling water from the canning pot into the bowl with the lids. Using a jar lifter, remove the sterilized jars from the canning pot, carefully pouring the water from each one back into the pot, and place them upright on a folded towel. Drain the water off the jar lids.

Ladle the hot jam into the jars, leaving ¼ inch headspace at the top. Use a damp paper towel to wipe the rims of the jars, then put a flat lid and ring on each jar, adjusting the ring so that it's just finger-tight. Return the jars to the water in the canning pot, making sure the water covers the jars by at least 1 inch. Bring to a boil, and boil for 5 minutes to process. Remove the jars to a folded towel and do not disturb for 12 hours. After 1 hour, check that the lids have sealed by pressing down on the center of each; if it can be pushed down, it hasn't sealed, and the jar should be refrigerated immediately. Label the sealed jars and store.

Raspberry Preserves

MAKES ABOUT 5 HALF-PINT JARS

◇◇

NOW, WE MUST DISCUSS SEEDS. I'm of the opinion that any kind of berry preserve labeled "seedless," whether raspberry, blackberry, or what have you, is an affront to nature and should be destroyed so that no human or animal will be at risk of consuming such an atrocity. The seeds not only add texture and let you know what you're eating, but also provide a certain slight bitterness that I think is absolutely necessary in a berry preserve (as well as in berry ice creams and frozen yogurts). That said, I understand that they can be a bit much for the ol' chompers to deal with. But I'd like to suggest a compromise: Instead of deseeding the jam completely, remove only half the seeds.

1 pound Granny Smith apples (about 4 small)
3 pounds raspberries, rinsed if necessary (about 10 cups)
2 cups sugar
3 tablespoons strained fresh lemon juice

Prepare for water-bath canning: Sterilize the jars and keep them hot in the canning pot, put a small plate in the freezer, and put the flat lids in a heat-proof bowl. (See page 21 for details.)

Quarter and core the apples, reserving the cores and seeds. Put as many of the apple trimmings in a jelly bag or 4 layers of cheesecloth as will fit, and tie the bag closed.

Put the raspberries and sugar in a wide, 6- to 8-quart preserving pan. Bring to a simmer, stirring frequently. (If you'd like fewer seeds, spoon half of the berries into a sieve held over the pan and press them to extract as much juice and pulp as possible, discarding the seeds.) Add the apples and the bag

with the trimmings, along with the lemon juice. Bring to a boil over high heat and cook, stirring frequently to prevent it from sticking, until a small dab of the jam spooned onto the chilled plate and returned to the freezer for a minute becomes somewhat firm (it will not gel), 15 to 20 minutes. Remove from the heat and stir gently for a few seconds to distribute the fruit in the liquid. Remove the bag and the apples. (Reserve the apples for another use; see page 94.)

Ladle boiling water from the canning pot into the bowl with the lids. Using a jar lifter, remove the sterilized jars from the canning pot, carefully pouring the water from each one back into the pot, and place them upright on a folded towel. Drain the water off the jar lids.

Ladle the hot jam into the jars, leaving ¼ inch headspace at the top. Use a damp paper towel to wipe the rims of the jars, then put a flat lid and ring on each jar, adjusting the ring so that it's just finger-tight. Return the jars to the water in the canning pot, making sure the water covers the jars by at least 1 inch. Bring to a boil, and boil for 5 minutes to process. Remove the jars to a folded towel and do not disturb for 12 hours. After 1 hour, check that the lids have sealed by pressing down on the center of each; if it can be pushed down, it hasn't sealed, and the jar should be refrigerated immediately. Label the sealed jars and store.

SUMMER VEGETABLES

Long-Fermented Kosher Dill Pickles

MAKES ABOUT 5 QUART JARS

THIS IS THE PICKLE, THE REAL THING. Two or three weeks may seem like a long time to tend to a crock of pickles, but the actual work involved is minimal, and the results are extraordinary. The mild, mellow tang from the lactic acid produced by fermentation is nothing like the sharp bite of vinegared pickles—it's a subtler and more complex flavor.

Choose perfectly fresh, firm, blemish-free pickling cucumbers—the small, nubby Kirby-type ones, not the kind you'd put in a salad. Cut open a couple cucumbers before you start the batch; if they're hollow on the inside, they're no good for fermented pickles, as bacteria can survive in the air pockets.

The grape or currant leaves are optional, but the tannins in the leaves will help keep the pickles crisp by deactivating the enzyme that causes softening.

As with all cucumber pickles, pasteurizing (heating the jars in water at 180°F for 30 minutes) rather than processing in boiling water for a shorter period will result in a slightly crisper pickle. However, I've given boiling-water processing instructions as well for those without a thermometer or who are short on time. Though really: You've spent weeks on these guys already . . .

½ cup pickling spice (see page 126)

1 bunch fresh dill

Several handfuls of fresh, untreated grape (or scuppernong) or black currant leaves (optional)

7 pounds pickling cucumbers (no longer than 4 inches, if possible, for easy packing)

4 cloves garlic, peeled but left whole

1 cup cider vinegar (5% acidity; optional)

¾ cup pure kosher salt

Cut off the blossom end of each cucumber. If you can't tell which end that is, cut off both ends.

Put half of the spices in the bottom of a clean 2- to 3-gallon crock or glass jar. Add half of the dill and half of the grape leaves, if using, then add the cucumbers, filling the jar no more than two thirds full. Top with the remaining spices, dill, and grape leaves and drop in the garlic.

In a large bowl, combine the vinegar, salt, and 1 gallon cold water. Pour over the cucumbers to just cover them (you may not use all of the liquid). Set a small plate on top of the cucumbers and place a weight on top to keep them submerged in the brine (a quart-size freezer bag filled with water or extra brine works well). Cover loosely and set aside in a cool spot in the house for 2 to 3 weeks, until the pickles are no longer white in the center when cut. After about 2 days, the mixture should start to ferment and bubble; skim the foam from the surface once every day or two.

Prepare for water-bath canning: Wash the jars and keep them hot in the canning pot, and put the flat lids in a heatproof bowl. (See page 21 for details.)

Put a fine-mesh sieve over a large nonreactive pot and ladle in as much of the brine as you can. Bring to a simmer.

Ladle boiling water from the canning pot into the bowl with the lids. Using a jar lifter, remove the hot jars from the canning pot, carefully pouring the water from each one back into the pot, and place them upright on a folded towel. Drain the water off the jar lids.

Working quickly, pack the pickles in the jars as snugly as you can without damaging them. Put a garlic clove and some of the dill in each jar, along with a grape leaf, if desired. Ladle in the hot brine, leaving ½ inch headspace at the top. Use a chopstick to remove the air bubbles around the inside of each jar. Use a damp paper towel to wipe the rims of the jars, then put a flat lid and ring on each jar, adjusting the ring so that it's just finger-tight. Return the jars to the water in the canning pot, making sure the water covers the jars by at least 1 inch. If pasteurizing, bring the water in the pot to 180°F, and keep it there, adjusting the burner as necessary, for 30 minutes. (Any time the water spends below 180°F must be added to the pasteurizing time so that the water is at 180°F for a total of 30 minutes.) If processing, bring to a full boil, and boil for 10 minutes. Remove the jars to a folded towel and do not disturb for 12 hours. After 1 hour, check that the lids have sealed by pressing down on the center of each; if it can be pushed down, it hasn't sealed, and the jar should be refrigerated immediately. Label the sealed jars and store.

PICKLING SPICE

To make your own pickling spice, combine all of the following (or some mustard seeds, peppercorns, and dill seeds, plus as many of the remaining spices as you have on hand) and store in an airtight container in a dark spot for up to 6 months:

1 tablespoon black mustard seeds
1 tablespoon yellow mustard seeds
1 tablespoon allspice berries, crushed
1 tablespoon dill seeds
½ tablespoon whole cloves
1 dried red chile, crushed
3 cinnamon sticks, crushed
½ nutmeg, crushed
3 bay leaves, crumbled
1 teaspoon black peppercorns
1 teaspoon whole coriander seeds
1 teaspoon cardamom pods, crushed
½ star anise pod, crushed

Quicker Kosher Dills

MAKES ABOUT 8 PINT JARS OR 4 QUART JARS

RATHER THAN A LONG FERMENTATION, THESE PICKLES GET THEIR SOURNESS FROM GOOD OLD VINEGAR. The overnight soak in salt water helps to firm up the cucumbers and flavor them before their rendezvous with the canning pot, but it doesn't allow for actual fermentation.

As with all cucumber pickles, pasteurizing (heating the jars in water at 180°F for 30 minutes) rather than processing in boiling water for a shorter period will result in a slightly crisper pickle.

6 pounds pickling cucumbers (3 to 4 inches long)

1 cup pure kosher salt

3⅔ cups cider vinegar (5% acidity)

1 tablespoon sugar

Fresh dill

8 cloves garlic

16 teaspoons pickling spice (see page 126)

8 dried hot red peppers, or 8 teaspoons grated fresh horseradish (optional)

Fresh, untreated grape (or scuppernong) or black currant leaves (optional)

Cut off the blossom end of each cucumber; cut into spears or leave whole.

In a large bowl, combine ¾ cup of the salt with 1 gallon water and stir to dissolve. Add the cucumbers and let sit at room temperature for 8 hours or overnight. Drain and rinse well.

In a nonreactive pot, combine the vinegar, 4 cups water, the sugar, and the remaining ¼ cup salt. If pasteurizing, bring the mixture to 160°F to 180°F on a candy thermometer. If processing, bring to a full boil.

Ladle boiling water from the canning pot into the bowl with the lids. Using a jar lifter, remove the hot jars from the canning pot, carefully pouring the water from each one back into the pot, and place them upright on a folded towel. Drain the water off the jar lids.

Working quickly, put a few dill sprigs in each jar and divide the garlic, spices, dried peppers, and scuppernong leaves among the jars. Pack the cucumbers in the jars as snugly as you can without damaging them. Ladle the hot vinegar mixture into the jars, leaving ½ inch headspace. Use a chopstick to remove air bubbles around the inside of each jar. Use a damp paper towel to wipe the rims of the jars, then put a flat lid and ring on each jar, adjusting the ring so that it's just finger-tight. Return the jars to the water in the canning pot, making sure the water covers the jars by at least 1 inch. If pasteurizing, bring the water in the pot to 180°F, and keep it there, adjusting the burner as necessary, for 30 minutes. (Any time the water spends below 180°F must be added to the pasteurizing time so that the water is at 180°F for a total of 30 minutes.) If processing, bring to a full boil, and boil for 10 minutes. Remove the jars to a folded towel and do not disturb for 12 hours. After 1 hour, check that the lids have sealed by pressing down on the center of each; if it can be pushed down, it hasn't sealed, and the jar should be refrigerated immediately. Label the sealed jars and store.

Quickest Kosher Dills

MAKES ABOUT 4 PINT JARS

◇◇

THESE ARE EXCEEDINGLY EASY AND QUICK, PERFECT FOR WHEN YOU COME INTO A SMALL BATCH OF PICKLING CUCUMBERS AND DON'T WANT TO GO TO THE TROUBLE OF BRINING THEM, MUCH LESS FERMENTING THEM.

As with all cucumber pickles, pasteurizing (heating the jars in water at 180°F for 30 minutes) rather than processing in boiling water for a shorter period will result in a slightly crisper pickle.

3 pounds pickling cucumbers (3 to 4 inches long)

2 cups cider vinegar (5% acidity)

2 tablespoons pure kosher salt

Fresh dill

4 cloves garlic

8 teaspoons pickling spice (see page 126)

4 dried hot red peppers, or 4 teaspoons grated fresh
    horseradish (optional)

Fresh young scuppernong, grape, or black currant
    leaves (optional)

Prepare for water-bath canning: Wash the jars and keep them hot in the canning pot, and put the flat lids in a heatproof bowl. (See page 21 for details.)

Cut off the blossom end of each cucumber; cut into spears.

In a nonreactive pot, combine the vinegar, 2 cups water, and the salt. If pasteurizing, bring the mixture to 160°F to 180°F on a candy thermometer. If processing, bring to a full boil.

Ladle boiling water from the canning pot into the bowl with the lids. Using a jar lifter, remove the hot jars from the canning pot, carefully pouring the water from each one back into the pot, and place them upright on a folded towel. Drain the water off the jar lids.

Working quickly, put a few dill sprigs in each jar and divide the garlic, spices, dried peppers, and scuppernong leaves among the jars. Pack the cucumbers in the jars as snugly as you can without damaging them. Ladle the hot vinegar mixture into the jars, leaving ½ inch headspace. Use a chopstick to remove air bubbles around the inside of each jar. Use a damp paper towel to wipe the rims of the jars, then put a flat lid and ring on each jar, adjusting the ring so that it's just finger-tight. Return the jars to the water in the canning pot, making sure the water covers the jars by at least 1 inch. If pasteurizing, bring the water in the pot to 180°F, and keep it there, adjusting the burner as necessary, for 30 minutes. (Any time the water spends below 180°F must be added to the pasteurizing time so that the water is at 180°F for a total of 30 minutes.) If processing, bring to a full boil, and boil for 10 minutes. Remove the jars to a folded towel and do not disturb for 12 hours. After 1 hour, check that the lids have sealed by pressing down on the center of each; if it can be pushed down, it hasn't sealed, and the jar should be refrigerated immediately. Label the sealed jars and store.

Honeyed Bread-and-Butter Pickles

MAKES ABOUT 7 PINT JARS

◇◇

TRADITIONAL B&BS ARE LOADED WITH WHITE SUGAR, AND TOO SWEET. Here, though, the combination of the golden honey with deep-tasting cider vinegar, a touch of spiciness, and sharp mustard in two forms makes the crisp cucumber rounds and onion slices almost addictive. For another variation on the style, see the Zucchini Bread-and-Butter Pickles with Ginger (page 162).

As with all cucumber pickles, pasteurizing (heating the jars in water at 180°F for 30 minutes) rather than processing in boiling water for a shorter period will result in a slightly crisper pickle.

3 pounds pickling cucumbers (3 to 4 inches long)
1 pound small onions (about 2)
¼ cup plus 1 tablespoon pure kosher salt
2 tablespoons yellow mustard seeds
1 tablespoon celery seeds
2 teaspoons crushed red pepper flakes
6 cups cider vinegar (5% acidity)
¾ cup mild honey
1½ teaspoons turmeric
1½ teaspoons dry mustard powder

Cut off the blossom end of each cucumber; cut into ¼-inch rounds. Cut the onions in half lengthwise and thinly slice them into half-circles. Put the cucumbers and onions in a large bowl and sprinkle with the ¼ cup salt, tossing to combine. Cover with a layer of ice cubes and refrigerate for 8 hours or overnight. Pick out any unmelted ice, drain well, and rinse under cold running water. Toss with the mustard seeds, celery seeds, and red pepper flakes and set aside.

Prepare for water-bath canning: Wash the jars and keep them hot in the canning pot, and put the flat lids in a heatproof bowl. (See page 21 for details.)

In a nonreactive pot, combine the vinegar, 1½ cups water, the honey, turmeric, mustard powder, and the remaining 1 tablespoon salt. If pasteurizing, bring the mixture to 160°F to 180°F on a candy thermometer. If processing, bring to a full boil.

Ladle boiling water from the canning pot into the bowl with the lids. Using a jar lifter, remove the hot jars from the canning pot, carefully pouring the water from each one back into the pot, and place them upright on a folded towel. Drain the water off the jar lids.

Working quickly, pack the cucumbers and onions into the jars (not too tightly). Ladle the hot vinegar mixture into the jars, leaving ½ inch headspace at the top. Use a chopstick to remove air bubbles around the inside of each jar. Use a damp paper towel to wipe the rims of the jars, then put a flat lid and ring on each jar, adjusting the ring so that it's just finger-tight. Return the jars to the water in the canning pot, making sure the water covers the jars by at least 1 inch. If pasteurizing, bring the water in the pot to 180°F, and keep it there, adjusting the burner as necessary, for 30 minutes. (Any time the water spends below 180°F must be added to the pasteurizing time so that the water is at 180°F for a total of 30 minutes.) If processing, bring to a full boil, and boil for 15 minutes. Remove the jars to a folded towel and do not disturb for 12 hours. After 1 hour, check that the lids have sealed by pressing down on the center of each; if it can be pushed down, it hasn't sealed, and the jar should be refrigerated immediately. Label the sealed jars and store.

Classic Cucumber Relish

MAKES ABOUT 6 PINT JARS

◇◇

IF YOU'VE GOT A KID IN THE HOUSE, AS I DO—EVEN ONE WITH A FAIRLY REFINED PALATE—HOT DOGS ARE LIKELY TO BE A FACT OF LIFE FOR A WHILE. This relish, based on a recipe from the National Center for Home Food Preservation, is exactly like the one my mom and dad always had in the door of the fridge—when they didn't have Grandma's—and it's miles more interesting than standard store-bought. While today my preferred frankfurter condiments are spicy mustard and sauerkraut, I still occasionally revert to the relish of my youth, and it makes me happy that we get to eat hot dogs several times a week. Also try folding a few spoonfuls of it into a simple tuna salad with fresh lemon juice, a little mayonnaise and/or plain yogurt, and diced celery and sweet onion.

2 pounds cucumbers, unpeeled

12 ounces celery

1 medium green bell pepper, cored and seeded

1 medium red bell pepper, cored and seeded

3 cups diced onions (about 2 large)

¼ cup pure kosher salt

2¼ cups sugar

2½ cups distilled white vinegar (5% acidity)

1 tablespoon celery seeds

1 tablespoon mustard seeds

Trim and dice the cucumbers and celery and pulse in a food processor until finely chopped but not pureed. (Alternatively, use a blender or grind them in a food grinder.) Transfer to a very large bowl and repeat with the peppers and onions. Sprinkle in the salt and cover all the vegetables with cold water. Set aside at room temperature for 4 hours.

Working in batches, scoop the vegetables into a sieve to drain them, squeezing out as much of the liquid as possible. Dump them out into a bowl.

Prepare for water-bath canning: Wash the jars and keep them hot in the canning pot, and put the flat lids in a heatproof bowl. (See page 21 for details.)

In a wide, 6- to 8-quart preserving pan, combine the sugar, vinegar, celery seeds, and mustard seeds and bring to a boil, stirring to dissolve the sugar. Add the vegetables and bring to a boil; lower the heat and simmer, stirring occasionally, for 10 minutes.

Ladle boiling water from the canning pot into the bowl with the lids. Using a jar lifter, remove the hot jars from the canning pot, carefully pouring the water from each one back into the pot, and place them upright on a folded towel. Drain the water off the jar lids.

Ladle the hot relish into the jars, leaving ½ inch headspace at the top. Use a damp paper towel to wipe the rims of the jars, then put a flat lid and ring on each jar, adjusting the ring so that it's just finger-tight. Return the jars to the water in the canning pot, making sure the water covers the jars by at least 1 inch. Bring to a boil, and boil for 10 minutes to process. Remove the jars to a folded towel and do not disturb for 12 hours. After 1 hour, check that the lids have sealed by pressing down on the center of each; if it can be pushed down, it hasn't sealed, and the jar should be refrigerated immediately. Label the sealed jars and store.

Achar Segar (Indonesian Quick Pickle)

MAKES ABOUT 1 QUART

1 cucumber, julienned

1 carrot, peeled and julienned

3 large shallots, peeled and thinly sliced lengthwise

4 teaspoons sugar

1 tablespoon pure kosher salt

¾ cup distilled white vinegar (5% acidity)

Toss the vegetables together in a medium bowl, then transfer them to a quart-size glass jar. In a measuring cup or bowl, combine the sugar, salt, vinegar, and 1½ cups warm water and stir until the sugar and salt are dissolved. Pour over the vegetables in the jar and refrigerate for at least 3 hours before serving. The pickle will keep in the refrigerator for about 2 weeks.

Nasi Goreng (Indonesian Fried Rice)

SERVES 4

EVERY TIME I WENT TO MY FAVORITE INDONESIAN RESTAURANT IN NEW YORK, I HAD EITHER *NASI GORENG* OR *RENDANG PEDANG.* Both of those dishes were so good I was loath to order anything else. Unfortunately I'm left with a very limited knowledge of Indonesian food and, periodically, extremely powerful cravings for that fried rice and braised beef. The recipe below is how I try to replicate Indonesian fried rice at home here in Georgia. The pickles are served on the side, but they're absolutely essential to this dish.

1½ tablespoons fish sauce

1 teaspoon sugar

2 tablespoons vegetable oil

1 large egg, lightly beaten

2 large shallots, peeled and thinly sliced

2 cloves garlic, minced

1 hot red or green chile, seeded and minced

1 boneless, skinless chicken breast, cut into
  ½-inch pieces

4 cups cooked white or brown rice, chilled

Achar Segar (above), to serve

In a small cup, stir together the fish sauce and sugar until the sugar is dissolved.

In a large sauté pan, heat 1 tablespoon of the oil over medium-high heat. Pour in the egg and tilt the pan to coat the bottom as thinly as possible. Cook just until the top is set, about 1 minute, then transfer the egg to a cutting board and thinly shred it. Return the pan to medium-high heat, add the remaining 1 tablespoon of the oil, then add the shallots and cook, stirring, for 2 minutes. Add the garlic, chile, and chicken and cook, turning, until the chicken is cooked through, about 3 minutes. Increase the heat to high, then add the rice and the fish sauce mixture and cook, stirring constantly, until the rice is heated through and just beginning to brown, about 3 minutes. Garnish with the egg and serve immediately, with the *achar segar* alongside.

Persian Tarragon Pickles

MAKES ABOUT 2 QUART JARS

WHEN YOU CONSIDER THE INHERENT BEAUTY OF THINGS IN JARS, THIS IS WHAT YOU MIGHT BE IMAGINING: bright green, slender cucumbers, papery garlic cloves, deep red chiles, sprays of coriander heads, a tangle of oceanic-looking tarragon rising from the bottom of the jar—all surrounded by a clear, cold brine.

My mom and her friend Shalah Williams wrote down Shalah's recipe for the pickles she remembered from her family's home in Isfahan, Iran, and there's always a jar of them in my fridge now. If you love tarragon, as I do, try them—they taste like pure, uncut herb. You can use Kirby cucumbers or the narrow, ridged, sweet Persian cucumbers that are sometimes available in specialty markets. If your cucumbers are short (less than 5 inches long), you could fit them all in one half-gallon jar.

2 pounds small Persian seedless cucumbers or firm, fresh pickling cucumbers (no more than 5 inches long)
4 cloves garlic, unpeeled
4 sprigs fresh tarragon
1 tablespoon coriander seeds, or 4 heads fresh coriander seeds
4 fresh or dried hot chiles
¼ cup pure kosher salt
1 cup cider vinegar (5% acidity)

Cut off the blossom end of each cucumber. Put the cucumbers, garlic, tarragon, coriander, and chiles in two quart jars, being careful not to bruise the cucumbers.

In a large measuring cup or bowl, combine 4 cups water, the salt, and vinegar. Stir to dissolve the salt. Pour the mixture over the cucumbers. Put the lids on the jars. Refrigerate for 4 weeks.

Cut the pickles lengthwise into wedges to serve. The pickles will keep, in the refrigerator, for at least 3 months, though I've kept them for much longer.

Dilly Beans!

MAKES ABOUT 5 PINT JARS

YOU'LL RARELY SEE ANY REFERENCE TO THE SOUTH'S BELOVED DILLY BEANS (THESE ARE BASED ON THE OLD *BALL BLUE BOOK* RECIPE) WITHOUT AN EXCLAMATION POINT NEARBY. People in the know love them that much. It's true that they are worth getting loud and excited about. As spicy as you want them (add chile flakes, if you like them extra-hot), other dilly bean qualities include sourness, saltiness, and crispness. In short, the dilly bean is the perfect food.

4 cups cider vinegar (5% acidity)

3 tablespoons pure kosher salt

5 sprigs fresh dill

5 cloves garlic

5 or 10 dried hot red chiles

2½ to 5 teaspoons crushed red pepper flakes (optional)

2 pounds crisp green beans, ends trimmed, 4½ inches long

Prepare for water-bath canning: Wash the jars and keep them hot in the canning pot, and put the flat lids in a heatproof bowl. (See page 21 for details.)

In a wide, 6- to 8-quart preserving pan, combine the vinegar, 4 cups water, and the salt. Bring just to a boil, stirring to dissolve the salt.

Ladle boiling water from the canning pot into the bowl with the lids. Using a jar lifter, remove the hot jars from the canning pot, carefully pouring the water from each one back into the pot, and place them upright on a folded towel. Drain the water off the jar lids.

Working quickly, put a sprig of dill, a clove of garlic, 1 or 2 dried chiles, and ½ to 1 teaspoon red pepper flakes, if using, in each hot jar. Pack the beans in the jars, standing them upright. Ladle in the hot vinegar mixture, leaving ½ inch headspace at the top. Use a chopstick to remove air bubbles around the inside of each jar. Use a damp paper towel to wipe the rims of the jars, then put a flat lid and ring on each jar, adjusting the ring so that it's just finger-tight. Return the jars to the water in the canning pot, making sure the water covers the jars by at least 1 inch. Bring to a simmer, and simmer for 10 minutes to process. Remove the jars to a folded towel and do not disturb for 12 hours. After 1 hour, check that the lids have sealed by pressing down on the center of each; if it can be pushed down, it hasn't sealed, and the jar should be refrigerated immediately. Label the sealed jars and store.

Variation: Soy and Wasabi Pickled Beans
To approximate the popular and tasty (and pricey) Rick's Picks Windy City Wasabeans, replace the salt in the recipe with good-quality soy sauce, omit the dill, and to each jar, in addition to the garlic and dried chiles, add about 1½ teaspoons wasabi powder (I've done it quite successfully with only ½ teaspoon per jar—because I'm cheap that way), a couple thin slices of fresh ginger, and ½ teaspoon whole black peppercorns.

Pickled Romano Beans with Indian Spices

MAKES ABOUT 6 PINT JARS

WIDE, FLAT ROMANO BEANS WITH WHOLE SPICES AND SLIVERS OF TURMERIC-YELLOWED ONION MAKE A STUNNING ADDITION TO A DINNER OF VARIOUS INDIAN DISHES, OR EVEN TO A FALL OR SPRING COOKOUT. They pair surprisingly well with bold grilled meats and vegetables or, say, fresh ginger–spiked turkey burgers. When I was testing and developing the recipes for this book and my fridge was stuffed to its ceiling with every kind of pickle imaginable, these are the ones I kept reaching for between meals.

2 teaspoons cumin seeds
2 teaspoons coriander seeds
2 teaspoons yellow mustard seeds
1 teaspoon whole black peppercorns
1 teaspoon fennel seeds
2 pounds Romano (or flat pole) beans, trimmed
6 cups white wine vinegar (6% acidity)
4 teaspoons pure kosher salt
1 teaspoon turmeric
¼ onion, thinly sliced

Prepare for water-bath canning: Wash the jars and keep them hot in the canning pot, and put the flat lids in a heatproof bowl. (See page 21 for details.)

In a heavy skillet over medium heat, toast the cumin seeds, coriander seeds, mustard seeds, peppercorns, and fennel seeds until fragrant, about 2 minutes. Remove to a plate and let cool. In a large bowl, toss the whole spices with the beans.

In a wide, 6- to 8-quart preserving pan, combine the vinegar, 2 cups water, the salt, and turmeric. Bring just to a boil, stirring to dissolve the salt.

Ladle boiling water from the canning pot into the bowl with the lids. Using a jar lifter, remove the hot jars from the canning pot, carefully pouring the water from each one back into the pot, and place them upright on a folded towel. Drain the water off the jar lids.

Working quickly, pack the beans and spices in the jars, standing them upright. Fill in spaces between the beans with slivers of onion. Ladle in the hot vinegar mixture, leaving ½ inch headspace at the top. Use a chopstick to remove air bubbles around the inside of each jar. Use a damp paper towel to wipe the rims of the jars, then put a flat lid and ring on each jar, adjusting the ring so that it's just finger-tight. Return the jars to the water in the canning pot, making sure the water covers the jars by at least 1 inch. Bring to a simmer, and simmer for 10 minutes to process. Remove the jars to a folded towel and do not disturb for 12 hours. After 1 hour, check that the lids have sealed by pressing down on the center of each; if it can be pushed down, it hasn't sealed, and the jar should be refrigerated immediately. Label the sealed jars and store.

Fermented Yard-Long Beans

MAKES 1 POUND

◇◇◇

SINCE I LEFT NEW YORK, I'VE BEEN OBSESSED WITH FIGURING OUT HOW TO REPLICATE A CERTAIN HUNAN DISH THAT I'D BECOME ACCUSTOMED TO ORDERING ONCE OR TWICE A WEEK FROM MY FAVORITE NEIGHBORHOOD CHINESE RESTAURANT IN HELL'S KITCHEN. Until recently, I would go to great lengths to buy vacuum-packed sour long beans (ingredients: salt, beans), which are sometimes available in the refrigerated sections of Asian grocery stores, or fresh long beans, which I'd then pickle like Dilly Beans! (page 135), with vinegar but no dill. My various renditions were good, but never quite right. Then I learned how to ferment vegetables, and all the pieces fell into place.

This recipe is based on one in the fascinating *Wild Fermentation* by Sandor Ellix Katz. Like sauerkraut or old-fashioned cucumber pickles, it requires no vinegar; the lactic acid produced in the fermentation process is what makes the vegetables sour and also lowers the pH to a point that's sufficient to inhibit spoilage for a while.

1 pound yard-long beans
1 tablespoon crushed red pepper flakes
½ cup pure kosher salt

Wash the beans well and trim off the ends (see Note), as well as any soft or very dark areas. Cut them in half and put them in a large stainless-steel mixing bowl or pot, or a food-grade plastic tub. Sprinkle the red pepper flakes over the beans.

Combine the salt and 12 cups water, stirring to dissolve the salt. Pour enough brine over the beans to just cover them, then pour the rest of the brine into a gallon-size resealable plastic bag, seal, and place it on top of the beans to keep them submerged in the brine. Cover the container with a clean, heavy towel and let ferment at room temperature. After 2 or 3 days, scum will start to form on the surface; skim it off, and skim every day or two. When the beans are sour, after about 1 week, refrigerate them in the brine for several weeks, or drain them and freeze them in freezer bags for up to 6 months.

Note: You could spend all day lining up the ends of the beans to cut them off with a knife; easier to do that with one end (they're usually sold in rubber-banded bunches with ends flush anyway), then use scissors to snip off the other ends.

Chopped Sour Long Beans with Minced Pork

SERVES 2 OR 3

SOMETIMES I ADD SOME MINCED GINGER AND GARLIC TO THE PAN (OR FROZEN GINGER-GARLIC PASTE; SEE PAGE 70) WHEN THE PORK IS ALMOST COOKED THROUGH, BUT THEY AREN'T REALLY NECESSARY: The fermented long beans give the dish quite enough flavor on their own.

Chinese black vinegar, which is dark and syrupy (but not sweet), is available in most Asian grocery stores and is worth experimenting with. If you can't find it, balsamic makes a fine substitute, or you can add some of the sour bean fermenting liquid. The dish should be quite spicy, sour, and salty.

1 tablespoon chile oil
8 ounces lean ground pork
3 dried hot red chiles
2½ cups diced Fermented Yard-Long Beans (page 137)
6 scallions, trimmed and cut into ¼-inch lengths
2 tablespoons soy sauce
1 tablespoon Shaoxing (Chinese cooking wine)
1 tablespoon Chinese black vinegar
½ teaspoon crushed red pepper flakes, or to taste
Hot cooked white rice

In a large sauté pan, heat the oil over high heat. Add the pork and cook, stirring to break it up into small pieces, until lightly browned and no longer pink. Add the dried chiles, beans, and scallions and toss to combine. Cook, stirring frequently, until the beans are just tender, about 4 minutes. Add the soy sauce, Shaoxing, vinegar, and red pepper flakes and cook for 1 minute. Serve hot with rice.

Snack-Size Faux Tamales

MAKES 6 SMALL TAMALES

◇◇

I CONSIDER MYSELF A GREAT APPRECIA-TOR OF TAMALES—THE REAL ONES. The more tediously made, the better, wrapped in corn husks and lovingly steamed over simmering water (or, in the case of Delta-style hot tamales, simmered in a big pot of spicy, meat-scented tomato broth). I'll tell you, though, sometimes I just want something quick and easy for lunch or a snack, and if it resembles a tamale, so much the better. This recipe doubles handily.

2 large egg whites
2 tablespoons olive oil
½ cup frozen corn kernels (above), thawed
¼ cup salsa, such as Charred Tomato and Chile Salsa
   (page 169), plus more for serving
1 cup cornmeal or masa harina (either works fine)

Put the egg whites, oil, corn, and ¼ cup salsa in a blender or food processor and blend until smooth. Add the cornmeal, blending until incorporated.

Lay 6 (6-by-12-inch) sheets of waxed paper (or, as we did back in the day, plastic wrap) on a work surface and divide the dough among them, shaping each pile into a log about ¾ inch in diameter by lifting the long edges of the paper and shaking gently. Wrap each log tightly: Hold the long edges together and fold them over and over until you reach the dough log. Fold the ends of the paper up, turn the package seam side down, and tuck the ends of the paper underneath.

Arrange the packages in a bamboo steamer or steamer basket (or in a circle on the turntable of a microwave oven), and set over boiling water for about 5 minutes (or microwave on high power for 2½ to 3 minutes), until firm. (The internal temperature should reach about 160°F, if you're concerned about the egg whites.) Unwrap and serve with more salsa spooned over the top.

Smoky Corn Chowder

SERVES 8

THIS LIGHT BUT EXTREMELY SATISFYING
CORN CHOWDER GETS ITS SMOKINESS NOT
FROM BACON BUT FROM DRIED CHIPOTLE
CHILE FLAKES. Its creaminess comes from the
russet potatoes and the starch in the corn itself.
Miso paste, which, along with sweet corn, is a
staple in my freezer, gives the chowder depth.

1 tablespoon unsalted butter

1 sweet onion, such as Vidalia, diced

1 red bell pepper, diced

2 Russet potatoes, peeled and diced

1 tablespoon miso paste

2 teaspoons dried chipotle chile flakes

4 cups frozen sweet corn kernels (see below)

Pure kosher salt

In a large pot over medium-high heat, melt the butter, then add the onion and sauté until translucent,
about 5 minutes. Add the bell pepper, potatoes, 4
cups water, the miso paste, chile flakes, and corn
and bring to a boil over high heat. Skim the foam
from the surface, then lower the heat and simmer
until the potatoes are tender and beginning to
break apart, about 15 minutes. Smash some of the
potatoes against the side of the pot to thicken the
chowder. Season with salt to taste and serve hot.

FREEZING CORN

Opening your freezer on a dreary, gray day in Feb-
ruary and seeing neatly stacked (okay, who are we
kidding—a tumbling pile of) little cups of blanched
and cut sweet corn kernels has to be one of the most
uplifting of simple pleasures. Corn chowder awaits!
As does one of my favorite summer-in-winter dishes:
halved grape tomatoes (the only kind of fresh tomatoes worth buying in the off season, and usually
pretty good), thinly sliced shallot, corn kernels, and
lots of basil (a small indulgence), all sautéed for just
a few minutes in a bit of olive oil, and seasoned with
plenty of salt.

Frozen cut corn: Bring a large pot of water to a boil
and shuck as much corn as you care to. A few ears
at a time, blanch the corn for 2 minutes. Using tongs,
transfer the corn to a large bowl of ice water to cool.

Use a sharp chef's knife to cut the kernels from the
corn. Rather than holding the ear vertically, which
always results in about as many kernels on the floor
or in some dark corner of the counter, I prefer to rest
it flat—horizontally—on the cutting board and cut
straight down, holding the knife blade parallel to the
rows of kernels and rolling the cob an eighth of a turn
or so with each cut, so that all the action occurs close
to the board. After removing all the kernels from each
cob, hold the cob at a shallow angle to the cutting
board and use the blade of the knife to scrape as
much of the pulp from the cob as you can without
getting any of the tough cob fibers. Pack the corn
into small containers, leaving 1 inch headspace (corn
expands in the freezer!), or into small freezer bags,
and freeze for up to 1 year.

Pickled Garlic Scapes

MAKES ABOUT 4 PINT JARS

IN EARLY SUMMER, THESE CURLY, SPIRALLY, BRIGHT GREEN ALIEN THINGS PROTRUDE FROM THE STALKS OF SOME VARIETIES OF GARLIC, AND THEY CAN BE FOUND AT FARMERS' MARKETS AND IN ASIAN GROCERY STORES. These "scapes" have a mild, fresh garlic flavor. The curved tops, while pretty, tend to be tough, not to mention a pain to pack into canning jars; use only the bottom 4 to 8 inches. Pickled scapes are great served plain alongside grilled meats or vegetables, or diced and sprinkled over deviled eggs or into frittatas or quiches, or in the white bean puree below—my favorite use for them so far.

2½ pounds garlic scapes, rinsed
4 cups cider vinegar (5% acidity)
¼ cup pure kosher salt
2 teaspoons crushed red pepper flakes

Prepare for water-bath canning: Wash the jars and keep them hot in the canning pot, and put the flat lids in a heatproof bowl. (See page 21 for details.)

Line up the bottoms of the scapes and cut two 4-inch lengths from the tender bottom; the tops are usually pretty tough, but if another 4 inches' worth is tender enough to bite into without unpleasantness, by all means use it.

In a nonreactive pot, combine the vinegar, 2 cups water, and the salt and bring just to a boil.

Ladle boiling water from the canning pot into the bowl with the lids. Using a jar lifter, remove the hot jars from the canning pot, carefully pouring the water from each one back into the pot, and place them upright on a folded towel. Drain the water off the jar lids.

Working quickly, pack the scapes upright in the jars. Add ½ teaspoon red pepper flakes to each jar. Ladle the hot vinegar mixture into the jars, leaving ½ inch headspace at the top. Use a chopstick to remove air bubbles around the inside of each jar. Use a damp paper towel to wipe the rims of the jars, then put a flat lid and ring on each jar, adjusting the ring so that it's just finger-tight. Return the jars to the water in the canning pot, making sure the water covers the jars by at least 1 inch. Bring to a boil, and boil for 15 minutes to process. Remove the jars to a folded towel and do not disturb for 12 hours. After 1 hour, check that the lids have sealed by pressing down on the center of each; if it can be pushed down, it hasn't sealed, and the jar should be refrigerated immediately. Label the sealed jars and store.

WHITE BEAN PUREE

This tangy, creamy puree seems to call out for hot and fluffy pita bread, but as it's subtly reminiscent of tartar sauce, I think it's best dolloped on grilled or pan-seared fish. Makes 1¼ cups.

½ cup diced drained Pickled Garlic Scapes
1 (15-ounce) can white beans, drained and rinsed
3 tablespoons olive oil
1 tablespoon garlic scape pickling liquid
1 tablespoon chopped fresh parsley
Pinch of pure kosher salt
Pinch of ground cayenne

Put all the ingredients in a mini food processor and process to a slightly chunky puree. Serve.

Simple Pickled Jalapeño Slices

MAKES ABOUT 4 PINT JARS

◇◇◇

2½ pounds jalapeño chiles
4 cups cider vinegar (5% acidity)
2 tablespoons sugar or honey
1½ tablespoons pure kosher salt
4 cloves garlic

Prepare for water-bath canning: Wash the jars and keep them hot in the canning pot, and put the flat lids in a heatproof bowl. (See page 21 for details.)

Cut the chiles into ⅛-inch-thick rounds and rinse them in a colander under cold running water, shaking them to remove loose seeds. Pick out and discard any very dark-colored seeds. Drain well.

In a nonreactive pot, combine the vinegar, 1 cup water, the sugar, and salt and bring just to a boil, stirring to dissolve the sugar and salt.

Ladle boiling water from the canning pot into the bowl with the lids. Using a jar lifter, remove the hot jars from the canning pot, carefully pouring the water from each one back into the pot, and place them upright on a folded towel. Drain the water off the jar lids.

Working quickly, put a garlic clove in each jar and pack with the chiles, leaving 1 inch headspace at the top. Ladle the hot vinegar mixture into the jars, leaving ½ inch headspace. Use a chopstick to remove air bubbles around the inside of each jar. Use a damp paper towel to wipe the rims of the jars, then put a flat lid and ring on each jar, adjusting the ring so that it's just finger-tight. Return the jars to the water in the canning pot, making sure the water covers the jars by at least 1 inch. Bring to a boil, and boil for 10 minutes to process. Remove the jars to a folded towel and do not disturb for 12 hours. After 1 hour, check that the lids have sealed by pressing down on the center of each; if it can be pushed down, it hasn't sealed, and the jar should be refrigerated immediately. Label the sealed jars and store.

Sliced Braised Beef Sandwich

SERVES 8

◇◇

I'VE NEVER HAD A REAL ITALIAN BEEF, THE CHICAGO SANDWICH OF ROAST BEEF WITH PEPPERS, ONIONS, AND PROVOLONE ON A SPECIAL KIND OF ROLL. (Depending on the customer's wishes, the roll is or is not dipped, bread and all, back into the beef cooking liquid just before consumption.) So I feel perfectly free to offer this amazingly tasty and satisfying variation on it.

Well-marbled chuck roast is best here, but top or bottom round roasts, which are leaner, are fine too—they just won't crumble and disintegrate quite as nicely. You can also make this in a slow cooker: Brown the beef in a skillet, as below, then transfer it to the slow cooker; deglaze the skillet with the broth; pour the broth into the cooker and add the remaining braising ingredients. Cook, covered, on the low setting for about 8 hours, or until the meat is very tender and you're ready to tend to it again. Slice the meat and return it to the cooker to heat through.

1 (3-pound) chuck roast

Pure kosher salt and freshly ground black pepper

2 tablespoons olive oil

1 teaspoon dried oregano

1 teaspoon granulated garlic

1 teaspoon granulated onion

2 cups beef broth (see Note)

½ pint Simple Pickled Jalapeño Slices (opposite), with pickling liquid

4 large onions, thinly sliced

8 slices rye bread

8 slices provolone or white Cheddar cheese

Preheat the oven to 325°F.

Season the beef all over with salt and pepper. In a Dutch oven or flameproof casserole, heat 1 tablespoon of the oil over medium-high heat and add the beef. Cook, turning, until well browned on all sides, about 10 minutes total. Add the oregano, garlic, onion, and broth and bring to a boil. Cover and transfer to the oven. Cook until very tender, 1½ to 2 hours. Using tongs, transfer the meat to a cutting board and slice it very thinly across the grain; it should nearly crumble apart. Return the slices to the pot, along with the jalapeños and their liquid. Cover and return the pot to the oven until the beef is heated through and you're ready to eat.

In a skillet, heat the remaining 1 tablespoon oil over medium heat. Add the onions and cook, stirring frequently, until very soft and golden brown, about 10 minutes.

Arrange the bread slices on a baking sheet and toast under the broiler until well browned, then flip them over and toast until lightly browned. Use a slotted spoon to pile beef and jalapeños atop the slices, top with the onions, then lay a slice of cheese over each. Return to the oven and broil until the cheese is melted. Use a spatula to transfer the open-faced sandwiches to plates, then spoon some of the broth over the top and serve.

Note: Canned beef broth is fine (use one 14-ounce can), but you might wish to add a bay leaf, a chopped rib of celery, and a chopped carrot to deepen its flavor. Fish them out and discard them when you remove the meat to slice it.

Whole Jalapeños with Honey and Allspice

MAKES ABOUT 5 PINT JARS

◇◇

HERE HONEY AND A SWEET SPICE HELP TO TAME THE ALREADY FAIRLY MILD HEAT OF JALAPEÑOS. They're practically kid-friendly.

2½ pounds jalapeño chiles
6 cups cider vinegar (5% acidity)
2 tablespoons pure kosher salt
2 tablespoons honey
5 cloves garlic
5 small bay leaves
1 teaspoon whole allspice
½ teaspoon black peppercorns

Slit the chiles almost in half lengthwise from the bottom and set aside.

Prepare for water-bath canning: Wash the jars and keep them hot in the canning pot, and put the flat lids in a heatproof bowl. (See page 21 for details.)

In a nonreactive saucepan, combine the vinegar, 2 cups water, the salt, and honey. Bring just to a boil, stirring to dissolve the salt and honey.

Ladle boiling water from the canning pot into the bowl with the lids. Using a jar lifter, remove the hot jars from the canning pot, carefully pouring the water from each one back into the pot, and place them upright on a folded towel. Drain the water off the jar lids.

Working quickly, pack the chiles as tightly as possible into the hot jars (flattening them first with your palm if necessary), along with the garlic, bay leaves, and spices, leaving 1 inch headspace at the top. Ladle the hot vinegar mixture into the jars, leaving ½ inch headspace. Use a chopstick to remove air bubbles around the inside of each jar. Use a damp paper towel to wipe the rims of the jars, then put a flat lid and ring on each jar, adjusting the ring so that it's just finger-tight. Return the jars to the water in the canning pot, making sure the water covers the jars by at least 1 inch. Bring to a boil, and boil for 10 minutes to process. Remove the jars to a folded towel and do not disturb for 12 hours. After 1 hour, check that the lids have sealed by pressing down on the center of each; if it can be pushed down, it hasn't sealed, and the jar should be refrigerated immediately. Label the sealed jars and store.

OTHER PICKLED CHILES

Following the same method as for the jalapeños above, you can pickle any kind of hot chile: serranos, Hungarian wax peppers, banana peppers, little round red cherry peppers—you name it. For those, however, I omit the honey and allspice, and for pale green chiles I use distilled white vinegar (5% acidity) instead of the darker cider vinegar.

Escabeche Vegetables

MAKES ABOUT 7 PINT JARS

YOU CAN WARM A JAR OF THESE VEGETABLES IN THEIR PICKLING LIQUID AND POUR IT OVER CRUNCHY FRIED SMELTS OR ANCHOVIES; THIS WOULD BE A GOOD START TO A MEXICAN MEAL. Or just serve the vegetables in a little bowl alongside tacos or grilled flank steak.

This recipe is based on two pepper-and-mixed-vegetable recipes published online by the Colorado State University extension office, which offers an unusually interesting selection of pickled and marinated pepper recipes—perhaps because its constituent demographic is shifting as more immigrants from Mexico arrive.

1 pound carrots, trimmed and scrubbed
1 pound jalapeño chiles
1 small onion (about 4 ounces)
5 cups cider vinegar (5% acidity)
⅔ cup olive oil
4 teaspoons pure kosher salt
3 tablespoons dried oregano
1 tablespoon crumbled dried epazote (optional; see Note)
7 cloves garlic

Peel the carrots if desired, and cut into 1-inch lengths. Cut the chiles in half lengthwise, or make a slit in the bottom of the chiles and leave them whole. Thinly slice the onion.

Prepare for water-bath canning: Wash the jars and keep them hot in the canning pot, and put the flat lids in a heatproof bowl. (See page 21 for details.)

In a wide, 6- to 8-quart preserving pan, combine the vinegar, 1 cup water, the oil, salt, oregano, and epazote, if using. Bring to a boil, then simmer for 5 minutes. Add the carrots and cook until just crisp-tender, 8 to 10 minutes. Add the chiles and onion and bring just to a boil.

Ladle boiling water from the canning pot into the bowl with the lids. Using a jar lifter, remove the hot jars from the canning pot, carefully pouring the water from each one back into the pot, and place them upright on a folded towel. Drain the water off the jar lids.

Working quickly, put a garlic clove in each jar. Using a slotted spoon, transfer the hot vegetables to the jars (do not pack them too tightly). Ladle the hot pickling liquid into the jars, being sure that the oil is evenly distributed among them and leaving ½ inch headspace at the top. Use a chopstick to remove air bubbles around the inside of each jar. Use a damp paper towel to wipe the rims of the jars well, then put a flat lid and ring on each jar, adjusting the ring so that it's just finger-tight. Return the jars to the water in the canning pot, making sure the water covers the jars by at least 1 inch. Bring to a boil, and boil for 20 minutes to process. Remove the jars to a folded towel and do not disturb for 12 hours. After 1 hour, check that the lids have sealed by pressing down on the center of each; if it can be pushed down, it hasn't sealed, and the jar should be refrigerated immediately. Label the sealed jars and store.

Note: Epazote, a pungent herb commonly used in Mexican black bean preparations, is available fresh and dried in Latino markets. There's no good substitute, so if you can't find it just leave it out.

Catfish Fillets in Escabeche

SERVES 4

IF YOU'RE CONCERNED ABOUT THE DECLIN-ING POPULATIONS OF EDIBLE SEAFOOD SPECIES, IT'S OFTEN HARD TO KNOW WHAT FISH TO PUT YOUR DOLLARS BEHIND ON ANY GIVEN DAY. Catfish to the rescue! Channel catfish, *Ictalurus punctatus*, farmed in the United States—primarily in Mississippi, Arkansas, Alabama, and Louisiana—is described by Seafood Watch as "one of the most sustainable fish species available" and is listed as a "best choice." (Basa, *Pangasius bocourti*, a river catfish farmed in Southeast Asia, is becoming more widely available here and is often cheaper than its domestic cousin. It's listed as a "good alternative" to domestic catfish; it's raised in a relatively sustainable manner, but there are concerns about the lack of oversight of foreign producers.)

Catfish need not always be fried. In this dish, it's lightly poached in a sauce of tomatoes and tangy *Escabeche* Vegetables. If you'd like, add some chunks of summer squash or zucchini with the onion and garlic for a more substantial dish. Serve with steamed white rice or warm fresh corn tortillas. You could also use small whole cleaned catfish instead of fillets, or another "best choice," domestic farmed tilapia fillets.

4 catfish fillets
Pure kosher salt and freshly ground black pepper
¼ cup olive or other vegetable oil
½ onion, diced
2 cloves garlic, smashed
2 large tomatoes, grated (see Note)
1 pint *Escabeche* Vegetables (page 147), drained, liquid reserved

Pat the fish dry and season with salt and pepper. Heat the oil in a large sauté pan over medium-high heat. Add the fish and cook, without disturbing the fillets, for 2 minutes. Use a metal spatula to turn the fish over and cook on the other side for 1 minute. Remove to a plate and set aside.

Pour off all but 1 tablespoon of the oil and return the pan to medium-high heat. Add the onion and garlic and sauté until just softened, about 5 minutes. Add the tomatoes and 1 cup water and stir to scrape up any browned bits in the pan; bring to a simmer and cook, stirring frequently, until the sauce is somewhat thick, 4 to 6 minutes. Add the *escabeche* vegetables and cook until heated through. Nestle the fish in the sauce and simmer for 2 to 3 minutes, until just heated through. Taste the sauce and stir in a little of the *escabeche* liquid if it needs more tang. Serve hot.

Note: Grating fresh tomatoes is an easy way to make a quick, tomato-skin-free sauce. Cut the tomatoes in half (horizontally or vertically, it doesn't matter) and rub the cut sides over a large-holed cheese grater set over a bowl to remove the pulp, stopping when you get to the skin. Discard the skin.

Roasted Red Peppers with Lemon Juice

MAKES ABOUT 3 PINT JARS

◇◇

I BELIEVE IT WAS MY ESTEEMED EDITOR, LUISA WEISS, WHO ONCE WROTE A BLOG POST (IT WAS ESSENTIALLY A PROSE SIGH) DECRYING THE USE OF GAS BURNERS TO ROAST BELL PEPPERS. She patiently explained to her faithful readers that the only way to roast a pepper is slowly—very slowly—in the oven, so rather than remaining a basically raw pepper with charred skin, it practically collapses and melts into a silky mass of sweet vegetal-ness. That's really wonderful, but if you're going to process them in boiling water so they keep at room temperature, you need them to be peeled but still somewhat firm, so they can withstand the heat of the boiling-water processor without turning to mush.

The recipe here is based on one by Eugenia Bone, mistress of all preserves Italianate, in *Well-Preserved*, as well as one of the several really appealing pepper recipes developed by the Colorado State University extension office.

4 pounds red bell peppers (about 10)

1 cup bottled or strained fresh lemon juice

2 cups white wine vinegar (6% acidity)

1 cup extra-virgin olive oil

2 cloves garlic, sliced

2 teaspoons pure kosher salt

Roast the peppers directly on a gas burner or under the broiler until blistered all over, turning them frequently with tongs. Peel and seed the peppers, then rip them into large sections.

Prepare for water-bath canning: Wash the jars and keep them hot in the canning pot, and put the flat lids in a heatproof bowl. (See page 21 for details.)

In a wide, 6- to 8-quart preserving pan, combine the lemon juice, vinegar, oil, garlic, and salt. Bring just to a boil.

Ladle boiling water from the canning pot into the bowl with the lids. Using a jar lifter, remove the hot jars from the canning pot, carefully pouring the water from each one back into the pot, and place them upright on a folded towel. Drain the water off the jar lids.

Pack the roasted peppers into the jars and ladle in the hot liquid, leaving ½ inch headspace at the top. Use a chopstick to remove air bubbles around the inside of each jar (be diligent about removing the bubbles here). Use a damp paper towel to wipe the rims of the jars well, then put a flat lid and ring on each jar, adjusting the ring so that it's just finger-tight. Return the jars to the water in the canning pot, making sure the water covers the jars by at least 1 inch. Bring to a boil, and boil for 15 minutes to process. Remove the jars to a folded towel and do not disturb for 12 hours. After 1 hour, check that the lids have sealed by pressing down on the center of each; if it can be pushed down, it hasn't sealed, and the jar should be refrigerated immediately. Label the sealed jars and store.

Sweet Red Pepper Relish

MAKES ABOUT 3 HALF-PINT JARS

◇◇

THIS OLD CANNING STANDBY, PRETTY MUCH RIGHT OUT OF THE *BALL BLUE BOOK*, IS ESSENTIALLY CANDIED VINEGARED RED PEPPERS— AND I LIKE IT THAT WAY. I keep a few jars of it on hand for one reason, and one reason only: so my daughter will know what meatloaf is supposed to taste like. My mom spreads the top of hers (baked in a baking dish, not a loaf pan, so there's more surface area to brown) with a mixture of half red pepper relish—this one almost exactly—and half ketchup. The composition of the loaf itself matters not very much at all, in my opinion, as long as it has this sweet-tart crusty glaze on top. You could put it on hot dogs or hamburgers, or mix it into cream cheese and do whatnot with it, but that's up to you.

Mom says that a food processor is an unacceptable tool here and that you must use a meat grinder, but I don't pull out my meat grinder unless there's sausage in the offing, so mini food processor it is.

4 cups finely chopped red bell peppers (see Note)
1 tablespoon pure kosher salt
3 cups sugar
2 cups distilled white vinegar

Put the peppers in a large bowl and stir in the salt. Set aside for 2 to 3 hours.

Prepare for water-bath canning: Wash the jars and keep them hot in the canning pot, and put the flat lids in a heatproof bowl. (See page 21 for details.)

Working in batches, scoop the peppers into a sieve to drain them, squeezing out as much of the liquid as possible. Dump them out into a wide, 6- to 8-quart preserving pan and add the sugar and vinegar. Bring to a boil over high heat, stirring frequently, and cook until the larger pieces of pepper are translucent and the syrup is somewhat thick, about 35 minutes.

Ladle boiling water from the canning pot into the bowl with the lids. Using a jar lifter, remove the hot jars from the canning pot, carefully pouring the water from each one back into the pot, and place them upright on a folded towel. Drain the water off the jar lids.

Ladle the hot relish into the jars, leaving ½ inch headspace at the top. Use a damp paper towel to wipe the rims of the jars, then put a flat lid and ring on each jar, adjusting the ring so that it's just finger-tight. Return the jars to the water in the canning pot, making sure the water covers the jars by at least 1 inch. Bring to a boil, and boil for 10 minutes to process. Remove the jars to a folded towel and do not disturb for 12 hours. After 1 hour, check that the lids have sealed by pressing down on the center of each; if it can be pushed down, it hasn't sealed, and the jar should be refrigerated immediately. Label the sealed jars and store.

Note: You'll need about 2½ pounds of peppers, or about 5 large ones. Stem and seed the peppers, then dice them and put them in a food processor (I do this in batches in a mini processor). Pulse to finely chop but not puree. You can use all red peppers or a combination of red and yellow or orange.

FREEZING PEPPERS

My folks would simply dice up their homegrown summery bell peppers of every conceivable color, stuff them into plastic bags, and stash them in the freezer for the winter. I have vivid memories of Mom sending me to the chest freezer for peppers for this or that supper; when I opened the freezer, I was amazed at all the little bags of colorful diced peppers (and knew that we'd probably be having bell peppers in everything from now until eternity). Now that I'm on my own, I don't honestly have much use for peppers in quantity unless they're (1) roasted or (2) chiles, hot. When they're in season and plentiful in midsummer, I can roast red peppers in olive oil and lemon juice, but also freeze whole roasted poblanos so they're ready and waiting for chiles rellenos or *rajas* or chowders (or really anything that's cooked in a pot). Small hot chiles I freeze either whole or diced (I keep them in a little container with the other aromatics in the freezer door, and use a fork to pry out only as many as I need at a time).

Roasted poblano chiles: As with the Roasted Red Peppers with Lemon Juice on page 149, here I like to use a gas burner—in fact, all four of mine at once—to blister the skins of the peppers. You can also put them on sheet pans and pass them under the broiler, turning them over and moving the pans around occasionally, but I find the stovetop method to be much less labor intensive. I can blister a batch of 30 peppers in about 20 minutes on four gas burners. Peeling and seeding takes a good 45 minutes if you take the seeds out through a discreet slit in the side, less time if you just cut around the top and pull the seed pod out by the stem, which I think makes for a supremely silly-looking stuffed pepper. But by all means do it the quick way if you know you're going to use them for *rajas* or other dishes in which they'll be cut into pieces rather than left whole.

Rajas with Fresh Tortillas

SERVES 4 AS AN APPETIZER OR SIDE DISH

RAJAS CON CREMA, STRIPS OF SILKY ROASTED POBLANO, ALTERNATELY SPICY AND MILD, TANGLED UP WITH GOLDEN, ALMOST BUTTERY SAUTÉED ONION IN A WARM, SOOTHING, BUT TART CREAM SAUCE: it's true comfort food for me and mine, especially when served with a couple of fragrant fresh corn tortillas for scooping up every last bit of sauce. Gloriously simple, *rajas* are heavenly with grilled hamburgers, roasted winter squash, or roast chicken, or heated up for breakfast to accompany soft scrambled eggs.

If your grocery store has a refrigerated Mexican-foods section, it almost certainly carries *crema*, which is sort of a thin sour cream. (Also check the meat department; some stores put fresh Mexican cheeses and other dairy products in with the pork and poultry.) That said, I much prefer thicker and tastier homemade crème fraîche here.

For the tortillas:
2 cups masa harina
Pinch of pure kosher salt
Pinch of baking soda

For the *rajas*:
1 teaspoon olive oil
1 white onion, halved lengthwise and cut into ½-inch slices
Pure kosher salt and freshly ground black pepper
6 to 8 frozen roasted poblano chiles (page 151), thawed and cut into ½-inch strips (about 1 pound)
½ cup Crème Fraîche (page 289) or Mexican *crema*

Make the tortillas: In a medium bowl, combine the masa harina, salt, and baking soda. Stir in 1½ cups warm water to make a smooth dough; knead in the bowl or on a work surface for a couple minutes, then cover with plastic wrap and set aside to rest for 30 minutes.

Divide the dough into 8 balls and cover them with plastic wrap. Put 1 ball between sheets of heavy plastic wrap (or a cut-apart freezer bag) and press into a round using a tortilla press, or use a rolling pin to roll it out. Heat a heavy skillet or griddle over medium-high heat, then add the tortilla and cook for 30 seconds to 1 minute on each side, until just starting to brown; transfer to a plate and cover with plastic wrap while you cook the remaining tortillas.

Make the rajas: Heat a heavy skillet over medium heat. Add the oil and the onion, season with salt and pepper to taste, and cook, stirring frequently, until softened and beginning to brown, 5 to 7 minutes. Add the chiles and crème fraîche and bring to a simmer. Taste and add more salt and pepper if necessary. Remove from the heat and serve with the tortillas.

Hot Pickled Okra

MAKES ABOUT 5 PINT JARS

CRISP, SPICY, AND NOT VERY SLIMY AT ALL,
PICKLED OKRA IS A REAL CLASS ACT.

1 tablespoon dill seeds
2½ teaspoons crushed red pepper flakes
4 cups cider vinegar (5% acidity)
2 tablespoons pure kosher salt
2 pounds okra, stems trimmed
5 dried hot red chiles
5 cloves garlic, crushed

Prepare for water-bath canning: Wash the jars and keep them hot in the canning pot, and put the flat lids in a heatproof bowl. (See page 21 for details.)

In a small cup, combine the dill seeds and red pepper flakes.

In a nonreactive pot, combine the vinegar, 4 cups water, and the salt. Bring just to a boil.

Ladle boiling water from the canning pot into the bowl with the lids. Using a jar lifter, remove the hot jars from the canning pot, carefully pouring the water from each one back into the pot, and place them upright on a folded towel. Drain the water off the jar lids.

Working quickly, pack the okra into the jars, and divide the chiles, garlic, and spices among the jars. Ladle the hot vinegar mixture into the jars, leaving ½ inch headspace at the top. Use a chopstick to remove air bubbles around the inside of each jar. Use a damp paper towel to wipe the rims of the jars, then put a flat lid and ring on each jar, adjusting the ring so that it's just finger-tight. Return the jars to the water in the canning pot, making sure the water covers the jars by at least 1 inch. Bring to a boil, and boil for 15 minutes to process. Remove the jars to a folded towel and do not disturb for 12 hours. After 1 hour, check that the lids have sealed by pressing down on the center of each; if it can be pushed down, it hasn't sealed, and the jar should be refrigerated immediately. Label the sealed jars and store.

Creole-Spiced Pickled Okra

MAKES ABOUT 5 PINT JARS

YOU KNOW ABOUT OPEN-REFRIGERATOR-DOOR PICKLES, RIGHT? The pickles you eat one after another while standing in front of the refrigerator with the door open? This is one of those.

4 cups cider vinegar (5% acidity)

2 tablespoons pure kosher salt

2 pounds okra, stems trimmed

5 teaspoons Creole Spice Blend, with no salt added (below)

2½ teaspoons dried onion flakes

CREOLE SPICE BLEND

This is my mom's much improved version of an old *Southern Living* recipe. You can add 2 tablespoons salt, if you'd like, but I find it's more versatile without it—for example, I like to marinate mushrooms in a mixture of Chinese light (not "lite") soy sauce, lime juice, olive oil, and this spice mix before pan-searing or grilling them. Mix all the ingredients in a spice jar and store in a dark spot. Makes about ⅔ cup.

¼ cup ground cayenne

1 tablespoon paprika

1 tablespoon ground coriander

1 tablespoon freshly ground black pepper

2 teaspoons ground cloves

1½ teaspoons garlic powder

1 teaspoon dried thyme, crumbled

Prepare for water-bath canning: Wash the jars and keep them hot in the canning pot, and put the flat lids in a heatproof bowl. (See page 21 for details.)

In a nonreactive pot, combine the vinegar, 4 cups water, and the salt. Bring just to a boil.

Ladle boiling water from the canning pot into the bowl with the lids. Using a jar lifter, remove the hot jars from the canning pot, carefully pouring the water from each one back into the pot, and place them upright on a folded towel. Drain the water off the jar lids.

Working quickly, pack the okra into the jars, and put 1 teaspoon spice blend and ½ teaspoon onion flakes in each jar. Ladle the hot vinegar mixture into the jars, leaving ½ inch headspace at the top. Use a chopstick to remove air bubbles around the inside of each jar. Use a damp paper towel to wipe the rims of the jars, then put a flat lid and ring on each jar, adjusting the ring so that it's just finger-tight. Return the jars to the water in the canning pot, making sure the water covers the jars by at least 1 inch. Bring to a boil, and boil for 15 minutes to process. Remove the jars to a folded towel and do not disturb for 12 hours. After 1 hour, check that the lids have sealed by pressing down on the center of each; if it can be pushed down, it hasn't sealed, and the jar should be refrigerated immediately. Label the sealed jars and store.

"Gumbo" with Chicken and Smoked Sausage

SERES 4

I KNOW THIS ISN'T THE WAY YOU'RE REALLY SUPPOSED TO MAKE TRUE, AUTHENTIC LOUISIANA GUMBO. But it's a foolproof and very tasty approximation for a Tuesday night, so I don't care. You can use frozen okra or pickled okra here.

2 tablespoons vegetable oil

2 tablespoons all-purpose flour

2 cups sliced frozen plain okra (right; do not thaw); or ½ pint jar Creole-Spiced Pickled Okra (page 155), drained and sliced

1 pound boneless, skinless chicken breasts or thighs, or a combination, trimmed and cut into 1-inch pieces

1 teaspoon dried thyme

1 pint Crushed Tomatoes (page 166); or 1 (28-ounce) can whole tomatoes, broken apart with your hands

Pure kosher salt and freshly ground black pepper

6 ounces smoked pork sausage such as andouille or kielbasa, sliced ½ inch thick on the bias

Hot cooked white rice

In a heavy skillet, combine the oil and flour and cook, stirring, over medium heat until caramel colored, about 5 minutes. Add the okra and chicken and sprinkle with the thyme; stir well, then add the tomatoes and their juices. Season with salt and pepper to taste and bring to a simmer over medium-high heat. Simmer until the chicken is cooked through and the sauce is somewhat thick, about 5 minutes.

Meanwhile, in a small sauté pan over high heat, cook the sausage until browned on both sides, about 3 minutes. Stir the sausage into the gumbo, taste and season again if necessary, and serve hot, with a scoop of rice in the center of each serving.

FREEZING OKRA

Last year around okra time, some friends came out to the house for what became known as Okrapalooza—a day of cooking okra every which way we could. One favorite recipe was a beautiful summer succotash that would work very well with frozen vegetables: Fry some bacon. In the bacon fat, sauté onions and garlic. Add corn kernels, a chopped jalapeño, lima beans, sliced okra, halved cherry or grape tomatoes, a splash of vinegar, fresh basil, and salt and pepper. Crumble the bacon over the top and serve.

Frozen plain okra: Bring a large pot of water to a boil and drop in a few handfuls of whole okra pod; after 3 minutes, remove them with a slotted spoon or sieve and put them in a bowl of ice water to cool. Drain, slice if desired, and freeze on a baking sheet in a shallow layer until just firm before transferring the okra to freezer bags.

Frozen cornmeal-breaded okra: Blanch the okra pods and cool them in an ice-water bath as above, then cut them into ½-inch slices and dredge them in a mixture of half cornmeal and half flour seasoned with salt and pepper to taste. Freeze on a baking sheet, then transfer to bags.

Fried Okra with Black-Eyed Pea Relish

SERVES 4

◇◇◇

I LOVE HOW THE LEMON VINAIGRETTE AND THE CHIPOTLE MAYONNAISE MINGLE ON THE PLATE AS THE MEAL PROGRESSES. The contrasting textures of crisp, very lightly breaded okra and creamy little black-eyed peas make for a fun combination.

For the black-eyed peas:

Juice of 1 lemon

1 teaspoon agave nectar or honey

¾ teaspoon pure kosher salt, or more to taste

¼ teaspoon freshly ground black pepper

2 tablespoons olive oil

2 (15.5-ounce) cans black-eyed peas, drained and
   rinsed

½ red bell pepper, diced

½ red onion, diced

2 tablespoons chopped fresh basil or parsley, or a
   combination

For the sauce:

⅓ cup good-quality mayonnaise

1 to 2 chipotle chiles in adobo, finely minced

For the okra:

Vegetable oil

1 pound frozen cornmeal-breaded okra (opposite;
   do not thaw)

Pure kosher salt

Make the black-eyed peas: In a large bowl, whisk together the lemon juice, agave nectar, salt, pepper, and oil. Add the remaining ingredients and toss to combine. Set aside.

Make the sauce: In a small bowl, stir together the mayonnaise and chiles. Set aside.

Make the okra: In a large skillet, heat ½ inch oil over medium-high heat until it shimmers. Add the breaded okra and cook, turning with a slotted spoon or tongs, until golden brown on all sides, about 5 minutes. Remove to a baking sheet lined with paper towels to drain. Sprinkle with salt to taste.

On each of 4 serving plates, spoon a mound of the black-eyed peas. Surround with okra and a few dollops of the sauce. Serve immediately.

Quick French Onion Soup

SERVES 2

THIS MAKES AN ABSOLUTELY LOVELY WINTER-TIME LUNCH, HOMEY AND COMFORTING, OR AN OPENER TO A HEARTIER MAIN COURSE AT SUPPER, AND IT COULD NOT BE EASIER: Just put the frozen onions right in the broth as it heats. I like to add a splash of red wine to the broth, since I'm usually drinking it anyway, but it's certainly not necessary.

1 cup frozen melted sweet onions (below)

4 cups good-quality beef broth or stock (see Note)

3 tablespoons red wine (optional)

Pure kosher salt and freshly ground black pepper

2 slices French bread, cut on a bias

Olive oil

½ cup grated melting cheese such as Gruyère, Emmentaler, Swiss, or Fol Epi

½ teaspoon fresh thyme leaves

Put the onions, broth, and wine, if using, in a medium saucepan and bring to a simmer. Cook until the onions are thawed and heated through, then season with salt and pepper to taste.

Meanwhile, preheat the broiler. Brush one side of the bread slices lightly with oil and toast the oiled side until nicely browned. Flip and toast until the top is just dry. Pile the cheese on top and broil until melted.

Ladle the soup into serving bowls, set the toasts on top, and sprinkle with the thyme. Serve immediately.

Note: If using store-bought broth, you can give it more layers of flavor by simmering it gently for 10 minutes with a bay leaf and a few whole black peppercorns; fish them out, then add the onions.

FREEZING SWEET ONIONS

To my mind, the best way to preserve sweet onions like fresh summer Vidalias or Walla Wallas is to cook them low and slow, then freeze them in small, easy-to-use portions. It's so simple it's almost not a recipe, but these soft, golden onions can be used in many ways to make quick meals. Spread thawed onions over fingertip-dimpled focaccia dough (if you're in a hurry, use pizza dough from a local pizzeria, or from the bakery of a good supermarket), drizzle with olive oil, and sprinkle with cracked black pepper, coarse salt, and rosemary, then bake. Or thaw and warm the onions and spoon a mound of them over cinnamon- and cumin-spiced brown lentils.

Melted sweet onions: Peel 5 pounds onions, cut them in half, then cut lengthwise into ½-inch slices. Put the onions, 2 tablespoons olive oil, and 1 teaspoon pure kosher salt in a wide, 6- to 8-quart preserving pan over medium-low heat and sauté, stirring occasionally, until most of the liquid is evaporated and the onions are silky in texture and deep golden, about 1½ hours. Let cool to room temperature, then spoon 1-cup portions into small sealable plastic containers or freezer bags and freeze. This will make about 3 cups.

Hot Cumin-Pickled Summer Squash

MAKES ABOUT 7 PINT JARS

THE FAMILY AND I WENT TO WILMINGTON, NORTH CAROLINA, THIS PAST SUMMER FOR A WEEKEND OF OUR FAVORITE ACTIVITIES, NEW-TOWN EXPLORING AND NEW-FOOD FINDING. I bought a couple jars of Angela's Pickles at the farmers' market on the river, and when I opened them in the car to taste them (we often eat entire meals—messy tacos, whole cold-smoked mackerels, barbecue, etc.—on our laps in the car when we travel), I was blown away. This is a rough approximation of Angela's squash pickles, a great way to use up a glut of summer squash; check out the Pickled Greens with Fresh Chiles on page 231, inspired by her collards.

4 pounds yellow summer squash or zucchini

8 ounces sweet onion (about 1 medium)

¼ cup plus 1 tablespoon pure kosher salt

2 tablespoons cumin seeds

1 tablespoon yellow mustard seeds

1 tablespoon hot red pepper flakes

1 teaspoon ground cumin

6 cups cider vinegar (5% acidity)

2 tablespoons mild honey

7 cloves garlic

7 small fresh serrano chiles (optional)

Scrub the squash and cut it into ¼-inch rounds. Cut the onion in half lengthwise and thinly slice it into half-circles. Put the squash and onion in a large bowl and sprinkle with the ¼ cup salt, tossing to combine. Cover with a layer of ice cubes and refrigerate for 8 hours or overnight. Pick out any unmelted ice, drain well, and rinse under cold running water. Toss with the cumin seeds, mustard seeds, red pepper flakes, and ground cumin and set aside.

Prepare for water-bath canning: Wash the jars and keep them hot in the canning pot, and put the flat lids in a heatproof bowl. (See page 21 for details.)

In a nonreactive pot, combine the vinegar, 1½ cups water, the honey, and the remaining 1 tablespoon salt. Bring to a boil.

Ladle boiling water from the canning pot into the bowl with the lids. Using a jar lifter, remove the hot jars from the canning pot, carefully pouring the water from each one back into the pot, and place them upright on a folded towel. Drain the water off the jar lids.

Working quickly, pack the squash, onion, garlic, and chiles into the jars (not too tightly). Ladle the hot vinegar mixture into the jars, leaving ½ inch headspace at the top. Use a chopstick to remove air bubbles around the inside of each jar. Use a damp paper towel to wipe the rims of the jars, then put a flat lid and ring on each jar, adjusting the ring so that it's just finger-tight. Return the jars to the water in the canning pot, making sure the water covers the jars by at least 1 inch. Bring to a boil, and boil for 15 minutes to process. Remove the jars to a folded towel and do not disturb for 12 hours. After 1 hour, check that the lids have sealed by pressing down on the center of each; if it can be pushed down, it hasn't sealed, and the jar should be refrigerated immediately. Label the sealed jars and store.

* TOP: Squash- and Rice-Stuffed Roasted Poblanos
BOTTOM, LEFT TO RIGHT: Cumin and Paprika Pickled Turnips
(page 235), Dilly Beans! (page 135), Hot Cumin-Pickled Summer
Squash (page 159)

Squash- and Rice-Stuffed Roasted Poblanos

SERVES 4

IS THERE ANYTHING BETTER THAN CHILES
RELLENOS? No, probably not. I am a real sucker for
the traditional New Mexico–style egg-white-puffy
battered ones stuffed with strips of Jack cheese like
my mom makes, but I actually might prefer lighter
renditions like this one, which is neither battered
nor fried, but simply filled with fluffy rice, cubes of
cuminy squash, and lots of cilantro; it does feature
Mom's signature tomato sauce, complete with the
whole spices that so annoyed me as a kid. If you
have any of the prepared ingredients on hand—the
squash pickles, roasted chiles, or tomato sauce—you
really must try this, as it's quick to pull together
even if you have to roast the chiles or whip up a
makeshift tomato sauce (or use store-bought!). You
could also sauté fresh squash or zucchini in a little
olive oil and use it in place of the pickles.

1 cup raw long-grain white rice

Pure kosher salt

½ pint Hot Cumin-Pickled Summer Squash (page 159),
  drained and diced

¼ cup chopped fresh cilantro

8 roasted poblano chiles (page 151; thawed if frozen)

1 pint All-Purpose Tomato Sauce (page 165), or
  crushed tomatoes simmered with sautéed onion

1 cinnamon stick

½ teaspoon whole black peppercorns

½ teaspoon whole cloves

1 bay leaf

Warmed corn tortillas (page 152)

Preheat the oven to 350°F and lightly oil a baking
dish.

Rinse the rice well in cold water, drain, and put in
a small saucepan with 1¼ cups cold water and ½
teaspoon salt. Bring to a boil, uncovered, over high
heat, then stir once, cover the pot, and reduce the
heat to low. Cook for 14 to 15 minutes, until the
rice is tender and the water is absorbed. Fluff with
a spatula and add the pickled squash and cilantro. Cover the pot and let steam off the heat for 5
minutes.

Arrange the chiles in the baking dish. Spoon the
rice mixture into the chiles. Cover the dish with
aluminum foil and bake for 10 to 15 minutes, until
heated through.

Meanwhile, put the tomato sauce in a small saucepan and add the cinnamon stick, peppercorns,
cloves, and bay leaf. Bring to a boil, then lower the
heat and simmer for 15 minutes. Season with salt to
taste.

Spoon some of the sauce onto serving plates and
use a spatula to transfer two stuffed chiles to each
plate. Tuck a corn tortilla next to the chiles and
serve hot.

Zucchini Bread-and-Butter Pickles with Ginger

MAKES ABOUT 6 PINT JARS

I DEVELOPED THIS RECIPE BASED ON AN EMAIL CORRESPONDENCE WITH MY FRIEND DAVID CENTNER, A.K.A. FATHER KITCHEN (WHOM I MET VIA CHOWHOUND). He said he likes B&Bs with coriander, and also ones made with zucchini instead of cucumbers. For health reasons he prefers not to eat sweet things, though, so I made these much less sweet than standard versions, which can be extremely cloying, and used agave nectar, which purportedly does not raise blood sugar as much as sugar or honey.

4 pounds zucchini

1 pound small sweet onions (about 2)

¼ cup plus 1 tablespoon pure kosher salt

2 tablespoons coriander seeds

1 tablespoon yellow mustard seeds

2 teaspoons crushed red pepper flakes

6 cups cider vinegar (5% acidity)

½ cup light agave nectar, or ¾ cup mild honey

1½ teaspoons turmeric

1½ teaspoons dry mustard powder

6 thin rounds fresh ginger

Scrub the zucchini and cut them into ¼-inch rounds. Cut the onions in half lengthwise and thinly slice them into half-circles. Put the zucchini and onions in a large bowl and sprinkle with the ¼ cup salt, tossing to combine. Cover with a layer of ice cubes and refrigerate for 8 hours or overnight. Pick out any unmelted ice, drain well, and rinse under cold running water. Toss with the coriander seeds, mustard seeds, and red pepper flakes and set aside.

Prepare for water-bath canning: Wash the jars and keep them hot in the canning pot, and put the flat lids in a heatproof bowl. (See page 21 for details.)

In a nonreactive pot, combine the vinegar, 1½ cups water, the agave nectar, turmeric, mustard powder, and the remaining 1 tablespoon salt. Bring to a boil.

Ladle boiling water from the canning pot into the bowl with the lids. Using a jar lifter, remove the hot jars from the canning pot, carefully pouring the water from each one back into the pot, and place them upright on a folded towel. Drain the water off the jar lids.

Working quickly, put a slice of ginger in each jar, then pack the zucchini and onions into the jars (not too tightly). Ladle the hot vinegar mixture into the jars, leaving ½ inch headspace at the top. Use a chopstick to remove air bubbles around the inside of each jar. Use a damp paper towel to wipe the rims of the jars, then put a flat lid and ring on each jar, adjusting the ring so that it's just finger-tight. Return the jars to the water in the canning pot, making sure the water covers the jars by at least 1 inch. Bring to a boil, and boil for 15 minutes to process. Remove the jars to a folded towel and do not disturb for 12 hours. After 1 hour, check that the lids have sealed by pressing down on the center of each; if it can be pushed down, it hasn't sealed, and the jar should be refrigerated immediately. Label the sealed jars and store.

Salsa Verde

MAKES ABOUT 4 PINT JARS

◇◇

BROILING ALL THE VEGETABLES BEFORE BLENDING THEM TOGETHER, AS RICK BAYLESS DESCRIBES IN *MEXICAN KITCHEN*, ADDS A KIND OF SMOKINESS TO THIS CLASSIC TOMATILLO-BASED SAUCE. And Beverly Cox and Martin Jacobs, in their exhaustively researched book of Latin American indigenous foods *Spirit of the Earth*, point out that roasting the tomatillos (traditionally on a *comal*, or heavy griddle) tempers their acidity.

Look for firm, bright green tomatillos in Latin and Asian markets in high summer, when they're only about as expensive as red tomatoes—and more reliably ripe.

3½ pounds tomatillos, papery husks and stems removed, rinsed

1 medium white onion (4 ounces), peeled and cut into 1-inch chunks

5 large serrano chiles (2 ounces)

5 large cloves garlic, peeled

1 firmly packed cup roughly chopped fresh cilantro

⅔ cup fresh lime juice

1 tablespoon pure kosher salt, or to taste

Preheat the oven to 500°F.

Prepare for water-bath canning: Sterilize the jars and keep them hot in the canning pot, and put the flat lids in a heatproof bowl. (See page 21 for details.)

Put all the vegetables in a single layer in baking dishes or on rimmed baking sheets and roast for 20 to 35 minutes, turning occasionally, until blackened in spots and the tomatillos are soft, collapsed, and leaking. Working in batches, puree the vegetables and their juices, along with the cilantro, in a blender, covering the lid with a towel to prevent the hot liquid from erupting. Put the puree in a wide, 6- to 8-quart preserving pan or other nonreactive pot and stir in the lime juice and salt. Bring to a boil.

Ladle boiling water from the canning pot into the bowl with the lids. Using a jar lifter, remove the sterilized jars from the canning pot, carefully pouring the water from each one back into the pot, and place them upright on a folded towel. Drain the water off the jar lids.

Ladle the hot salsa into the jars, leaving ½ inch headspace at the top. Use a damp paper towel to wipe the rims of the jars, then put a flat lid and ring on each jar, adjusting the ring so that it's just finger-tight. Return the jars to the water in the canning pot, making sure the water covers the jars by at least 1 inch. Bring to a boil, and boil for 5 minutes to process. Remove the jars to a folded towel and do not disturb for 12 hours. After 1 hour, check that the lids have sealed by pressing down on the center of each; if it can be pushed down, it hasn't sealed, and the jar should be refrigerated immediately. Label the sealed jars and store.

Enchiladas Verdes

SERVES 4

◇◇

4 chicken leg quarters (about 3½ pounds)
Pure kosher salt and freshly ground black pepper
1 pint Salsa Verde (page 163)
8 corn tortillas (page 152)
½ cup chicken stock or water
2 cups grated Monterey Jack cheese, or 1 cup crumbled *queso fresco*
½ cup Mexican *crema* or whisked sour cream (optional)

Preheat the oven to 400°F.

Put the chicken in a baking dish and season lightly with salt and pepper. Roast until well browned and the juices run clear, about 1 hour. Leave the oven on. When the chicken is cool enough to handle, pull the meat off the bones and put it in a large bowl, discarding the bones, skin, and large pieces of fat. Shred the meat with your hands, then pour ½ cup of the salsa over the meat and toss to coat. Taste, and season with salt and pepper if necessary. Set aside.

Heat a skillet over medium-high heat. One or two at a time, cook the tortillas until just tender and pliable, about 1 minute on each side, stacking them on a plate and covering with a clean towel as they cook. Lightly oil a clean 9-by-11-inch baking dish. Fill each tortilla with some of the chicken and roll it closed. Arrange the filled tortillas seam side down in the baking dish; they should fit snugly. (The enchiladas can be prepared to this point up to 8 hours in advance, covered with plastic wrap, and refrigerated.)

Stir the stock into the remaining salsa, season with salt and pepper if necessary, and pour it over the stuffed tortillas. If using Monterey Jack, sprinkle the cheese all over the top. Bake until the salsa is bubbling and the cheese is melted, about 30 minutes. (If using *queso fresco*, sprinkle it on top just before serving.) Drizzle with *crema*, if using, and serve hot.

DEPARTMENT OF NOT WASTING ANYTHING: DRIED TOMATO PEELS

Put the tomato peels left over from a canning session in one layer on baking sheets lined with parchment paper. Try to spread the pieces out flat, but it's fine if they're doubled over or twisted in places. Bake in a 200°F oven for about 1½ hours, until the peels are dry and crisp, then let them cool to room temperature in the oven. Crumble them up or grind them to a finer powder in a spice mill and store in an airtight jar in a cool, dry, dark spot (preferably next to your canisters of algin and calcic, ha). I've sprinkled it on homemade vanilla ice cream, to which it adds a subtle tartness; and tossed it with cauliflower, along with mustard seeds, cumin seeds, turmeric, salt, and olive oil for roasting. Use larger shards of dried peels as pretty garnishes atop vegetable purees or pan-seared fish.

All-Purpose Tomato Sauce

MAKES ABOUT 4 PINT JARS

◇◇

MY FOLKS USED TO PUT UP JAR AFTER JAR OF EVERY KIND OF TOMATO SAUCE IMAGINABLE: "SPAGHETTI SAUCE," "PIZZA SAUCE," "ENCHILADA SAUCE," "CHILES RELLENOS SAUCE," AND SO ON. They had bushels of tomatoes to process, so I guess it made sense for them to anticipate all the different things they'd do with tomato sauce throughout the year. For me, this all-purpose sauce is much more practical, and I try to put up as much of it as possible in the summertime. (I do wish I had a couple of propane burners and some giant nonreactive cauldrons so I could make it in industrial-size amounts instead of measly 4-pint batches, but even so it's well worth the time.)

About 12 pounds tomatoes, preferably Roma, peeled (see Note)
1 tablespoon olive oil
12 ounces onion, diced (about 2 small)
2 large cloves garlic
2 teaspoons pure kosher salt, or to taste
About 2 teaspoons citric acid

Break the tomatoes apart and use your fingers to scrape out the seeds. Working in batches, put the flesh in a blender or food processor and puree until very smooth. You should have 12 cups puree; reserve any extra for another use. Set aside.

In a wide, 6- to 8-quart preserving pan, heat the oil over medium-high heat. Add the onion and sauté until translucent, about 5 minutes. Add the garlic and sauté, stirring constantly, for 1 minute. Pour in the 12 cups tomato puree and bring to a boil over high heat. Lower the heat and simmer, stirring occasionally, until the sauce darkens a shade and is reduced by one third, about 45 minutes. Season with salt to taste.

Meanwhile, prepare for water-bath canning: Wash the jars and keep them hot in the canning pot, and put the flat lids in a heatproof bowl. (See page 21 for details.)

Ladle boiling water from the canning pot into the bowl with the lids. Using a jar lifter, remove the hot jars from the canning pot, carefully pouring the water from each one back into the pot, and place them upright on a folded towel. Drain the water off the jar lids.

Put ½ teaspoon citric acid in each jar. Spoon the hot sauce into the jars, leaving ½ inch headspace at the top. Use a damp paper towel to wipe the rims of the jars, then put a flat lid and ring on each jar, adjusting the ring so that it's just finger-tight. Return the jars to the water in the canning pot, making sure the water covers the jars by at least 1 inch. Bring to a boil, and boil for 35 minutes to process. Remove the jars to a folded towel and do not disturb for 12 hours. After 1 hour, check that the lids have sealed by pressing down on the center of each; if it can be pushed down, it hasn't sealed, and the jar should be refrigerated immediately. Label the sealed jars and store.

Note: To peel tomatoes: Bring a large pot of water to a boil. Fill a large bowl with ice water. Near the bowl of ice water, have ready a medium bowl (for the peels and seeds) and another bowl (for the peeled tomatoes).

A few at a time, drop the tomatoes into the water; after 30 seconds, remove them with a slotted spoon to the ice bath to cool. Pull off the peels and cut out the core (or dig it out with your thumbnail).

Crushed Tomatoes

MAKES ABOUT 7 PINT JARS

I HAVE VIVID MEMORIES MOSTLY OF TRYING TO STAY OUT OF MY PARENTS' KITCHEN ON CANNING DAYS. Not one but two huge canning pots would be full and boiling morning to night. They'd set up a propane burner out in the herb garden next to the kitchen door so they could have several pots of sauce simmering at once. There was one legendary weekend we all still remember. My mom was out of town for some reason (though the reason may have been anticipation of what followed), and my dad and his buddy Buster, a rancher from Montana who was living with us at the time, took it upon themselves to can every ripe tomato in the garden. They put up two hundred quarts—quarts—in two days. My mom limited my dad to a single tomato plant the next year, even though he also built custom shelves in the two pantry closets to hold all the jars.

In a big canning pot you can process up to 7 pint jars at a time. Since 1 pound of tomatoes will yield about 1 pint of crushed seeded tomatoes, I work with tomatoes in 7-pound batches, which is also about as much as my stainless-steel preserving pan will hold at once. I peel, seed, crush, boil, and pack one batch of tomatoes, then begin peeling and seeding the next batch while the first 7 jars are processing in the canner. I've found this to be the most efficient way to can tomatoes by myself, and I can do about three canner loads in a long morning—not a bad way to end up with 21 pints of tomatoes (plus a handful of jars of tomato juice, which I either process right away in a fourth canner load or after a shower and a cold beer).

Salt and basil are optional; I rarely add either. Citric acid, on the other hand, is not optional: Your tomatoes, depending on their variety, at what point in the season they were harvested, and the particu-lar conditions under which they were grown, may not be quite acidic enough to be safely preserved in a boiling-water bath. Citric acid, which is sold as a fine white powder, will lower the pH to an acceptable level. Some folks put 1 tablespoon bottled lemon juice in each jar instead of citric acid, but I find the citric acid to be easier to use, and its flavor less intrusive, than lemon juice. Citric acid can be found in the canning section of some grocery stores or online (see Sources, page 291). (Fruit Fresh, usually used to prevent discoloration of fruits, is a combination of citric and ascorbic acids, cut with an anti-caking agent.)

7 pounds ripe tomatoes, preferably Roma
Citric acid (¼ teaspoon per pint jar), Fruit Fresh
    (½ teaspoon per pint jar), or bottled lemon juice
    (1 tablespoon per pint jar)
Pure kosher salt (optional)
7 fresh basil leaves (optional)

Bring a large pot of water to a boil. Fill a large bowl with ice water. Near the bowl of ice water, have ready a medium bowl (for the peels and seeds) and a 6- to 8-quart preserving pan (for the crushed tomatoes).

A few at a time, drop the tomatoes into the water; after 30 seconds, remove them with a slotted spoon to the ice bath to cool. Pull off the peels and cut out the core (or dig it out with your thumbnail). Rip each tomato into pieces and scrape most of the seeds out into a bowl with the peels. Put the seeded tomatoes in the preserving pan. Repeat with the remaining tomatoes. (Reserve the peels and seeds for another use; see below.)

Prepare for water-bath canning: Wash the jars and keep them hot in the canning pot, and put the flat lids in a heatproof bowl. (See page 21 for details.)

Set the pan with the tomatoes over medium-high heat and bring to a boil. Boil for 5 minutes.

Ladle boiling water from the canning pot into the bowl with the lids. Using a jar lifter, remove the hot jars from the canning pot, carefully pouring the water from each one back into the pot, and place them upright on a folded towel. Drain the water off the jar lids.

Put ¼ teaspoon citric acid (or ½ teaspoon Fruit Fresh, or 1 tablespoon bottled lemon juice) and ½ teaspoon salt, if using, in each jar. Ladle the hot tomatoes into the jars, leaving ½ inch headspace at the top. If desired, tuck a basil leaf into each jar. Use a chopstick to remove air bubbles around the inside of each jar. Use a damp paper towel to wipe the rims of the jars, then put a flat lid and ring on each jar, adjusting the ring so that it's just finger-tight. Return the jars to the water in the canning pot, making sure the water covers the jars by at least 1 inch. Bring to a boil, and boil for 35 minutes to process. Remove the jars to a folded towel and do not disturb for 12 hours. After 1 hour, check that the lids have sealed by pressing down on the center of each; if it can be pushed down, it hasn't sealed, and the jar should be refrigerated immediately. Label the sealed jars and store.

Tomato Juice

MAKES ABOUT 4 PINT JARS

◇◇◇

I TEND TO MAKE TOMATO JUICE ONLY AS A BYPRODUCT OF TOMATO CANNING. It's thinner than the juice made from tomatoes that have been simmered until soft and then passed through a food mill, but to my mind more refreshing and just as intensely tomato flavored. I usually get about 4 pints of juice per morning of canning—not a lot, but well worth loading up the canner one more time.

Seeds and peels from canning 21 pints tomatoes
¼ teaspoon citric acid, ½ teaspoon Fruit Fresh, or
  1 tablespoon bottled lemon juice per pint jar
½ teaspoon pure kosher salt per pint jar (optional)

Pass the seeds and peels through a food mill fitted with the fine screen into a nonreactive saucepan, or put them in a sieve and use a spatula or spoon to push as much juice through as possible. Bring the juice to a boil; boil for 1 minute. Heat pint jars in the canning pot of boiling water, then remove them to a folded towel. Put the citric acid and salt, if desired, in each jar. Ladle in the boiling tomato juice, put the lids on, and process for 35 minutes in a boiling-water bath as described on page 167.

Note: If you'd prefer a thicker juice, pass roughly chopped raw tomatoes through a Squeezo strainer or a food mill fitted with the disk with the finest holes to get rid of the skins and seeds (or most of them). Bring the juice and pulp to a boil and boil, stirring frequently, for 5 minutes. Put the citric acid and salt, if desired, in each pint jar, or twice as much in quart jars. Ladle in the boiling tomato juice, put the lids on, and process pints or quarts for 35 minutes in a boiling-water bath.

THINGS TO PUT IN A BLOODY MARY IN ADDITION TO VODKA

Tomato juice seasoned with:

* Worcestershire sauce or soy sauce

* Balsamic vinegar or pickle juice

* Grated fresh horseradish

* Coarsely ground black pepper

* Fresh lime or lemon juice

* Hot sauce

* Dried ground habanero chiles (see page 103)

* Ground cayenne

Garnishes—I believe the more the better:

* Celery sticks

* Green olives

* Lemon or lime wedges

* Hot Pickled Okra (page 154)

* Dilly Beans! (page 135)

* Whole Jalapeños with Honey and Allspice (page 146)

* Pickled Garlic Scapes (page 142)

* Pickled peppers (see page 144)

Charred Tomato and Chile Salsa

MAKES ABOUT 5 PINT JARS

◇◇

MY LATE UNCLE LLOYD, WHO WAS A SEABEE IN VIETNAM AND PROBABLY THE TOUGHEST PERSON I'VE EVER KNOWN, WAS ALSO A BONA-FIDE CHILE FANATIC, ALWAYS TESTING THE LIMITS OF HIS AND HIS FAMILY'S TOLERANCE WITH EVER HOTTER CONCOCTIONS. This salsa, which my dad has been making for decades and which has become legendary in our family, is based on Lloyd's best salsa, although I've cut down the heat and the sugar a fair amount. Ten jalapeños makes a hot but not unbearable salsa. If you want to make it hotter, use a hotter variety of chile rather than adding more jalapeños, lest the additional non-acid ingredients push the pH too high for boiling-water-bath canning.

5 pounds tomatoes, halved lengthwise, cores cut out

8 ounces red jalapeño chiles (about 10), stemmed and halved lengthwise

2 ounces garlic (about 12 cloves), peeled

1 pound, 6 ounces onions (about 3 small), peeled and quartered

½ cup cider vinegar (5% acidity)

1 tablespoon salt, or more to taste

2 tablespoons sugar

Prepare for water-bath canning: Wash the jars and keep them hot in the canning pot, and put the flat lids in a heatproof bowl. (See page 21 for details.)

Preheat the broiler to high and set a rack about 4 inches from the heating element. Line a rimmed baking sheet with aluminum foil.

Working in batches, put the tomatoes cut side down on the baking sheet and broil for about 10 minutes, until the skin is blistered and black in places. Put the tomatoes in a large bowl and set aside. Broil the chiles, garlic, and onions until blackened. When the tomatoes are cool enough to handle, pull off the skins and return only the charred bits to the bowl. In three batches, put all the broiled vegetables in a blender and pulse until just coarsely chopped; transfer to a wide, 6- to 8-quart preserving pan and add the remaining ingredients. Bring to a boil and boil for 5 minutes.

Ladle boiling water from the canning pot into the bowl with the lids. Using a jar lifter, remove the hot jars from the canning pot, carefully pouring the water from each one back into the pot, and place them upright on a folded towel. Drain the water off the jar lids.

Spoon the hot salsa into the jars, leaving ½ inch headspace at the top. Use a damp paper towel to wipe the rims of the jars, then put a flat lid and ring on each jar, adjusting the ring so that it's just finger-tight. Return the jars to the water in the canning pot, making sure the water covers the jars by at least 1 inch. Bring to a boil, and boil for 40 minutes to process. Remove the jars to a folded towel and do not disturb for 12 hours. After 1 hour, check that the lids have sealed by pressing down on the center of each; if it can be pushed down, it hasn't sealed, and the jar should be refrigerated immediately. Label the sealed jars and store.

✳ Bloody Mary fixings, including Mango and Peach Habanero Hot Sauce
(page 102), Dilly Beans! (page 135), and Tomato Juice (page 168)

Chili

SERVES 6 TO 8

IN MY FANTASY WORLD, EVERY FAMILY IN AMERICA WOULD COOK FOR THEMSELVES MOST NIGHTS OF THE WEEK, AND EVERY FAMILY WOULD HAVE ITS OWN VERSION OF A SLOW-SIMMERED WINTER-SUNDAY CHILI. The following is my mom and dad's—the one my brother and I grew up with. It was always made with lean venison (we rarely had beef in our house because our neighbors and friends were always so generous with their deer and because my dad, who "hunted" in his bathrobe from a recliner next to the window in his second-floor bedroom, occasionally got lucky), but now I just use beef—a well-marbled slab of chuck is best here.

Try the chili spooned over the Snack-Size Faux Tamales on page 140.

1½ tablespoons cumin seeds

1 teaspoon allspice berries

2 tablespoons olive oil

2 large onions, chopped

3 cloves garlic, minced

2½ pounds well-trimmed beef chuck or venison shoulder, cut into ½-inch pieces

1 pint Crushed Tomatoes (page 166); or 1 (28-ounce) can whole tomatoes with their juices, crushed with your hands

1 pint Charred Tomato and Chile Salsa page 169)

2 teaspoons pure kosher salt, or more to taste

2 ribs celery, chopped

2 (15-ounce) cans dark red kidney beans, drained and rinsed

In a heavy skillet over medium-high heat, toast the cumin, stirring constantly, until fragrant, about 3 minutes. Grind it, along with the allspice, with a mortar and pestle; set aside.

In a Dutch oven or heavy pot over medium-high heat, heat 1 tablespoon of the oil. Add the onions and garlic and cook, stirring frequently, until lightly browned, about 8 minutes. Transfer to a large bowl and return the pot to high heat. Add ½ tablespoon of the oil and half of the beef or venison and cook, turning occasionally, until well browned all over, about 10 minutes. Transfer to the bowl with the onion mixture. Brown the remaining meat in the remaining ½ tablespoon oil, then return the onions, garlic, and first batch of meat to the pot. Stir in the cumin and allspice, then add the tomatoes, salsa, and salt. Cover and bring to a boil, then lower the heat and simmer, stirring occasionally, until the meat is very tender and falling apart, 2½ to 3 hours, adding a cupful of water now and then if it becomes too thick and uncovering the pot for the last 30 minutes of simmering to thicken it.

Add the celery and beans and cook, uncovered, until the celery is tender, about 20 minutes. Taste and season with more salt, if necessary. Serve.

Good Ketchup

MAKES ABOUT 4 HALF-PINT JARS

THIS IS A BASIC, NO-FRILLS TOMATO KETCHUP, SWEET AND TANGY BUT A BIT LESS OF EITHER THAN STORE-BOUGHT—AND SIGNIFICANTLY MORE AT HOME TOWARD THE BOTTOM OF THE FOOD PYRAMID. If you're like me, you'll want to futz around and add things like smoked paprika, a couple of canned chipotle chiles, a tablespoon or two of chopped fresh ginger or a fresh chile. You could also replace a few of the tomatoes with nectarines or peaches and reduce the amount of sugar you add.

1 tablespoon olive oil

8 ounces onion (about 1 large), chopped

3 cloves garlic, chopped

7 pounds tomatoes, preferably Roma, chopped

½ cup cider vinegar (5% acidity), or more to taste

½ cup packed brown sugar or honey, or ⅓ cup agave nectar, or more to taste

2 teaspoons pure kosher salt

1 teaspoon paprika

1 teaspoon ground cinnamon

½ teaspoon ground cloves

½ teaspoon ground allspice

¼ teaspoon ground cayenne

In a wide, 6- to 8-quart preserving pan, heat the oil over medium heat. Add the onion and garlic and sauté, stirring frequently, until the onion is translucent and soft but not browned, 5 to 7 minutes. Add the remaining ingredients and cook, stirring occasionally, until the tomatoes are very soft, about 30 minutes. Pass the mixture through a Squeezo strainer or a food mill fitted with the disk with the smallest holes to remove the seeds, or puree the mixture in a blender in batches then push it through a sieve.

Prepare for water-bath canning: Wash the jars and keep them hot in the canning pot, and put the flat lids in a heatproof bowl. (See page 21 for details.)

Rinse out the preserving pan and return the puree to the pan. Bring to a boil, then lower the heat and simmer, stirring frequently to prevent the solids from sticking at the bottom, until thick; this could take as long as 2 hours, depending on your patience and your need for thickness. (I confess I never manage to keep mine going quite long enough to make a very viscous condiment.) Taste, and add more vinegar or sugar as necessary.

Ladle boiling water from the canning pot into the bowl with the lids. Using a jar lifter, remove the sterilized jars from the canning pot, carefully pouring the water from each one back into the pot, and place them upright on a folded towel. Drain the water off the jar lids.

Ladle the hot ketchup into the jars, leaving ¼ inch headspace at the top. Use a damp paper towel to wipe the rims of the jars, then put a flat lid and ring on each jar, adjusting the ring so that it's just finger-tight. Return the jars to the water in the canning pot, making sure the water covers the jars by at least 1 inch. Bring to a boil, and boil for 20 minutes to process. Remove the jars to a folded towel and do not disturb for 12 hours. After 1 hour, check that the lids have sealed by pressing down on the center of each; if it can be pushed down, it hasn't sealed, and the jar should be refrigerated immediately. Label the sealed jars and store.

Tomato and Cashew Chutney

MAKES ABOUT 7 HALF-PINT JARS

THERE ARE A THOUSAND TOMATO CHUT-
NEYS IN THE WORLD, AND I LOVE THEM ALL—
FROM THE SIMPLEST (CHOPPED TOMATOES,
CHILES, ONION, AND GINGER, COOKED WITH
MUSTARD SEEDS AND CUMIN AND SHOW-
ERED WITH FRESH CILANTRO) TO THE MORE
COMPLEX, LIKE THIS ONE. Though not quite as
sweet as similar chutneys, with the sugar and dried
mangoes (plus the maple-syrup note sounded by
the fenugreek, and the sweetness of the chewy-soft
cashews), it's jammy enough to balance the heat of
fresh chiles and ground cayenne—in fact, feel free
to add more of the latter to suit your taste—and
provide a luxurious counterpoint to a spicy dal.
Serve it with plain rice or a pilaf, or spoon a bit over
an omelet as you would salsa (okay, as my dad and
I would) and sprinkle the whole thing with fresh
cilantro.

1 tablespoon vegetable oil

6 ounces diced onion (about 1 small)

2 tablespoons minced fresh ginger

1 tablespoon minced garlic

2 teaspoons brown mustard seeds

1 teaspoon cumin seeds

1 teaspoon crushed fenugreek

1 cup coarsely chopped unroasted cashews

½ cup diced dried mangoes, golden raisins, or diced
   dried apricots

3 pounds tomatoes, preferably Roma, peeled (see
   Note, page 165) and diced (about 6 cups)

3 jalapeño chiles, seeded and diced

½ teaspoon ground cayenne

4 teaspoons pure kosher salt

¾ cup sugar

½ cup cider vinegar (5% acidity)

Prepare for water-bath canning: Wash the jars and
keep them hot in the canning pot, and put the flat
lids in a heatproof bowl. (See page 21 for details.)

In a wide, 6- to 8-quart preserving pan, heat the oil
over medium-high heat. Add the onion and sauté,
stirring, until just soft, about 3 minutes. Add the
ginger and garlic and sauté for 30 seconds. Add the
mustard seeds, cumin seeds, fenugreek, cashews,
and mangoes and sauté for 1 minute. Add the
remaining ingredients, bring to a boil, then lower
the heat and simmer briskly until the vegetables are
tender but still hold their shape and the chutney is
somewhat thick, 10 to 15 minutes.

Ladle boiling water from the canning pot into the
bowl with the lids. Using a jar lifter, remove the hot
jars from the canning pot, carefully pouring the
water from each one back into the pot, and place
them upright on a folded towel. Drain the water off
the jar lids.

Ladle the hot chutney into the jars, leaving ¼ inch
headspace at the top. Use a damp paper towel to
wipe the rims of the jars, then put a flat lid and ring
on each jar, adjusting the ring so that it's just finger-
tight. Return the jars to the water in the canning
pot, making sure the water covers the jars by at
least 1 inch. Bring to a boil, and boil for 35 minutes
to process. Remove the jars to a folded towel and do
not disturb for 12 hours. After 1 hour, check that the
lids have sealed by pressing down on the center of
each; if it can be pushed down, it hasn't sealed, and
the jar should be refrigerated immediately. Label
the sealed jars and store.

FREEZING TOMATOES

For whatever reason—overbuying, a spontaneous trip out of town that precludes a weekend of canning, or a good harvest despite the neglect I tend to lavish on my tomato plants—I occasionally find myself (and if you're lucky, you do too) in the midst of a tomato emergency. Tomatoes rotting in boxes on the dining room table, tomatoes rotting on the vine, tomatoes rotting on the porch! Here are a couple ways I deal with them when I don't have the time or energy for canning.

Slow-roasted tomatoes: Find as many rimmed baking sheets as will fit in your oven or will hold all your tomatoes, halved, in one layer. (You can fit about 8 pounds of Roma-type tomatoes on four quarter-sheet pans or similar. The tomatoes won't release a lot of juices into the pan, so if all you have are flat baking sheets, you can jury-rig them by lining them with aluminum foil and folding the edges up to make rims.) Drizzle some olive oil in the bottom of each pan and sprinkle it with pure kosher salt, freshly ground black pepper, and dried herbs: basil, thyme, oregano, ground fennel, parsley—I think this works best with Italianate herbs, but be creative. (For four quarter-sheet pans, you'd use about 2 tablespoons oil, 2 teaspoons salt, ½ teaspoon pepper, and 1 teaspoon each dried herb.) Halve the tomatoes lengthwise and arrange them cut side down over the oil in a single layer. Tuck a few unpeeled garlic cloves among them and drizzle with a touch more oil. Roast at 200°F for about 10 hours, until the tomatoes are collapsed, the peels are shriveled and look blistered, and the cut sides are lightly browned; the garlic will be very soft.

Pick off the peels, then pack the tomatoes tightly into small freezer bags, sucking out as much air as possible before you seal them. Label (they look a bit freakish when frozen, and in a couple months you might not remember what the heck they are) and freeze.

Whole frozen tomatoes: Despite what the old books say, raw tomatoes freeze remarkably well, if you don't peel them. Rinse them off, pat them dry, stick them in freezer bags, and freeze—simple as that. No need to freeze separately on baking sheets or anything. When you're ready to use them—and they can be plucked out of the bag two or three at a time; so convenient!—put them in a colander and run cold water over them. The peels will slip right off. Thaw the rest of the way in a bowl to catch the juices. They're not quite as good as fresh, but just about as good as canned.

USES FOR SLOW-ROASTED TOMATOES

* Smashed onto slices of grilled bread, and in sandwiches.

* As a nice low-moisture pizza topping, natch.

* Pureed and stirred into brothy vegetarian or vegan soups to give them body and depth.

* Sliced and sautéed with a little chicken and strips of roasted red peppers or poblano chiles and tossed with pasta.

* Diced and stuffed into *onigiri* (page 225).

* Pureed into a sort of pesto with lots of basil or parsley, some hard cheese, toasted nuts, and a drizzle of olive oil.

* Diced and tossed into hot brown rice.

Tomato and Basil Jam with Sherry Vinegar

MAKES ABOUT 4 HALF-PINT JARS

◇◇

THERE'S ALMOST NOTHING MORE APPEALING THAN A TOASTED AND BUTTERED ENGLISH MUFFIN SPREAD WITH THE HERBAL SWEET-TART GOODNESS OF TOMATO AND BASIL JAM. Except that there is: a toasted and *cream-cheesed* English muffin with tomato and basil jam.

This version of the old Ball Blue Book standby is intensely tomato-flavored because no commercial pectin is used, but is nevertheless just similar enough to the Ball jam—the one I remember from my childhood—that those who remember it fondly will not be disappointed by what follows. You'll need a colander and a large bowl for draining the tomatoes and catching their juices, and also a sieve—fine or medium—to push the juice and apple pulp through after it's cooked down.

3 pounds ripe tomatoes, peeled (see Note, page 165), cored, and diced

2 pounds Granny Smith apples, diced but not peeled or cored

1 lemon, chopped

2 cups sugar

¼ cup sherry vinegar (7% acidity)

¼ cup chopped fresh basil

Prepare for water-bath canning: Sterilize the jars and keep them hot in the canning pot, put a small plate in the freezer, and put the flat lids in a heat-proof bowl. (See page 21 for details.)

Put the tomatoes in a wide, 6- to 8-quart preserving pan. Bring to a boil over high heat and cook until the juices cover the tomatoes, about 5 minutes. Pour into a colander set over a large bowl. Return the juice to the pan and add the apples and lemon. Bring to a boil over high heat. Boil, stirring occasionally, until the apples are completely broken down and the peels have separated from the pulp, about 15 minutes.

Dump the tomato solids into the bowl and place a sieve over the bowl. Pour the apple and lemon mixture into the sieve and press as much of the juice and apple pulp through the sieve as you can. Discard the solids in the sieve.

Rinse the preserving pan and pour in the tomato mixture; add the sugar and vinegar. Bring to a boil over high heat and boil, stirring frequently, until a small dab of the jam spooned onto the cold plate and set in the freezer for a minute wrinkles when you nudge it, about 15 minutes. Remove from the heat and stir in the basil.

Ladle boiling water from the canning pot into the bowl with the lids. Using a jar lifter, remove the sterilized jars from the canning pot, carefully pouring the water from each one back into the pot, and place them upright on a folded towel. Drain the water off the jar lids.

Ladle the hot jam into the jars, leaving ¼ inch headspace at the top. Use a damp paper towel to wipe the rims of the jars, then put a flat lid and ring on each jar, adjusting the ring so that it's just finger-tight. Return the jars to the water in the canning pot, making sure the water covers the jars by at least 1 inch. Bring to a boil, and boil for 5 minutes to process. Remove the jars to a folded towel and do not disturb for 12 hours. After 1 hour, check that the lids have sealed by pressing down on the center of each; if it can be pushed down, it hasn't sealed, and the jar should be refrigerated immediately. Label the sealed jars and store.

Extra-Crisp Watermelon Rind Pickles

MAKES 4 PINT JARS, OR 8 HALF-PINT JARS

THIS AND GRANDMA BARRON'S GREEN TOMATO RELISH ARE THE ONLY RECIPES IN THIS BOOK IN WHICH I USE PICKLING LIME TO KEEP THE PICKLES CRISP. I use it here because to my mind a soft watermelon-rind pickle is an absolute travesty of nature.

Pickling lime, which is food-grade calcium hydroxide, is perfectly safe, and can be found in the canning-supplies section of any grocery store. It's very important, though, to *soak and rinse the rinds several times* after treating them with lime: If any lime remains, it will neutralize the acid necessary for preservation, and the pickle will spoil.

All that said, these are wonderful pickles, and you should make lots of them! One or two little squares make a perfect sweet-sour treat, especially if they're ice-cold, straight out of the fridge.

Rind from 1 small watermelon
2 tablespoons pickling lime (see above)
3 cups distilled white vinegar (5% acidity)
3 cups sugar
1 lemon, coarsely chopped
1 inch fresh ginger, peeled and coarsely chopped
1½ teaspoons whole allspice
1½ teaspoons whole cloves
2 cinnamon sticks

Trim off the pink flesh and the green and pale green outer portion of the watermelon rind and cut the rind into 1-inch squares or other shapes. You should have about 2 pounds prepared rind. Put the rind in a large bowl with 7 cups water and the pickling lime and stir to combine. Cover the bowl and set aside at room temperature for 8 hours or overnight.

Drain in a colander, rinse well, and cover with cold water. Let soak for 1 hour, then drain. Repeat the soaking and draining two more times to remove all of the lime; do not skip this step.

In a wide, 6- to 8-quart preserving pan, combine the vinegar, 3 cups water, and the sugar. Put the lemon, ginger, allspice, cloves, and cinnamon in a cheesecloth bag and add it to the pan. Bring to a boil, stirring to dissolve the sugar. Add the rind, then remove from the heat and let soak for at least 4 hours and up to 12 hours. Bring to a boil, then lower the heat and simmer until the rind is evenly translucent and tender but still crisp, about 1 hour and 15 minutes. Remove the cheesecloth bag.

Prepare for water-bath canning: Wash the jars and keep them hot in the canning pot, and put the flat lids in a heatproof bowl. (See page 21 for details.)

Ladle boiling water from the canning pot into the bowl with the lids. Using a jar lifter, remove the hot jars from the canning pot, carefully pouring the water from each one back into the pot, and place them upright on a folded towel. Drain the water off the jar lids.

Ladle the hot rinds and syrup into the jars, leaving ½ inch headspace at the top. Use a damp paper towel to wipe the rims of the jars, then put a flat lid and ring on each jar, adjusting the ring so that it's just finger-tight. Return the jars to the water in the canning pot, making sure the water covers the jars by at least 1 inch. Bring to a boil, and boil for 10 minutes to process. Remove the jars to a folded towel and do not disturb for 12 hours. After 1 hour, check that the lids have sealed by pressing down on the center of each; if it can be pushed down, it hasn't sealed, and the jar should be refrigerated immediately. Label the sealed jars and store.

Fall

There's a wonderful illustrated children's book, which I first read with Thalia last fall at the height of apple season, called *The Seven Silly Eaters*, by Mary Ann Hoberman and Marla Frazee, about a weary mom who has one kid after another who will each eat only one food. My favorite pages were the ones devoted to Jack—"a happy baby, never cross, but all *he'd* eat was applesauce." You can practically hear the New Englandy foliage crunching under the wheels of the kids' red wagon and Mrs. Peters's knife scraping as she sits outside on the front steps "peeling apples by the peck," smell the earth being turned over by Mr. Peters (planting a seedling apple tree), and feel the crisp north wind that's fluttering through the pages of a coloring book left open on the porch.

This is what fall is like for me. Somehow the season corresponds to a heightening of the senses: The quality of the daylight changes, the sky appears a deeper blue, the air is harder and more distinct. Our dog, Cooper, a furry black shepherd mix who was born in a swamp in Florida, is suddenly even more attuned to every movement of squirrel or rabbit (or falling leaf) as he bounds with renewed energy around his domain, the backyard.

I wait and wait for the good new-crop apples, the misshapen, knobby, and amazingly delicious ones the local countrified grocery store independently trucks down from the mountains of North Carolina and sells from huge cardboard crates for less than half the price I'd readily pay for them. Mutsu, Red Roma, Staymen-Winesap, Gala, and tart and hilariously enormous Kinglicious—I can never get out of the place without a bag or two of every variety they have on offer that day. We dehydrate the sweet ones, make the streaky-fleshed Red Romas (mixed with other varieties for flavor) into as much applesauce as possible, make a pie or two (warming the old house in the process), and eat the rest out of hand as the weather finally allows us to venture outside after what is always a long and draining summer. We toss the cores into the chicken tractor if it happens to be nearby, and everybody wins.

FALL FRUITS

Green Apple Pectin Stock

MAKES 3 CUPS

◇◇◇

THIS STOCK CAN BE USED AS THE BASIS FOR ANY JELLY WHOSE MAIN INGREDIENT DOESN'T CONTAIN ENOUGH PECTIN TO SET FULLY ON ITS OWN. It can also be added to jams, a cup at a time, if you prefer a thicker spread.

To strain the apple juice, I use an 8-inch conical bouillon strainer—like a *chinois*, but with wire mesh instead of punched holes—that I got at a restaurant supply store, a good investment if you plan to make a more than few jellies each year (it's also ideal for straining, well, bouillon, or *stock* stock). It's fine enough that you don't have to use cheesecloth or a jelly bag to get a pectin stock that yields a clear jelly. If your sieve isn't very fine, line it with a few layers of rinsed and squeezed cheesecloth. Make sure it's large enough to hold all the apple mixture in one batch, though, because straining in batches can be messy and frustrating.

3 pounds Granny Smith apples

Cut the apples into eighths, removing the stems, and put the apples—peels, cores, seeds, and all—in a 6- to 8-quart preserving pan. Add 6 cups water, cover, and bring to a boil over high heat. Boil, stirring occasionally, until the apples are completely broken down and the peels have separated from the pulp, 30 to 40 minutes.

Set a large, very-fine-mesh sieve (or jelly bag) over a deep bowl or pot. Pour the apples and their juice into the sieve and let drain for at least 30 minutes, stirring occasionally but not pressing down too hard on the solids; discard the solids (or see below). You should have about 5½ cups juice.

Rinse the preserving pan and pour in the apple juice. Bring to a boil over high heat and cook until the juice is reduced to about 3 cups (pour it into a large heatproof measuring cup to check it), about 20 minutes. Transfer the stock to a clean container and store in the refrigerator for up to 2 weeks, or in the freezer for several months.

GRANNY SMITH APPLESAUCE

Don't tell your compost pile, but you stole its apple pulp. Pass the apple solids through a Squeezo strainer or a food mill fitted with the disk with the finest holes, and you have a very tart applesauce. Sweeten with a little sugar or honey, or freeze it to use in cakes and quick breads—a favorite of mine is on page 182.

Afternoon Applesauce Spice Cake

MAKES ONE 9-INCH SQUARE CAKE

THIS MOIST, LIGHTLY SPICED, NOT-TOO-SWEET CAKE IS AN IDEAL AFTERNOON SNACK. Quick, no-mess, and comforting, it's also vegan—in case you have friends who are. If you want to make this with regular applesauce rather than Granny Smith pulp, add 1 teaspoon vinegar to the batter to help activate the baking soda, and reduce the brown sugar to ¾ cup.

2½ cups all-purpose flour
1 cup packed light brown sugar
1 teaspoon ground cinnamon
½ teaspoon freshly grated nutmeg
¼ teaspoon ground cloves
1½ teaspoons baking soda
½ teaspoon pure kosher salt
1 cup Granny Smith applesauce (from making Green Apple Pectin Stock, page 181)
½ cup vegetable oil
½ cup nuts, toasted and chopped
½ cup raisins (optional)

Preheat the oven to 350°F.

In a medium bowl, use a fork to combine the flour, brown sugar, spices, baking soda, and salt. Add the remaining ingredients and ½ cup water and stir until the dry ingredients are just moistened. Scrape the batter into a 9-inch square cake pan and smooth the top. Bake in the middle of the oven for 30 to 35 minutes, until a toothpick inserted in the center comes out clean. Cool on a wire rack for at least 15 minutes before cutting into squares and serving.

Applesauce

MAKES ABOUT 5 PINT JARS

◇◇◇

FOR PLAIN, UNSWEETENED APPLESAUCE, I LIKE TO USE A COMBINATION OF SEVERAL TYPES OF APPLES: Red Romas for the lovely pink they impart, some good crisp eating apples like Galas or Winesaps for their natural sweetness, and maybe a tart apple like a Granny Smith for a bit of acidity. They all cook at different rates, some puffing up and gently exploding as they simmer, some retaining their shape to the very end, but they all get pureed together into the humblest of fruit dishes so it doesn't matter. I don't think applesauce needs sweetening or spicing at all, but you can add a bit if you think yours needs it.

The best tool for applesauce making is a Squeezo strainer. No peeling or coring is neces-sary. A food mill is another option. I happen to have an unhealthy relationship with mine (I've given it to my parents twice, and they have then sent it back to me when I mentioned missing it). I find it awkward, slow, and ineffective for most tasks—but if you have one that is better made than mine is, with a disk with very fine holes, it'll work just fine for applesauce. (You might wish to core the apples before you cook them, though, to prevent any hard bits from making their way through the mill.) A third option is to peel and core the apples, cook them until soft, then mash them or puree them in a blender or food processor. The yields will vary depending on the method you use.

6 pounds apples, peeled and cored only if necessary (see above)

Cut the apples into 1-inch chunks, removing the stems, and put the apples in a 6- to 8-quart preserv-ing pan. Add 1½ cups water, cover, and bring to a boil over high heat. Boil, stirring occasionally, until the apples are broken down and the peels have separated from the pulp, 30 to 40 minutes.

Pass the apples through a Squeezo strainer or food mill to remove the peels and cores. (Or, if you cored and peeled the apples, puree them in batches in a food processor or blender.) Rinse out the preserving pan and return the puree to the pan. Bring to a boil and cook for 5 minutes.

Meanwhile, prepare for water-bath canning: Wash the jars and keep them hot in the canning pot, and put the flat lids in a heatproof bowl. (See page 21 for details.)

Ladle boiling water from the canning pot into the bowl with the lids. Using a jar lifter, remove the hot jars from the canning pot, carefully pouring the water from each one back into the pot, and place them upright on a folded towel. Drain the water off the jar lids.

Ladle the hot applesauce into the jars, leaving ½ inch headspace at the top. Use a damp paper towel to wipe the rims of the jars, then put a flat lid and ring on each jar, adjusting the ring so that it's just finger-tight. Return the jars to the water in the can-ning pot, making sure the water covers the jars by at least 1 inch. Bring to a boil, and boil for 15 min-utes to process. Remove the jars to a folded towel and do not disturb for 12 hours. After 1 hour, check that the lids have sealed by pressing down on the center of each; if it can be pushed down, it hasn't sealed, and the jar should be refrigerated immedi-ately. Label the sealed jars and store.

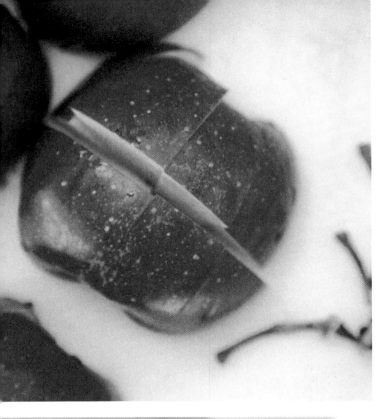

Spiced Apple Butter

MAKES ABOUT 6 HALF-PINT JARS OR 3 PINT JARS

◇◇◇

MY MOM IS A PURIST WHEN IT COMES TO APPLE BUTTER, AND SHE HAS THE COOKING-APPLE-BUTTER-OVER-AN-OPEN-FIRE PEDIGREE TO LEND HEFT TO HER CONTENTION THAT, MADE PROPERLY, APPLE BUTTER NEEDS NOTHING MORE THAN APPLES. Period. No vinegar, no sugar, no spices—just apples. It's damn hard work making it the old-fashioned way, though, with the hockey-stick-shaped stirrer and the iron cauldron—oh, yes—and the open fire that has to be kept at just the right temperature for something like eighty-two hours. The following is a fair compromise, I think.

There are two things about apple butter: First, it's best when it's cooked for a long, long time, so that the sugars in the apples caramelize and darken and take on a flavor that is not at all like that of thick, sweet applesauce. I've done apple butter on the stovetop (where it takes hours, and lots of stirring to keep it from scorching), in the oven (ditto), and in a slow cooker (bingo). By far the easiest and most trouble-free way to *slowly cook* apple butter is in a *slow cooker*. No stirring unless you want to, and the end result is just as good—no, better, because it ain't even remotely scorched, and neither is your stirrin' arm.

Second, apple butter's best when it's very smooth—you know, like butter. Some folks, after passing the apple pulp through a Squeezo-type strainer or a food mill, then push it through a fine-mesh sieve. Messy and time consuming. The easiest, neatest, and quickest path to the hallowed land of velvety smooth apple butter is via the immersion blender, that great, unassuming workhorse. Whir it around in the apple puree for a couple minutes at any point in the cooking process, and maybe again at the very end. To review: Slow cooker + immersion blender = perfect apple butter, sane and happy apple butter maker.

6 pounds apples, cored and peeled only if necessary (see Note), cut into 1-inch chunks

2 cups apple cider or water

About 1½ cups sugar

1½ teaspoons ground cinnamon

½ teaspoon ground cloves

½ teaspoon ground allspice

½ teaspoon ground aniseed (optional)

Put the apples in a 6- to 8-quart preserving pan. Add the cider and 4 cups water and bring to a boil over high heat. Boil, stirring occasionally, until the apples are completely broken down and the peels have separated from the pulp, 30 to 40 minutes.

Pass the mixture through a Squeezo strainer or food mill to remove the peels and cores. (Or, if you cored and peeled the apples—bless your heart, as they'd say here in Georgia—puree it in batches in a food processor or blender.) Measure the puree.

If using the stovetop: Rinse out the preserving pan and return the puree to the pan. Add 2 tablespoons sugar per cup of puree, and add the spices. (Puree with an immersion blender, if you want an extra-smooth apple butter.) Bring to a boil, then lower the heat and simmer, stirring carefully every 10 minutes or so with a long-handled spoon or spatula, for several hours, until the puree is dark and thick enough that it mounds up in a teaspoon, and you can dollop a bit of it onto a plate and no liquid seeps out around the edges of the dollop.

If using the oven: Pour the puree into a large, deep baking dish, stir in the sugar and spices, and bake in a 300°F oven, stirring occasionally, for several hours, until thick and dark. (Transfer to a large pot or bowl and puree with an immersion blender if desired.)

If using a slow cooker: Pour the puree into a 4- to 6-quart slow cooker and stir in the sugar and spices. (Puree with an immersion blender if desired.) Cook on the low setting, with the lid propped up on chopsticks or set askew to allow the liquid to evaporate but still keep the splatters in the pot, for 9 to 12 hours, stirring occasionally when you can, keeping in mind that different models of slow cookers cook at different temperatures, until thick and dark.

Prepare for water-bath canning: Wash the jars and keep them hot in the canning pot, and put the flat lids in a heatproof bowl. (See page 21 for details.)

Bring the apple butter to a boil (transfer to a pan on the stovetop if it's not fully boiling in the oven or slow cooker; usually if you turn the slow cooker up to high for 10 or 15 minutes it'll come to a boil).

Ladle boiling water from the canning pot into the bowl with the lids. Using a jar lifter, remove the hot jars from the canning pot, carefully pouring the water from each one back into the pot, and place them upright on a folded towel. Drain the water off the jar lids.

Ladle the hot apple butter into the jars, leaving ½ inch headspace at the top. Use a damp paper towel to wipe the rims of the jars, then put a flat lid and ring on each jar, adjusting the ring so that it's just finger-tight. Return the jars to the water in the canning pot, making sure the water covers the jars by at least 1 inch. Bring to a boil, and boil half-pints or pints for 10 minutes to process. Remove the jars to a folded towel and do not disturb for 12 hours. After 1 hour, check that the lids have sealed by pressing down on the center of each; if it can be pushed down, it hasn't sealed, and the jar should be refrigerated immediately. Label the sealed jars and store.

Note: If you're using a Squeezo or similar strainer with a very fine screen, there's no need to core or peel the apples (yay!). If you're using a food mill, don't bother peeling them, but do core them; even the fine-holed disk will tend to let bits of core through (boo!). If you're pureeing the apples in a food processor or blender rather than passing them through a mill, core and peel them (sorry).

APPLE BUTTER SAVES THE DAY

* Substitute up to half of the fat in cakes, muffins, and cookies with apple butter.

* Stir it into oatmeal, cottage cheese, or yogurt.

* Smear on hot biscuits, or serve warm with waffles or pancakes. Make French toast, sandwiching two slices together with apple butter and fresh cheese or cottage cheese.

* Use it in sandwiches. Winners include but are not limited to: thinly sliced Black Forest ham and cheddar on rye; grilled brie and fresh roast turkey on apple-butter- and *butter*-buttered sourdough; apple butter spread on rounds of French bread and topped with thin slices of Gruyère; natural peanut butter and apple butter; cream cheese and apple butter.

* Put frozen roasted squash puree (page 229) and 1 cup water in a pan and heat until the squash is thawed. Add apple butter, season with salt and pepper, and bring to a simmer. Stir in a few tablespoons of crème fraîche. Serve in wide soup bowls with fresh croutons.

* Mix apple butter and mustard and use as a glaze for pork loin or ribs.

* Use apple butter instead of frosting between spice cake layers.

Candied-Pickled Apples with Star Anise

MAKES ABOUT 4 HALF-PINT JARS

◇◇◇

THIS SPICED APPLE PRESERVE IS BASED ON A RECIPE I TESTED FOR THE REPRINT OF *TOP CHEF: THE COOKBOOK.* There intensely sweet-sour apples were served alongside rich *pain perdu,* seared foie gras, sugary nuts, and some other things, including, as you might expect, a foam. In addition to using it as a glaze on the Ham Loaf on page 190, it would be excellent with a simply cooked slab of good ham, or you could serve it with pan-roasted steak.

I love how the colors of the red apple peels and creamy flesh equalize into a beautiful coppery pink and the apples gradually become translucent as they absorb the sugar and cider vinegar. Use any kind of firm, crisp, sweet red apples, such as Gala, Honeycrisp, or Staymen-Winesap.

3 pieces star anise, broken up

2 cinnamon sticks, broken up

½ teaspoon whole black peppercorns

2 pounds crisp red apples, cored and diced (no need to peel)

2 cups cider vinegar (5% acidity)

1¼ cups sugar

Prepare for water-bath canning: Wash the jars and keep them hot in the canning pot, and put the flat lids in a heatproof bowl. (See page 21 for details.)

Put the spices in a cheesecloth or muslin bag and tie it shut. Put the bag and all the remaining ingredients in a wide, 6- to 8-quart preserving pan. Bring to a boil over high heat, then lower the heat and simmer, stirring occasionally very gently to keep from breaking apart the apples too much, until the apples are translucent and the syrup is thick, about 45 minutes. Discard the spices.

Ladle boiling water from the canning pot into the bowl with the lids. Using a jar lifter, remove the hot jars from the canning pot, carefully pouring the water from each one back into the pot, and place them upright on a folded towel. Drain the water off the jar lids.

Ladle the hot apples into the jars, leaving ¼ inch headspace at the top. Use a chopstick to remove air bubbles around the inside of each jar. Use a damp paper towel to wipe the rims of the jars, then put a flat lid and ring on each jar, adjusting the ring so that it's just finger-tight. Return the jars to the water in the canning pot, making sure the water covers the jars by at least 1 inch. Bring to a boil, and boil for 10 minutes to process. Remove the jars to a folded towel and do not disturb for 12 hours. After 1 hour, check that the lids have sealed by pressing down on the center of each; if it can be pushed down, it hasn't sealed, and the jar should be refrigerated immediately. Label the sealed jars and store.

Ham Loaf

SERVES 4 TO 6

◇◇

DO YOU SOMETIMES FORGET ABOUT CITY
HAM? Living in a part of the United States where
country ham rules all, I do, and then suddenly
I can't stop thinking about ham loaf made with
regular old city ham. It's true comfort food: a little
sweet and a little salty, with familiar flavors, easy to
pull together at the end of the day, and even easier
to serve. I'm sorry I couldn't think of a more elegant
name for this . . . loaf. Because while *pain perdu* and
foie gras are fine and everything, I'll take ham loaf,
clunky name and all.

1 pound good-quality cooked city (wet-cured) ham,
    coarsely chopped
1 pound ground turkey
1 cup fresh bread crumbs
2 large eggs, lightly beaten
1 teaspoon freshly ground black pepper
¾ cup Candied-Pickled Apples with Star Anise
    (page 189)
¼ cup brown sugar
1 tablespoon Dijon-style mustard

Preheat the oven to 350°F. Lightly oil a 9-by-13-inch
baking dish.

Put the ham in a food processor and pulse to finely
chop. In a large bowl, use your hands to combine
the ham, turkey, bread crumbs, eggs, and pepper.
Dump the mixture out into the baking dish and pat
it into a loaf shape.

In a small bowl, combine the apples, brown sugar,
and mustard, then spread the mixture over the top
and sides of the loaf. Bake until the top is crusty
and browned and the loaf is cooked through, about
1½ hours. Let cool for 5 minutes, then slice and
serve.

Mint Jelly

MAKES ABOUT 3 HALF-PINT JARS, OR 7 FOUR-OUNCE JARS

NOT THE MOST BEAUTIFUL JELLY YOU'LL EVER MAKE, PERHAPS (IT LOOKS LIKE PLAIN OLD APPLE JELLY). But it's tangy, fresh-tasting, and just reminiscent enough of the stuff many folks have been dutifully setting out with the lamb every spring that you won't miss the bright green. That said, the last time I made mint jelly, I happened to have a tube of green gel food coloring (something about cupcakes my three-year-old simply *had* to make), so I dripped in a few drops just for the hell of it. And you know what? It actually looked pretty good—not the horrid fluorescent green I was expecting, but a sort of *leafy* green. It almost looked, dare I say, *natural*. So. Something to consider.

4 pounds Granny Smith Apples
1½ cups roughly chopped fresh mint
About 2¼ cups sugar
3 tablespoons strained fresh lemon juice

Cut the apples into eighths, removing the stems. Put the apples—peels, cores, seeds, and all—in a 6- to 8-quart preserving pan. Add the mint and 6 cups water and bring to a boil over high heat. Boil, stirring occasionally, until the apples are completely broken down and the peels have separated from the pulp, 20 to 30 minutes.

Set a large, very-fine-mesh sieve (or jelly bag) over a deep bowl or pot. Pour the apples and their juice into the sieve and let drain for at least 30 minutes, stirring occasionally but not pressing down too hard on the solids; discard the solids. Measure the juice; you should have about 4 cups. If you have less, stir a little water into the solids and continue to drain.

Prepare for water-bath canning: Sterilize the jars and keep them hot in the canning pot, put a small plate in the freezer, and put the flat lids in a heat-proof bowl. (See page 21 for details.)

Rinse the preserving pan and pour in the juice. Add ¾ cup sugar per cup of juice, and stir in the lemon juice. Bring to a boil over high heat and cook, stirring occasionally, until the mixture registers about 220°F on a candy thermometer or a small dab of it spooned onto the chilled plate and returned to the freezer for a minute wrinkles when you nudge it, 15 to 20 minutes.

Ladle boiling water from the canning pot into the bowl with the lids. Using a jar lifter, remove the sterilized jars from the canning pot, carefully pouring the water from each one back into the pot, and place them upright on a folded towel. Drain the water off the jar lids.

Ladle the hot jelly into the jars, leaving ¼ inch headspace at the top. Use a damp paper towel to wipe the rims of the jars, then put a flat lid and ring on each jar, adjusting the ring so that it's just finger-tight. Return the jars to the water in the canning pot, making sure the water covers the jars by at least 1 inch. Bring to a boil, and boil for 5 minutes to process. Remove the jars to a folded towel and do not disturb for 12 hours. After 1 hour, check that the lids have sealed by pressing down on the center of each; if it can be pushed down, it hasn't sealed, and the jar should be refrigerated immediately. Label the sealed jars and store.

Herb-Glazed Grilled Pork

SERVES 4

THIS IS A SUPER-EASY PANTRY DISH PER-
FECT FOR AN UNSEASONABLY WARM WINTER
EVENING WHEN YOU CAN GET OUTSIDE AND
USE THE GRILL—THOUGH YOU CAN ALSO USE
A GRILL PAN INDOORS. Really all you need to
buy fresh are the lime (I almost always have a few
nestled in the crisper drawer), pork, and herbs.

Serve these strips of grilled pork with fluffy
steamed rice and simply braised greens: Sauté very
thinly sliced onion and garlic in a little oil, add
chopped winter greens, splash in a little soy sauce
and water, cover, and simmer until tender, about 10
minutes. Uncover the pan and cook over high heat
until the liquid is mostly evaporated.

1¼ pounds thinly sliced center-cut pork chops
3 tablespoons Mint Jelly (page 191)
1 cube frozen ginger-garlic paste (page 70), thawed
    and drained; or 2 teaspoons minced ginger plus 1
    teaspoon minced garlic
1½ tablespoons fish sauce or soy sauce
1 tablespoon Chinese chile paste (sambal oelek)
1 tablespoon vegetable oil
½ cup chopped fresh cilantro
¼ cup minced fresh basil
Lime wedges

Trim any visible fat from the pork and cut it into
1-inch-wide strips.

In a small saucepan over low heat, heat the jelly
until it liquefies. (Or heat it for a few seconds in a
microwave oven.) In a medium bowl, combine the
jelly with all the remaining ingredients except the
lime wedges, tossing to coat the pork well.

Prepare a charcoal fire and set the grate about 4
inches above the coals, or preheat a cast-iron grill
pan over medium-high heat. When the coals are
hot and white and the grate is very hot, put the
pork strips on the grill and cook, turning once, until
nicely browned on both sides, about 3 minutes
per side. (If using a grill pan, cook the strips in
batches.) Serve hot, with the lime wedges.

GROWING CILANTRO

I used to think that cilantro tasted like licking a
stainless-steel bowl, but around the age of eigh-
teen I suddenly decided it was the best herb on
the face of the planet. It can be grown year round
just about anywhere.

Okay, first go to an Indian grocery store and
pick up a nice, cheap bag of whole coriander
seeds—so much more economical than buying
tiny packets of seeds at a garden store. (Incidentally, you can do this with cumin seeds, mustard
seeds, fenugreek . . .) Whenever the ground is
soft enough, scratch the dirt to rough it up a little. If you have any, mix in a bit of old compost.
Sprinkle the seeds all over, not worrying about
spacing—just toss them out. Cover with a little
loose dirt, and water it well. Try to water it every
few days for the first week or so. Soon you'll very
likely have a bed of tiny cilantro sprouts. Don't
bother thinning. The plants will grow slowly in
cold weather, then explode when it gets warm.
To harvest, mow off as much as you need with a
pair of kitchen shears, and it'll come right back.
When the plants flower, you'll end up with coriander seeds; when they're dry, shake them off
and repeat.

Red Onion Marmalade

MAKES ABOUT 4 HALF-PINT JARS

◇◇

HERE, RED ONION SLIVERS MINGLE WITH LEMON ZEST IN AN APPLE-TANGY, LOOSE JELLY WITH A THROAT-TINGLING, CINNAMONY SWEETNESS. This marmalade would make a nice counterpoint to a rich roasted or grilled meat dish, or spread it on slices of crusty bread with a thick slab of aged Cheddar. When you gather your red onions for this, be sure to scoop up as many of the papery peels as you can—the onion vendor may look at you strangely, but those peels will dye your preserve a beautiful red.

4 pounds Granny Smith apples
1 pound red onions, with papery peels
1 lemon, zest cut into thin strips
2 cinnamon sticks
2½ cups distilled white vinegar (5% acidity)
About 3 cups sugar

Cut the apples into eighths, removing the stems. Cut the root ends off the onions and rinse. Peel and thinly slice enough onions to make 1 cup, and set the slices aside. Roughly chop the remaining onions, with their peels. Put the lemon zest with the sliced onions. Roughly chop the lemon.

Put the apples—peels, cores, seeds, and all—along with the roughly chopped onions and lemon, and the cinnamon sticks, in a 6- to 8-quart preserving pan. Add 3 cups water and the vinegar and bring to a boil over high heat. Boil, stirring occasionally, until the apples are completely broken down, 20 to 30 minutes.

Set a large, very-fine-mesh sieve (or jelly bag) over a deep bowl or pot. Pour the apple mixture into the sieve and let drain for at least 30 minutes, stirring occasionally; discard the solids. Measure the juice; you should have about 4 cups. If you have less, stir a little water into the solids and continue to drain.

Prepare for water-bath canning: Sterilize the jars and keep them hot in the canning pot, put a small plate in the freezer, and put the flat lids in a heat-proof bowl. (See page 21 for details.)

Rinse the preserving pan and pour in the juice. Add ¾ cup sugar per cup of juice, and add the reserved lemon zest and sliced onions. Bring to a boil over high heat and cook, stirring occasionally, until the mixture registers about 220°F on a candy thermometer or a small dab of it spooned onto the chilled plate and returned to the freezer for a minute wrinkles when you nudge it, 15 to 20 minutes.

Ladle boiling water from the canning pot into the bowl with the lids. Using a jar lifter, remove the sterilized jars from the canning pot, carefully pouring the water from each one back into the pot, and place them upright on a folded towel. Drain the water off the jar lids.

Ladle the hot jelly into the jars, leaving ¼ inch headspace at the top. Use a damp paper towel to wipe the rims of the jars, then put a flat lid and ring on each jar, adjusting the ring so that it's just finger-tight. Return the jars to the water in the canning pot, making sure the water covers the jars by at least 1 inch. Bring to a boil, and boil for 5 minutes to process. Remove the jars to a folded towel and do not disturb for 12 hours. After 1 hour, check that the lids have sealed by pressing down on the center of each; if it can be pushed down, it hasn't sealed, and the jar should be refrigerated immediately. Label the sealed jars and store.

Hot Chile Jelly

MAKES ABOUT 4 HALF-PINT JARS

◇◇◇

DAMN, IS THIS GOOD. Rosy pink, spicy, sweet, and a little bit tart, it's a beautiful and classic jelly. Most recipes for jalapeño jelly ask you to use purchased pectin and maybe a couple drops of food coloring, and that is indeed a slightly easier method than this one, in which the cores and peel of tart green early-fall apples provide the pectin (as they do in other jelly recipes). But there are at least two tangible benefits to doing it this way. First, the apple flavor, while subtle, plays nicely against the heat of the chiles and the savory vegetable flavor of the bell pepper. Second, the gel created by the pectin to be found in whole apples simply feels better on the palate—which is why I started using apples for all my pectin needs in the first place.

To achieve an especially bright red jelly, I use either black plums (sometimes I just pull a few handfuls of sliced plums out of the freezer and toss them in with the apples) or some papery red onion skins, but if you use red chiles, that will subtly color the jelly. One recipe—it's almost the same as this one, which I developed independently—by Elise Bauer of the excellent Simply Recipes website, suggests adding pectin-rich cranberries in late fall, when the pectin content of green apples declines somewhat as they become riper; cranberries will not only infuse the jelly with color but also increase the pectin in the juice so it gels reliably. I haven't tried this yet, but it's a brilliant idea.

A quarter pound of chiles makes a hot but by no means incendiary jelly. If you'd like it hotter, use serranos or even habaneros rather than jalapeños; if you prefer a milder jelly, remove the seeds and membranes from some of the chiles before putting them in the pan with the apples. For a plain old sweet pepper jelly, omit the hot chiles and use 3 red bell peppers instead.

Serve with cream cheese and crackers, or Crème Fraîche (page 289) and toasted English Muffin Bread (page 282), or alongside pan-fried Kimchi and Pork Dumplings (page 273), or use in the recipe for Herb-Glazed Grilled Pork (page 192).

4 pounds Granny Smith apples

4 ounces hot chiles, preferably red (about 8 medium jalapeños or 10 serranos)

1 red bell pepper, cored and roughly chopped (about 2 cups)

1 cup sliced black plums, 1 cup cranberries, or a handful of papery red-onion skins (optional)

1 lemon, sliced

3 cups distilled white vinegar (5% acidity)

About 3 cups sugar

Cut the apples into eighths, removing the stems. Roughly chop the hot chiles and bell pepper.

Put the apples—peels, cores, seeds, and all—in a 6- to 8-quart preserving pan. Add the plums, if using, the chiles, bell pepper, and lemon. Add 3 cups water and the vinegar and bring to a boil over high heat. Boil, stirring occasionally, until the apples are completely broken down and the peels have separated from the pulp, 20 to 30 minutes.

Set a large, very-fine-mesh sieve (or jelly bag) over a deep bowl or pot. Pour the apples and their juice into the sieve and let drain for at least 30 minutes, stirring occasionally but not pressing down too hard on the solids; discard the solids. Measure the juice; you should have about 4 cups. If you have less, stir a little water into the solids and continue to drain.

Prepare for water-bath canning: Sterilize the jars and keep them hot in the canning pot, put a small plate in the freezer, and put the flat lids in a heat-proof bowl. (See page 21 for details.)

Rinse the preserving pan and pour in the juice. Add ¾ cup sugar per cup of juice. Bring to a boil over high heat and cook, stirring occasionally, until the mixture registers about 220°F on a candy thermometer or a small dab of it spooned onto the chilled plate and returned to the freezer for a minute wrinkles when you nudge it, 15 to 20 minutes.

Ladle boiling water from the canning pot into the bowl with the lids. Using a jar lifter, remove the sterilized jars from the canning pot, carefully pouring the water from each one back into the pot, and place them upright on a folded towel. Drain the water off the jar lids.

Ladle the hot jelly into the jars, leaving ¼ inch headspace at the top. Use a damp paper towel to wipe the rims of the jars, then put a flat lid and ring on each jar, adjusting the ring so that it's just finger-tight. Return the jars to the water in the canning pot, making sure the water covers the jars by at least 1 inch. Bring to a boil, and boil for 5 minutes to process. Remove the jars to a folded towel and do not disturb for 12 hours. After 1 hour, check that the lids have sealed by pressing down on the center of each; if it can be pushed down, it hasn't sealed, and the jar should be refrigerated immediately. Label the sealed jars and store.

Slow-Roasted Fig Preserves with Lemon

MAKES ABOUT 4 HALF-PINT JARS

◇◇

MY WORLDLY FRIEND REGAN HUFF TOLD ME ABOUT SLOW-ROASTING FIGS AT HER FAMILY'S HOUSE IN FRANCE, AND I HAD TO TRY IT AS A PRESERVE. The figs roast very, very slowly, which gives them time to gradually absorb the sugar before they start to caramelize.

Regan also remembered that those roasted figs were served with ricotta. Spoon a bit of cold, creamy Fresh Cheese (page 284) and warmed preserves onto a small plate, sprinkle with savory salted and toasted pine nuts and rosemary, and call it dessert.

I can this preserve in a boiling-water bath with great success (5 minutes in half-pint jars), but since it isn't completely sugar-saturated it's probably best to store it in the refrigerator, where it will keep for ages.

1 small lemon, quartered and thinly sliced, seeds removed

3 pounds ripe figs, stemmed and rinsed, left whole if small, halved if larger

1½ cups sugar

Preheat the oven to 300°F.

Scatter the lemon slices over the bottom of a large roasting pan, then spread the figs in the pan. Sprinkle with the sugar and pour in 1 cup water.

Cover the pan with aluminum foil and roast for 2 hours, then uncover the pan, increase the oven temperature to 400°F, and roast for about 1½ hours more, until the figs are dark, the lemon slices are translucent, and the juices are bubbling and have reduced to a dark, somewhat thick syrup.

Ladle the preserves into preheated nonreactive jars, then put the lids on, let cool, and refrigerate. The preserves will keep for at least a month.

Honeyed Fig Jam with Sesame Seeds

MAKES ABOUT 4 HALF-PINT JARS

◇◇◇

ANY TYPE OF FIG WILL DO HERE, BUT A LIGHT-COLORED VARIETY, SUCH AS THE BRIGHT GREEN SIERRA OR ROSY BROWN TURKEY FIGS, WILL MAKE AN ESPECIALLY PRETTY JAM. I like a mild honey such as orange blossom in this jam so it doesn't overpower the delicate-tasting figs.

I can this preserve in a boiling-water bath with great success (5 minutes in half-pint jars), but since it isn't sugar-saturated it's probably best to store it in the refrigerator. It's a wonderful thing to have on hand for a fall cheese plate or to spoon into mini puff-pastry tartlet shells as a quick but very special dessert.

3 tablespoons white sesame seeds
3 pounds figs, quartered, peeled if desired (see Note)
½ cup sugar
¼ cup honey
3 tablespoons strained fresh lemon juice
Grated zest of 2 lemons

In a small skillet over medium-high heat, toast the sesame seeds, stirring constantly, until golden brown and fragrant, about 3 minutes. Remove to a plate and set aside.

In a wide, 6- to 8-quart preserving pan, combine the figs, sugar, honey, lemon juice, and lemon zest. Bring to a boil and cook until the figs are tender and broken down, the jam is a shade darker in color, and a small dab of the jam spooned onto the chilled plate and returned to the freezer for a minute becomes somewhat firm (it will not gel), 10 to 15 minutes. Stir in the sesame seeds.

Ladle the preserves into preheated nonreactive jars, then put the lids on, let cool, and refrigerate. The preserves will keep for several weeks.

Note: You certainly don't have to peel the figs, but if the skin is at all tough, and if you have time, it will make for a slightly more spreadable spread: Quarter the figs first, then gently pull the peel from each piece, starting at the stem end.

Minted Cranberry Relish with Walnuts

MAKES ABOUT 4 PINT JARS

◇◇

THIS IS A COOKED AND CANNED VERSION OF MY FAVORITE FRESH CRANBERRY RELISH, WHICH IS ONE OF THOSE DISHES I FEEL I MUST HAVE ON THANKSGIVING. (Lest you think the Krissoffs are traditionalists, pierogies are another.) Just barely sweet and more than barely tart, the relish is a bright alternative to jelled cranberry sauce.

9 cups cranberries (three 12-ounce bags), washed and drained
2 navel oranges, scrubbed and coarsely chopped (peel included)
1 cup freshly squeezed orange juice
3 tablespoons strained fresh lemon juice
2 cups sugar
1 apple, peeled, cored, and coarsely chopped
1 cup walnuts, toasted and coarsely chopped
2 tablespoons chopped fresh mint

Prepare for water-bath canning: Wash the jars and keep them hot in the canning pot, and put the flat lids in a heatproof bowl. (See page 21 for details.)

In a food processor or blender, working in batches, pulse the cranberries and oranges until finely chopped. Put them in a wide, 6- to 8-quart preserving pan and stir in the orange juice, lemon juice, and sugar. Bring to a boil over high heat, stirring frequently, and cook for 5 minutes.

Meanwhile, pulse the apple and walnuts until finely chopped. Add them, along with the mint, to the preserving pan. Return the relish to a boil, stirring frequently. Remove from the heat.

Ladle boiling water from the canning pot into the bowl with the lids. Using a jar lifter, remove the hot jars from the canning pot, carefully pouring the water from each one back into the pot, and place them upright on a folded towel. Drain the water off the jar lids.

Ladle the hot relish into the jars, leaving ½ inch headspace at the top. Use a chopstick to remove air bubbles around the inside of each jar. Use a damp paper towel to wipe the rims of the jars, then put a flat lid and ring on each jar, adjusting the ring so that it's just finger-tight. Return the jars to the water in the canning pot, making sure the water covers the jars by at least 1 inch. Bring to a boil, and boil for 15 minutes to process. Remove the jars to a folded towel and do not disturb for 12 hours. After 1 hour, check that the lids have sealed by pressing down on the center of each; if it can be pushed down, it hasn't sealed, and the jar should be refrigerated immediately. Label the sealed jars and store.

Spiced Cranberries

MAKES ABOUT 6 HALF-PINT JARS

◇◇

DEEP RED AND INTENSELY TART CRANBERRIES ARE HERE AGGRESSIVELY SPICED TO MAKE A RICH PRESERVE BEST ENJOYED IN THE COMPANY OF CHEESE. Any kind will do, really, from a schmear of cream cheese to a wedge of blue. The liqueur adds a boozy note and, if you use Cointreau, a vague and pleasant bitterness, but you can leave it out if you prefer.

6 cups fresh cranberries (two 12-ounce bags), washed and drained
3 cups sugar
1 cup freshly squeezed orange juice
½ cup orange liqueur such as Cointreau, Grand Marnier, or triple sec
1 teaspoon ground cinnamon
1 teaspoon ground cloves
½ teaspoon freshly grated nutmeg

Prepare for water-bath canning: Sterilize the jars and keep them hot in the canning pot, put a small plate in the freezer, and put the flat lids in a heat-proof bowl. (See page 21 for details.)

Put all the ingredients in a wide, 6- to 8-quart preserving pan. Bring to a boil over high heat. Lower the heat and simmer, stirring frequently, until a small dab of the syrup spooned onto the cold plate and set in the freezer for a minute wrinkles when you nudge it, about 15 minutes. Remove from the heat.

Ladle boiling water from the canning pot into the bowl with the lids. Using a jar lifter, remove the sterilized jars from the canning pot, carefully pouring the water from each one back into the pot, and place them upright on a folded towel. Drain the water off the jar lids.

Ladle the hot cranberries into the jars, leaving ¼ inch headspace at the top. Use a damp paper towel to wipe the rims of the jars, then put a flat lid and ring on each jar, adjusting the ring so that it's just finger-tight. Return the jars to the water in the canning pot, making sure the water covers the jars by at least 1 inch. Bring to a boil, and boil for 5 minutes to process. Remove the jars to a folded towel and do not disturb for 12 hours. After 1 hour, check that the lids have sealed by pressing down on the center of each; if it can be pushed down, it hasn't sealed, and the jar should be refrigerated immediately. Label the sealed jars and store.

Cranberry Juice

MAKES 4 PINT OR 2 QUART JARS

◇◇

9 cups fresh cranberries (three 12-ounce bags),
    washed and drained
About 1½ cups sugar

Prepare for water-bath canning: Wash the jars and keep them hot in the canning pot, and put the flat lids in a heatproof bowl. (See page 21 for details.)

Put the cranberries and 9 cups water in a wide, 6- to 8-quart preserving pan. Bring to a boil over high heat. Boil, stirring frequently, until the cranberries burst and are soft, 4 to 5 minutes. Hang a jelly bag or set a colander lined with four layers of rinsed and squeezed cheesecloth over a large pot. Working in batches, ladle the cranberries and their juice into the cheesecloth and let the juice drain into the bowl; do not squeeze the cheesecloth or the juice will be cloudy. Discard the solids.

Stir in the sugar to taste and bring the juice to a boil over high heat. Boil for 1 minute.

Ladle boiling water from the canning pot into the bowl with the lids. Using a jar lifter, remove the hot jars from the canning pot, carefully pouring the water from each one back into the pot, and place them upright on a folded towel. Drain the water off the jar lids.

Ladle the hot juice into the jars, leaving ¼ inch headspace at the top. Use a damp paper towel to wipe the rims of the jars, then put a flat lid and ring on each jar, adjusting the ring so that it's just finger-tight. Return the jars to the water in the canning pot, making sure the water covers the jars by at least 1 inch. Bring to a boil, and boil for 15 minutes to process. Remove the jars to a folded towel and do not disturb for 12 hours. After 1 hour, check that the lids have sealed by pressing down on the center of each; if it can be pushed down, it hasn't sealed, and the jar should be refrigerated immediately. Label the sealed jars and store.

CRANBERRY AND VERBENA SPRITZER

Tart, herbal, and not too sweet, this simple, summery refresher is also good with mint. Serves 4.

3 cups Cranberry Juice (above)
6 sprigs fresh lemon verbena
Seltzer or sparkling water

In a small saucepan, bring the cranberry juice and 2 sprigs lemon verbena to a boil. Remove from the heat and let steep for 15 minutes. Remove and discard the lemon verbena, and chill the juice.

Fill tall glasses with ice and add the cranberry juice. Top off with seltzer and garnish with the fresh lemon verbena sprigs.

Pear and Ginger Preserves

MAKES ABOUT 5 HALF-PINT JARS

◇◇◇

CUTTING THE GINGER INTO *BRUNOISE* RATHER THAN FINELY MINCING IT OR DICING IT MORE COARSELY GIVES YOU A PLEASANTLY SPICY BUT NOT OBNOXIOUS HIT OF GINGER IN EACH BITE. Peel the ginger (about 1½ inches) and cut it into ¹⁄₁₆-inch-thick rounds, stack the rounds and cut into matchsticks, then finally into tiny cubes.

3 pounds pears, peeled, cored, and diced
   (about 7 cups)
3 tablespoons finely diced fresh ginger
Grated zest of 1 lemon
3 tablespoons strained fresh lemon juice
1½ cups sugar

Prepare for water-bath canning: Sterilize the jars and keep them hot in the canning pot, put a small plate in the freezer, and put the flat lids in a heat-proof bowl. (See page 21 for details.)

Put the pears, ginger, lemon zest and juice, and sugar in a wide, 6- to 8-quart preserving pan. Bring to a boil over high heat and cook, stirring occasionally, until the pears are very soft and translucent and a small dab of the jam spooned onto the chilled plate and returned to the freezer for a minute becomes somewhat firm (it will not gel), 15 to 20 minutes. Remove from the heat and stir gently for a few seconds to distribute the fruit in the liquid.

Ladle boiling water from the canning pot into the bowl with the lids. Using a jar lifter, remove the sterilized jars from the canning pot, carefully pouring the water from each one back into the pot, and place them upright on a folded towel. Drain the water off the jar lids.

Ladle the hot jam into the jars, leaving ¼ inch headspace at the top. Use a damp paper towel to wipe the rims of the jars, then put a flat lid and ring on each jar, adjusting the ring so that it's just finger-tight. Return the jars to the water in the canning pot, making sure the water covers the jars by at least 1 inch. Bring to a boil, and boil for 5 minutes to process. Remove the jars to a folded towel and do not disturb for 12 hours. After 1 hour, check that the lids have sealed by pressing down on the center of each; if it can be pushed down, it hasn't sealed, and the jar should be refrigerated immediately. Label the sealed jars and store.

Pear Juice

MAKES ABOUT 4 PINT JARS, OR 2 QUART JARS

◇◇

OR "NECTAR"? I never have been able to parse the difference. Most recipes for pear juice have you making a thick and pulpy puree (maybe *that's* a nectar), but I much prefer a lighter, more refreshing juice—and the resulting pear puree, which can be canned as pearsauce or pear butter. Try substituting pears in the recipe for Applesauce (page 183) or Spiced Apple Butter (page 186), adding a bit of ground ginger and cardamom to the pear versions. Iced pear juice is great on its own, but is also an excellent addition to cocktails—try it in bourbon- or rum-based drinks—or to alcohol-free cold or hot punches. Any variety of pear would be fine here, but the red ones yield the most attractive blush-colored juice.

4 pounds pears (preferably red), cored and cut into
   1-inch chunks

Put the pears in a wide, 6- to 8-quart preserving pot. Add 8 cups water, cover, and bring to a boil over high heat. Boil, stirring occasionally, until the pears are broken down and soft, about 20 minutes.

Working in batches, puree the pears in a blender. Set a large, fine-mesh sieve over a deep bowl or pot. Pour the pear puree into the sieve and let drain for at least 30 minutes, stirring occasionally to extract the juice. Reserve the puree for pearsauce or pear butter.

Prepare for water-bath canning: Wash the jars and keep them hot in the canning pot, and put the flat lids in a heatproof bowl. (See page 21 for details.)

Rinse the preserving pan and pour in the pear juice. Bring to a boil over high heat and boil for 5 minutes.

Ladle boiling water from the canning pot into the bowl with the lids. Using a jar lifter, remove the hot jars from the canning pot, carefully pouring the water from each one back into the pot, and place them upright on a folded towel. Drain the water off the jar lids.

Ladle the hot juice into the jars, leaving ½ inch headspace at the top. Use a damp paper towel to wipe the rims of the jars, then put a flat lid and ring on each jar, adjusting the ring so that it's just finger-tight. Return the jars to the water in the canning pot, making sure the water covers the jars by at least 1 inch. Bring to a boil, and boil pints or quarts for 10 minutes to process. Remove the jars to a folded towel and do not disturb for 12 hours. After 1 hour, check that the lids have sealed by pressing down on the center of each; if it can be pushed down, it hasn't sealed, and the jar should be refrigerated immediately. Label the sealed jars and store.

Spiced Seckel Pears with Red Wine

MAKES ABOUT 4 PINT JARS

◇◇◇

POACHED IN A SWEET VINEGAR-AND-WINE BRINE WITH GINGER AND WINTRY SPICES, THIS IS AN ODD PRESERVE, TO BE SURE. But it would be as appropriate as an informal after-dinner treat (just a tiny pickled pear to close off the meal) as it would on a loaded-up Thanksgiving supper table (in my Pennsylvania grandmother's house it would have counted as one of the seven sours but probably not one of the seven sweets traditionally offered at big family gatherings).

Juice of ½ lemon
3½ pounds ripe but firm seckel or fiorella pears
4 slices peeled fresh ginger
4 cinnamon sticks
2 teaspoons whole cloves
2 teaspoons whole allspice
1½ cups sugar
2¼ cups distilled white vinegar (5% acidity)
1 cup red wine

Prepare for water-bath canning: Wash the jars and keep them hot in the canning pot, and put the flat lids in a heatproof bowl. (See page 21 for details.)

Fill a large bowl with water and stir in the lemon juice. Peel the pears and remove the blossom end, halving and coring them if they're large; drop them into the water. Put the ginger, cinnamon, cloves, and allspice in a cheesecloth bag.

Put the sugar, vinegar, wine, 1 cup water, and the spice bag in a wide, 6- to 8-quart preserving pan. Bring to a boil over high heat, then lower the heat and simmer for 10 minutes. Discard the spices.

Ladle boiling water from the canning pot into the bowl with the lids. Using a jar lifter, remove the hot jars from the canning pot, carefully pouring the water from each one back into the pot, and place them upright on a folded towel. Drain the water off the jar lids.

Working quickly, drain the pears and pack them into the hot jars, leaving 1 inch headspace at the top. Ladle in the hot syrup, leaving ½ inch headspace. Use a chopstick to remove air bubbles around the inside of each jar. Use a damp paper towel to wipe the rims of the jars, then put a flat lid and ring on each jar, adjusting the ring so that it's just finger-tight. Return the jars to the water in the canning pot, making sure the water covers the jars by at least 1 inch. Bring to a boil, and boil for 15 minutes to process. Remove the jars to a folded towel and do not disturb for 12 hours. After 1 hour, check that the lids have sealed by pressing down on the center of each; if it can be pushed down, it hasn't sealed, and the jar should be refrigerated immediately. Label the sealed jars and store.

Pear, Clementine, and Pecan Conserve

MAKES ABOUT 6 HALF-PINT JARS

◇◇◇

AS SOON AS THE PEARS AND CLEMENTINES START TO SIMMER, AND THE AROMA OF FRESHLY TOASTED PECANS FILLS THE HOUSE, YOU'LL KNOW IT'S OFFICIALLY FALL. Here, pale, nearly translucent slices of pear are surrounded by pretty bits of clementine in a thick, fragrant syrup studded with naturally sweet pecans. Serve a spoonful—perhaps still on the spoon—at the end of a winter meal alongside a good hard cheese.

You could certainly use oranges here, but I prefer clementines because they're a little subtler and don't overpower the delicate pear flavor (any kind of pear will work fine; I usually use Bartlett, since so many generous people near me have Bartlett trees). In addition, the membranes surrounding the segments of a clementine are not as coarse as those in oranges, so you can just peel and chop—no careful segmenting, as I do in my marmalade recipes, is required.

3 pounds pears, peeled, cored, and cut into ⅛-inch slices (about 7 cups)

1 pound clementines (about 5), peeled and diced (about 1¼ cups), peel of 2 reserved and thinly sliced (about ¼ cup)

2 cups sugar

⅔ cup chopped pecans, toasted

Prepare for water-bath canning: Sterilize the jars and keep them hot in the canning pot, put a small plate in the freezer, and put the flat lids in a heatproof bowl. (See page 21 for details.)

Put the pears, clementines and sliced peel, and sugar in a wide, 6- to 8-quart preserving pan. Bring to a boil over high heat and cook, stirring occasionally, until the pears are very soft and translucent and a small dab of the conserve spooned onto the chilled plate and returned to the freezer for a minute becomes somewhat firm (it will not gel), about 25 minutes. Remove from the heat and stir in the pecans.

Ladle boiling water from the canning pot into the bowl with the lids. Using a jar lifter, remove the sterilized jars from the canning pot, carefully pouring the water from each one back into the pot, and place them upright on a folded towel. Drain the water off the jar lids.

Ladle the hot conserve into the jars, leaving ¼ inch headspace at the top. Use a chopstick to remove air bubbles around the inside of each jar. Use a damp paper towel to wipe the rims of the jars, then put a flat lid and ring on each jar, adjusting the ring so that it's just finger-tight. Return the jars to the water in the canning pot, making sure the water covers the jars by at least 1 inch. Bring to a boil, and boil for 5 minutes to process. Remove the jars to a folded towel and do not disturb for 12 hours. After 1 hour, check that the lids have sealed by pressing down on the center of each; if it can be pushed down, it hasn't sealed, and the jar should be refrigerated immediately. Label the sealed jars and store.

Old-Fashioned Concord Grape Jelly

MAKES ABOUT 3 HALF-PINT JARS

◇◇

GRAPE JELLY IS TRICKY—OR, AT ANY RATE, IT HAS BEEN FOR ME. You really need to have at least some partly unripe grapes in the mix so that there's enough pectin in the juice to set it into jelly and also so that the resulting spread is not too cloying. However, I am such a fan of plain old grape jelly (and few things pair so nicely with natural peanut butter—one of the many pleasures I've come to appreciate again as my daughter discovers them) that if I come across Concords that are tasty but fully ripe, I'm not above tossing a packet of powdered pectin in the pot. Do that if you want—just follow the instructions for grape jelly that come in the box of pectin. Or see the recipe that follows.

4 pounds Concord grapes, stemmed and rinsed, at
    least a quarter of them not quite ripe
About 2¼ cups sugar

Put the grapes in a wide, 6- to 8-quart preserving pan and use your hands to squeeze and crush them so that all the hulls have been slipped off. Add ½ cup water. Bring to a boil, then lower the heat and simmer for about 10 minutes, until the seeds start to separate from the pulp and the pulp is dark purple.

Set a large, very-fine-mesh sieve (or jelly bag) over a deep bowl or pot. Pour the grapes into the sieve and let drain for at least 1 hour, stirring occasionally but not pressing down too hard on the solids; discard the solids. Cover the bowl and put it in the refrigerator for 8 hours, or overnight. (This will ensure a clearer jelly.) Strain the juice again, leaving any sediment behind in the bowl. Measure the juice; you should have about 3 cups.

Prepare for water-bath canning: Sterilize the jars and keep them hot in the canning pot, put a small plate in the freezer, and put the flat lids in a heatproof bowl. (See page 21 for details.)

Rinse the preserving pan and pour in the grape juice. Add ¾ cup sugar for each cup of juice. Bring to a boil over high heat and cook, stirring occasionally, until the mixture registers about 220°F on a candy thermometer or a small dab of it spooned onto the chilled plate and returned to the freezer for a minute wrinkles when you nudge it, about 15 minutes.

Ladle boiling water from the canning pot into the bowl with the lids. Using a jar lifter, remove the sterilized jars from the canning pot, carefully pouring the water from each one back into the pot, and place them upright on a folded towel. Drain the water off the jar lids.

Ladle the hot jelly into the jars, leaving ¼ inch headspace at the top. Use a damp paper towel to wipe the rims of the jars, then put a flat lid and ring on each jar, adjusting the ring so that it's just finger-tight. Return the jars to the water in the canning pot, making sure the water covers the jars by at least 1 inch. Bring to a boil, and boil for 5 minutes to process. Remove the jars to a folded towel and do not disturb for 12 hours. After 1 hour, check that the lids have sealed by pressing down on the center of each; if it can be pushed down, it hasn't sealed, and the jar should be refrigerated immediately. Label the sealed jars and store.

Concord Grape Jelly with Green Apples

MAKES ABOUT 3 HALF-PINT JARS

◇◇

IF YOU'RE NOT SURE YOUR CONCORD GRAPES ARE PECTIN-RICH—THAT IS, IF THEY'RE ALL FULLY RIPE—TRY THIS RECIPE. Here the lemon and the peels and cores of green apples provide an extra shot of pectin and tartness. The grape flavor is not quite as intense as it is in jelly made with partly unripe grapes, but it will certainly satisfy any grape-jelly craving you might have.

3½ pounds Concord grapes, stemmed and rinsed
1 pound Granny Smith apples (about 3 large)
1 lemon
2¼ cups sugar

Put the grapes in a wide, 6- to 8-quart preserving pan and use your hands to squeeze and crush them so that all the hulls have been slipped off; add 1 cup water. Roughly chop the apples (do not peel or core them) and slice the lemon. Add the apples and lemon to the grapes. Bring to a boil, then lower the heat and simmer for about 20 minutes, until the apples are soft.

Set a large, very-fine-mesh sieve (or jelly bag) over a deep bowl or pot. Pour the grape mixture into the sieve and let drain for at least 1 hour, stirring occasionally but not pressing down too hard on the solids; discard the solids. Cover the bowl and put it in the refrigerator for 8 hours, or overnight. (This will ensure a clearer jelly.) Strain the juice again, leaving any sediment behind in the bowl. Measure the juice; you should have about 3 cups.

Prepare for water-bath canning: Sterilize the jars and keep them hot in the canning pot, put a small plate in the freezer, and put the flat lids in a heat-proof bowl. (See page 21 for details.)

Rinse the preserving pan and pour in the juice. Add ¾ cup sugar for each cup of juice. Bring to a boil over high heat and cook, stirring occasionally, until the mixture registers about 220°F on a candy thermometer or a small dab of it spooned onto the chilled plate and returned to the freezer for a minute wrinkles when you nudge it, about 15 minutes.

Ladle boiling water from the canning pot into the bowl with the lids. Using a jar lifter, remove the sterilized jars from the canning pot, carefully pouring the water from each one back into the pot, and place them upright on a folded towel. Drain the water off the jar lids.

Ladle the hot jelly into the jars, leaving ¼ inch headspace at the top. Use a damp paper towel to wipe the rims of the jars, then put a flat lid and ring on each jar, adjusting the ring so that it's just finger-tight. Return the jars to the water in the canning pot, making sure the water covers the jars by at least 1 inch. Bring to a boil, and boil for 5 minutes to process. Remove the jars to a folded towel and do not disturb for 12 hours. After 1 hour, check that the lids have sealed by pressing down on the center of each; if it can be pushed down, it hasn't sealed, and the jar should be refrigerated immediately. Label the sealed jars and store.

Spiced Concord Grape Jam

MAKES ABOUT 4 HALF-PINT JARS

◇◇◇

HUMBLE GRAPE JAM ISN'T SOMETHING YOU SEE ALL THAT OFTEN—IT'S ALMOST COMPLETELY ECLIPSED BY ITS STIFFER, CLEARER COUSIN. But that's a shame. The hulls are here made tender with simmering in the rich grape juice and are allowed to take center stage. Also, with Concord grapes it's easier to achieve a jamlike spread than a jellylike one: Jam doesn't have to set firmly to be usable, so you can use fully ripe fruit here with no pectin-related repercussions.

4 pounds Concord grapes, stemmed and rinsed
2 cups sugar
3 tablespoons fresh lemon juice
Grated zest of 1 lemon
1 teaspoon ground cinnamon
¼ teaspoon ground cloves

Prepare for water-bath canning: Sterilize the jars and keep them hot in the canning pot, put a small plate in the freezer, and put the flat lids in a heat-proof bowl. (See page 21 for details.)

Squeeze the grapes and put the pulp in a large saucepan and the hulls in a wide, 6- to 8-quart preserving pan. Bring the pulp to a boil, then lower the heat and simmer for about 10 minutes, until the seeds start to separate from the pulp. Ladle into a sieve set over the preserving pan and use a rubber spatula to push as much pulp and juice through as possible; discard the seeds. Add the remaining ingredients. Bring to a boil over high heat and boil, stirring occasionally, until a small dab of the jam spooned onto the chilled plate and returned to the freezer for a minute becomes somewhat firm, about 15 minutes. Remove from the heat and stir gently for a few seconds to distribute the hulls in the liquid.

Ladle boiling water from the canning pot into the bowl with the lids. Using a jar lifter, remove the sterilized jars from the canning pot, carefully pouring the water from each one back into the pot, and place them upright on a folded towel. Drain the water off the jar lids.

Ladle the hot jam into the jars, leaving ¼ inch headspace at the top. Use a damp paper towel to wipe the rims of the jars, then put a flat lid and ring on each jar, adjusting the ring so that it's just finger-tight. Return the jars to the water in the canning pot, making sure the water covers the jars by at least 1 inch. Bring to a boil, and boil for 5 minutes to process. Remove the jars to a folded towel and do not disturb for 12 hours. After 1 hour, check that the lids have sealed by pressing down on the center of each; if it can be pushed down, it hasn't sealed, and the jar should be refrigerated immediately. Label the sealed jars and store.

GRAPE JUICE

To make grape juice (for quaffing rather than for jelly), crush the grapes, simmer them (with some whole spices or herb sprigs, if you'd like), strain, let sit overnight, and strain again. Return the juice to the pan and add water to dilute it (pure grape juice can be a little intense), add sugar if it needs it (it probably won't), and a bit of lemon juice if desired. Bring to a boil, then ladle into sterilized pint or quart jars, leaving ½ inch headspace, put the lids and rings on, and process in a boiling-water bath, as above, for 5 minutes.

Muscadine and Plum Pie and Cobbler Filling

MAKES 3 QUART JARS, ENOUGH FOR 3 (9-INCH) PIES OR 3 COBBLERS

◇◇

YOU CAN USE TART AND FUNKY PURPLE MUSCADINES, GOLDEN SCUPPERNONGS, OR BLUEISH CONCORD-TYPE GRAPES—THE KIND WITH SEEDS AND A TOUGH SKIN, OR HULL— FOR PIES AND COBBLERS. As you're smushing the grapes (this might call to mind, for normal people, a Lucille Ball moment, but personally I always think of Rock Hudson and Salome Jens in *Seconds*), play them off one another, pressing a few of them together in your hand.

6 pounds muscadines, rinsed

1 pound red-fleshed plums, pitted and sliced ½ inch thick

3 tablespoons strained fresh lemon juice

2 cups sugar

Prepare for water-bath canning: Wash the jars and keep them hot in the canning pot, and put the flat lids in a heatproof bowl. (See page 21 for details.)

Squeeze the grapes and put the pulp in a large saucepan and the hulls in a wide, 6- to 8-quart preserving pan. Bring the pulp to a boil, then lower the heat and simmer for about 10 minutes, until the seeds start to separate from the pulp. Ladle into a sieve set over the preserving pan and use a rubber spatula to push as much pulp and juice through as possible; discard the seeds. Rinse out the preserving pan and return the pulp and juice to the pan. Bring to a boil over high heat and boil, stirring occasionally, until the hulls are tender, 5 to 7 minutes. Add the plums, lemon juice, and sugar. Bring to a boil and boil for 1 minute.

Ladle boiling water from the canning pot into the bowl with the lids. Using a jar lifter, remove the hot jars from the canning pot, carefully pouring the water from each one back into the pot, and place them upright on a folded towel. Drain the water off the jar lids.

Ladle the hot fruit and juice into the jars, leaving ½ inch headspace at the top. Use a chopstick to remove air bubbles around the inside of each jar. Use a damp paper towel to wipe the rims of the jars, then put a flat lid and ring on each jar, adjusting the ring so that it's just finger-tight. Return the jars to the water in the canning pot, making sure the water covers the jars by at least 1 inch. Bring to a boil, and boil for 25 minutes to process. Remove the jars to a folded towel and do not disturb for 12 hours. After 1 hour, check that the lids have sealed by pressing down on the center of each; if it can be pushed down, it hasn't sealed, and the jar should be refrigerated immediately. Label the sealed jars and store.

> ## CONCORD GRAPE FILLING
>
> To make grape filling, reduce the sugar to 1 cup (or to taste), and boil the pulp, hulls, and remaining ingredients together just until the hulls are tender, about 10 minutes. Ladle into a hot quart jar, put the lid and ring on, and process in a boiling-water bath, as above, for 10 minutes; alternatively, put it in a freezer bag or jar and freeze. When ready to use the filling, thaw it and stir in 3 tablespoons instant tapioca. The recipe above makes a bit more than 1 quart. See the Muscadine and Plum Pie recipe on page 000 for instructions on pie making, and the Muscadine and Plum Cobbler recipe on page 212 for a cornmeal-enhanced cobbler topping.

Easy Pie Dough

MAKES ENOUGH FOR 1 DOUBLE-CRUST 9-INCH PIE

THIS IS MY FAMILY'S GO-TO SHORT CRUST, USED FOR SAVORY AS WELL AS SWEET FILLINGS. I don't usually add any sugar to the dough because, first, the filling (and a bit of sugar sprinkled on top) makes the pie sweet enough for me, and second, if I have any leftover scraps of dough for the freezer, I want them to be as versatile as possible so that I can use them for a small batch of meat turnovers or whatever.

The egg and vinegar make the crust tender and the dough easy to roll out and work with. While a combination of vegetable shortening (for tenderness and ease of use) and butter (for flavor) will make a fantastic crust, leaf lard—the pure, snowy-white fat surrounding pigs' kidneys—gives it a slight crunch and a richer, darker flavor than I've ever achieved with vegetable shortening or butter and is well worth asking your butcher for. (I wouldn't use just plain lard or rendered pork fat for sweet pie crusts, as it tends to impart a meatiness that isn't exactly welcome in a dessert context.)

3 cups all-purpose flour

½ teaspoon pure kosher salt

1¼ cups cold leaf lard, or 1 cup cold vegetable shortening and ¼ cup (½ stick) unsalted butter

1 large egg

1 tablespoon vinegar

About 5 tablespoons ice water

In a large bowl, stir together the flour and salt. Using a pastry cutter, two table knives held in one hand, or your fingertips, cut in the lard until the largest pieces are the size of peas. Make a well in the center; add the egg and vinegar and stir them together with a fork or spatula. Sprinkle a few tablespoons of the ice water over the mixture and

toss just to combine. Using sharp folding and cutting motions with a wooden spoon or a spatula, stir just until the dough holds together. Turn out onto the counter and gather the dough into a very rough ball. Use the palm of your hand to smear the dough away from you. Use a bench knife to scrape it back into a rough ball. Repeat twice. (This flattens the pieces of fat into shards, which will melt into flaky goodness when the crust bakes.) Divide the dough into 2 roughly equal-size pieces. Wrap them tightly in plastic, smoothing each into an even, flat disk shape.

Chill in the freezer for about 20 minutes, or in the fridge for 30 minutes, until firm. The dough can be wrapped in a couple more layers of plastic and frozen for several months; defrost in the fridge for a couple hours before continuing.

Muscadine and Plum Pie

MAKES 1 (9-INCH) PIE; SERVES 6

◇◇

Easy Pie Dough (page 211)

1 quart Muscadine and Plum Pie and Cobber Filling
  (page 210)

3 tablespoons instant tapioca

1 tablespoon unsalted butter, cut into pieces

2 tablespoons milk

1 teaspoon coarse turbinado or Demerara sugar

Preheat the oven to 400°F.

On a lightly floured surface, roll out one disk of the pie dough into a rough circle about ⅛ inch thick. Transfer it to a 9-inch pie plate and trim the edges.

In a large bowl, stir together the pie filling and tapioca, then dump it into the dough-lined pie plate. Dot with the butter.

Roll out the second disk of dough and set it over the filling, sealing the edges. Cut slits in the top crust. Brush with the milk and sprinkle with the coarse sugar. Bake on the center rack of the oven until the filling starts to bubble up out of the slits and the crust is well browned, 45 minutes to 1 hour. Let cool on a wire rack for at least 1 hour, then slice and serve.

• •

Muscadine and Plum Cobbler

SERVES 6

◇◇

THIS RUSTIC, BISCUITY COBBLER TOPPING CAN BE USED WITH ANY FILLING. As a variation, drain a couple quarts of Peaches in Vanilla Syrup (page 108) and stir in sugar to taste, or thaw some frozen presweetened sliced fruit.

1 quart Muscadine and Plum Pie and Cobbler Filling
  (page 210)

3 tablespoons instant tapioca

¾ cup all-purpose flour

¼ cup fine cornmeal

1 tablespoon sugar

1½ teaspoons baking powder

½ teaspoon pure kosher salt

¼ cup (½ stick) unsalted butter

½ cup milk

Preheat the oven to 400°F.

In a 9-by-13-inch baking dish, combine the filling and tapioca and put the dish in the oven while you make the topping.

In a large bowl, whisk together the flour, cornmeal, sugar, baking powder, and salt. Using a pastry cutter, two table knives held in one hand, or your fingertips, cut in the butter until the largest pieces are the size of peas. Add the milk and stir until just combined; it will be lumpy—don't overmix. Drop spoonfuls of the topping onto the hot filling and bake until nicely browned, 25 to 30 minutes.

FREEZING PERSIMMONS

The first time my mom tasted the fruit of *Diospyros virginiana*, the native persimmon, she says, her mind could process only this phrase, over and over, to describe the flavor: *Long ago and far away*. She must've meant that in a good way, and she must've gotten lucky with a ripe one, for the tannins in a persimmon even slightly underripe, as Captain John Smith observed, "will draw a man's mouth awrie with much torment." He continued, "but when it is ripe, it is as delicious as an Apricock." Much more so, I'd say.

The wild persimmon is so unlike its cultivated Hachiya (heart-shaped, very mild, tannic when unripe) and Fuyu (round, squat, crisp, not tannic) cousins as to be almost not of the same family of fruit. Dark in color, with a frosted appearance, perhaps only an inch or so across, with a few large seeds, and, when ripe, slightly shriveled and collapsing upon itself, it has an almost Baroque look to it.

D. virginiana grows wild from Indiana to Georgia, where these days it seems only the old-timers and the interlopers like me know what pleasures await them in abandoned orchards and along country roads that haven't been visited by the DOT in a while. As early as 1979, Raymond Sokolov was advocating for commercial cultivation of the trees, but perhaps the right people still have not read his brilliant *Fading Feast*. And those people also must not have been sufficiently inspired by Marilyn Kluger's long and evocative piece in the October 1978 *Gourmet* about gathering wild persimmons. We still don't see native persimmons in farmers' markets with the regularity we should, so you'll have to get your own.

The trees are hard to spot until the leaves on the trees around them have fallen and the deep orange fruit becomes more apparent among the similarly colored foliage. Folkways insist that the fruit must be frozen at least once on the tree before it's suited for consumption, and that only the fallen fruit on the ground is sure to be ripe, but this is not true. Don't wait for the first frost; go out to collect them as soon as you notice that some have begun to soften. Slow down and scan the woods closely as you drive, then swerve onto the shoulder of the road when you see a tree. Here's hoping the fruit is as low and reachable as it appeared to be from the car. Pick all that you can reach, and any unsmushed ones from the ground; let the firm ones ripen on the counter at home.

If all you can scare up in the woods are a few wild persimmons, not enough for a pudding or to freeze for later, do this: Put the pulp in a mini food processor and drizzle in some cold heavy cream. Process until smooth and fluffy, and then simply eat it.

Freezing persimmon pulp: Remove the green-brown tops. Mash up whole wild persimmons with a spoon or fork, then push the pulp through a sieve or food mill to remove the seeds (the skin is tender and edible, so it's fine if some of it makes its way into the pulp). Freeze in 1-cup containers for up to 6 months. If you want to freeze Hachiya or Fuyu persimmons (the Fuyu variety isn't really freezable as pulp), just chop them up and puree them in a food processor—usually there aren't any seeds to deal with. There will be little bits of peel, but that's okay. The flavor won't be nearly as intense, but it has its own charm.

Persimmon Pudding

SERVES 4 TO 6

THIS IS MY MOM'S RECIPE. It makes a lightly spiced old-timey pudding-cake with a deep persimmon flavor—especially dark if you use wild native persimmon pulp, but also well worth doing with cultivated persimmons. The edges and bottom become a bit chewy and caramelized, while the moist interior falls. Be sure to call the kids into the kitchen to see the surface of the almost-done pudding trembling as the mass underneath bubbles in the heat of the oven. It's weird.

1 cup frozen persimmon pulp (opposite), thawed
1 cup sugar
1 large egg
2 tablespoons unsalted butter, melted or at room
    temperature
½ cup milk
1 cup all-purpose flour
1 teaspoon baking powder
1 teaspoon ground cinnamon
½ teaspoon baking soda
½ cup Yogurt (page 287) or buttermilk
Cold milk for serving

Preheat the oven to 350°F. Butter an 8- or 9-inch square baking dish.

In a large bowl, use a wooden spoon to beat the persimmon pulp, sugar, and egg until smooth. Beat in the butter and milk.

In a medium bowl, sift together the flour, baking powder, and cinnamon. In a small bowl, stir the baking soda into the yogurt. Add the flour mixture to the persimmon mixture alternately with the yogurt mixture, stirring until just incorporated. Scrape into the prepared pan and bake for 45 minutes, or until the edges start to pull away from the sides of the dish and the top is set and nicely browned; it will still be very moist inside. Serve warm, scooped into bowls with milk poured over.

FALL VEGETABLES

Pickled Garlic

MAKES ABOUT 5 PINT JARS

IT MIGHT SEEM OUT OF CHARACTER TO GIVE YOU A RECIPE THAT REQUIRES THE MAIN INGREDIENT TO BE PURCHASED PARTIALLY PREPARED. But pickled garlic is so good—and, many folks would claim, good for you—that I thought it worth including this recipe even though I can't imagine peeling (much less planting and harvesting) enough fresh garlic for three pounds of cloves. By all means, if you have the garlic and the time—and a proclivity for drudge work—peel the garlic yourself, but I cheat and get peeled garlic five pounds at a time from a huge Korean grocery store where the turnover is good and the garlic is clearly very fresh. I put the leftover cloves in a mini food processor, chop finely, put in a clean, dry container, and cover the garlic with olive oil. This keeps in the fridge for several weeks, and makes simple Italian-type dishes even simpler: Scoop some garlic and oil into a sauté pan, heat, add fresh greens of any kind, sprinkle with salt and some crushed red pepper flakes, and you've got something nice to go with a little piece of seared fish.

Mellow but spicy pickled garlic is surprisingly easy to snack on out of the jar (my friends the Adamses, not a large family, have been known to go through a pint in less than a week), but you can also use them in salads, or chopped up in a vinaigrette or hummus, or tossed into a Dutch oven with a chuck roast destined for hours and hours of cooking.

3 pounds peeled whole garlic cloves
6 cups distilled white vinegar (5% acidity)
½ cup sugar
1½ tablespoons pure kosher salt
Spices and/or dried herbs (see Note)

Bring a large pot of water to a boil. Add the garlic and blanch for 1 minute. Drain and set aside.

Prepare for water-bath canning: Wash the jars and keep them hot in the canning pot, and put the flat lids in a heatproof bowl. (See page 21 for details.)

In a nonreactive pot, combine the vinegar, sugar, and salt and bring just to a boil, stirring to dissolve the sugar and salt.

Ladle boiling water from the canning pot into the bowl with the lids. Using a jar lifter, remove the hot jars from the canning pot, carefully pouring the water from each one back into the pot, and place them upright on a folded towel. Drain the water off the jar lids.

Put desired spices in the jars, then pack with the blanched garlic, leaving 1 inch headspace at the top. Ladle the hot vinegar mixture into the jars, leaving ½ inch headspace. Use a chopstick to remove air bubbles around the inside of each jar. Use a damp paper towel to wipe the rims of the jars, then put a flat lid and ring on each jar, adjusting the ring so that it's just finger-tight. Return the jars to the water in the canning pot, making sure the water covers the jars by at least 1 inch. Bring to a boil, and boil for 15 minutes to process. Remove the jars to a folded towel and do not disturb for 12 hours. After 1 hour, check that the lids have sealed by pressing down on the center of each; if it can be pushed down, it hasn't sealed, and the jar should be refrigerated immediately. Label the sealed jars and store.

Note: Be creative! Just about anything goes with garlic. To give you a start, here are a few of my favorite combinations. *Spicy:* In each pint jar, put 1 teaspoon crushed red pepper flakes, ½ teaspoon celery seeds, ½ teaspoon dried oregano, and 1 dried crushed red chile. *Smoky:* In each pint jar, put 1 teaspoon chipotle pepper flakes, ¼ teaspoon cumin seeds, and 1 dried red chile. *Too Hot:* In each pint jar, put 1 fresh habanero or Scotch bonnet chile (split in half from the bottom almost to the stem). *For the Kids:* In each pint jar, put 1 teaspoon celery seeds, ½ teaspoon fennel seeds, and ½ teaspoon whole black peppercorns.

KEEPING GARLIC

Mature garlic is dug up usually in late summer, depending on the variety, and then hung up (with the stalks braided together in such a way that all sides of the bulbs are evenly exposed to air) in a cool, dark spot with good air circulation to dry, or cure, for several weeks. To keep garlic fresh, hang the bulbs in mesh bags in a dark spot—like a cool pantry, where it can keep for months. You can refrigerate garlic heads, but be aware that they'll sprout and become unusable fairly quickly upon their return to room temperature.

Dried garlic: Peel and thinly slice garlic cloves. Dry them in a single layer in a dehydrator until crisp, then put them in an airtight container and place it in the coldest part of the freezer for at least 48 hours—this will kill off any tiny bugs that might have gotten into the mix during drying. After that, the garlic can be stored at room temperature. Grind it to a powder, if you'd like, or leave it in larger chips to toss into soups and stews, or to use in spice rubs for smoking large cuts of meat.

Roasted garlic in oil: Cut several whole heads of garlic almost in half horizontally and put them on a large sheet of aluminum foil. Sprinkle the cut cloves with pure kosher salt, and drizzle with a little olive oil. Wrap tightly and roast in a 400°F oven for about 1 hour, until the cloves are very soft and caramel-colored. Squeeze the cloves out of the peel and pack them in a sealable plastic container or glass jar, pushing out any pockets of air between cloves. Sprinkle with lemon juice and cover the surface with a layer of olive oil. The garlic will keep, refrigerated, for several weeks and can be used in anything.

Frozen garlic: Roast garlic as above, and transfer the squeezed-out cloves to an ice-cube tray (one you don't plan to use again for plain ice); cover tightly with plastic wrap and aluminum foil and freeze until solid; transfer to freezer bags to store. Or make garlic butter: In a food processor, combine roasted peeled garlic cloves with room-temperature salted butter until smooth (salted butter keeps better than unsalted, and also tastes nice with roasted garlic). Scrape it out onto a sheet of waxed paper or plastic wrap, form into a log, wrap tightly, and freeze. (Wrap again in freezer paper if you plan to keep it for more than a month or so.)

Grandma Barron's Green Tomato Relish

MAKES ABOUT 5 PINT JARS

I RECENTLY FOUND MY MOM'S MOTHER'S OLD INDEX CARD—WELL USED AND EXTREMELY STAINED—CONTAINING THIS 4-H RELISH RECIPE. Here I've scaled the quantities down from pecks and bushels, down even from my mom's idiosyncratic scaling-down notes on the recipe: "tomatoes: large mixer bowl heaped." When I tried it, I remembered it from way back when I was a kid, before I was smart enough to realize that all the things I was eating had been *made by someone.* The recipe is similar to one published by the National Center for Home Food Preservation. If you're lucky enough to have access to a large, heaping bowlful of green tomatoes in the fall, do make some of this (you can scale it down even further, if you'd like). It's sweet and tart, as a relish should be, with just a hint of sweet spices. Spread it on a sandwich of lightly fried fish, sliced tomatoes, cilantro, and shredded lettuce. Combine it with mayonnaise and a little lemon juice to make a quick dipping sauce for shrimp. Use it in salmon cakes. Or just keep it handy for hot dogs.

5 pounds green tomatoes, chopped

12 ounces red bell peppers (about 2 medium), seeded and chopped

10 ounces onions (about 2 small), chopped

¼ cup pure kosher salt

2 cups distilled white vinegar (5% acidity)

1½ cups sugar

1 cinnamon stick

1 teaspoon whole cloves

1 teaspoon whole allspice

Working in batches, put the tomatoes, peppers, and onions in a food processor and pulse to finely chop. Transfer to a wide, 6- to 8-quart preserving pan and stir in the salt. Let stand for 8 hours, or overnight.

Prepare for water-bath canning: Wash the jars and keep them hot in the canning pot, and put the flat lids in a heatproof bowl. (See page 21 for details.)

Bring the vegetables to a boil over high heat and cook for 5 minutes. Scoop the vegetables into a sieve and press out as much of the liquid as possible. Return them to the preserving pan; set aside.

In a nonreactive pan, combine the vinegar, sugar, and spices and bring to a boil, stirring to dissolve the sugar. Boil for 5 minutes, then use a slotted spoon to remove and discard the spices. Pour the vinegar mixture over the vegetables and bring to a boil over high heat; lower the heat and simmer, stirring occasionally, for 5 minutes.

Ladle boiling water from the canning pot into the bowl with the lids. Using a jar lifter, remove the hot jars from the canning pot, carefully pouring the water from each one back into the pot, and place them upright on a folded towel. Drain the water off the jar lids.

Ladle the hot relish into the jars, leaving ½ inch headspace at the top. Use a damp paper towel to wipe the rims of the jars, then put a flat lid and ring on each jar, adjusting the ring so that it's just finger-tight. Return the jars to the water in the canning pot, making sure the water covers the jars by at least 1 inch. Bring to a boil, and boil for 10 minutes to process. Remove the jars to a folded towel and do not disturb for 12 hours. After 1 hour, check that the lids have sealed by pressing down on the center of each; if it can be pushed down, it hasn't sealed, and the jar should be refrigerated immediately. Label the sealed jars and store.

Sweet Green Tomato Pickles

MAKES ABOUT 6 WIDE-MOUTH PINT JARS

THESE LITTLE SUCKERS ARE ADDICTIVE. Not nearly as sweet as traditional green tomato pickles, but just sweet enough to satisfy some strange need you might not even know you had until you try one, they're good straight out of the jar (best chilled), but come closer to heavenly in a roast-turkey or chicken sandwich on sourdough bread with nothing more than a little mayonnaise and black pepper.

Use wide-mouth jars, and tomatoes no larger than 3 inches in diameter, so you can neatly stack the slices in the jars. If your tomatoes are bigger, slice them, then cut into quarters.

4 pounds green tomatoes (unripe)
¾ cup pickling lime (see page 177)
6 cups distilled white vinegar (5% acidity)
2½ cups sugar
2 tablespoons pure kosher salt
1 teaspoon celery seeds
½ cup minced celery (about 2 ribs)
2 tablespoons minced peeled fresh ginger
½ small sweet onion, very thinly sliced into rounds (optional)

Cut the tomatoes into ¼-inch rounds, cutting out the tough core in the top slices. In a large bowl, combine 3 quarts cold water with the pickling lime and add the tomatoes. Cover the bowl and set aside at room temperature for 8 hours or overnight.

Drain in a colander, rinse well, and cover with cold water. Let soak for 1 hour, then drain. Repeat the soaking and draining two more times to remove all of the lime; do not skip this step, as it's necessary to remove all of the lime so that the pickles will be acidic enough for preservation.

Prepare for water-bath canning: Wash the jars and keep them hot in the canning pot, and put the flat lids in a heatproof bowl. (See page 21 for details.)

In a wide, 6- to 8-quart preserving pan, combine the vinegar, sugar, salt, celery seeds, celery, and ginger. Bring to a boil, then add the drained tomatoes. Return to a boil and cook, gently pressing down on the tomatoes to keep them mostly submerged, for 15 minutes. The tomatoes will become somewhat translucent.

Ladle boiling water from the canning pot into the bowl with the lids. Using a jar lifter, remove the hot jars from the canning pot, carefully pouring the water from each one back into the pot, and place them upright on a folded towel. Drain the water off the jar lids.

Use a slotted spoon to transfer the hot tomatoes to the jars. (If you'd like, insert a round of onion or two between some of the tomato slices.) Ladle in the hot syrup, leaving ½ inch headspace at the top. Use a chopstick to remove air bubbles around the inside of each jar. Use a damp paper towel to wipe the rims of the jars, then put a flat lid and ring on each jar, adjusting the ring so that it's just finger-tight. Return the jars to the water in the canning pot, making sure the water covers the jars by at least 1 inch. Bring to a boil, and boil for 10 minutes to process. Remove the jars to a folded towel and do not disturb for 12 hours. After 1 hour, check that the lids have sealed by pressing down on the center of each; if it can be pushed down, it hasn't sealed, and the jar should be refrigerated immediately. Label the sealed jars and store.

Nuka (Japanese Fermented Bran Pickles)

MAKES AN INFINITE SUPPLY OF PICKLES

◇◇

NUKA ARE A TRADITIONAL JAPANESE PICKLE OFTEN SERVED AT THE END OF THE MEAL—I HAVE NO EVIDENCE THAT THEY DO IN FACT AID DIGESTION, BUT THAT'S THE IDEA. The pickles are made by burying vegetables in a bed of damp, salty rice or wheat bran until they are soured by fermentation. Two pickling books in particular go into great detail about *nuka*: Sandor Ellix Katz's weird and wonderful *Wild Fermentation* and the adorably quirky *Quick and Easy Tsukemono*, by Ikuko Hisamatsu (see Further Reading, page 292). I've only begun to delve into the world of *nuka*, but because it's so darn fun, I wanted to share some tips on what I've found to work well.

Look for wheat bran in the bulk bins at supermarkets, where it's usually pretty inexpensive. (Rice bran, which is more authentic, tends to be hard to come by.) Start these pickles in fall or early spring, when the weather's cool. When the weather warms up, empty the fermenting bed of pickles and store it in the refrigerator.

2 pounds wheat bran

2 (4-inch) pieces kombu seaweed

¾ cup pure kosher salt, plus more for each batch of
   vegetables

1 cup boiling water

¾ cup beer

¼ cup miso paste

¼ cup dry mustard powder

1-inch piece ginger, halved

2 cloves garlic, peeled but left whole

Vegetables, scrubbed, whole or cut into large pieces,
   peeled or not, such as carrots, cucumbers, turnips,
   daikon, red radishes, sunchokes, and turnip leaves
   (tied in a bunch)

In a large, deep sauté pan over medium heat, toast the bran, stirring constantly, until fragrant and a shade darker. Put in a 1-gallon pickling crock or other food-safe container and let cool completely.

Put the kombu and the ¾ cup salt in a large heatproof bowl and pour in the boiling water. Let stand for 30 minutes to hydrate the kombu. Stir in 3 cups water, the beer, miso paste, and dry mustard until well combined, then stir the liquid into the bran to make a paste; nestle the kombu, ginger, and garlic in the bran mixture. This is the fermenting bed, and will act like a brine.

Rub a few vegetables lightly with salt, then bury them in the fermenting bed, making sure that everything is completely surrounded by the bran, smoothing the surface and patting it down firmly to eliminate air pockets. Wipe the inside of the crock clean above the surface of the bran mixture with a paper towel. Cover the crock with a heavy towel and let ferment at cool room temperature for 24 hours. Remove the vegetables with clean hands and rinse them off; taste and serve them if you'd like—they will probably not be very sour yet. Stir the fermenting bed well to aerate it.

For several days, keep adding a few salt-rubbed vegetables at a time, leaving them for about 24 hours and then removing them, stirring the fermenting bed each time. After about a week, the pickles will start becoming more sour and will take on the flavors in the fermenting bed. Just keep tasting and experimenting to determine which vegetables you like and how long to leave them in. When the fermenting bed is well developed and a strong *Lactobacillus* culture is present, vegetables may sour to a point that you find ideal within a few hours; you can also try leaving some in the bed for weeks or months. Remember that each time you take out a pickled vegetable you're removing salt, so you need to salt new vegetables before you put them in the bed (or stir a little salt into the fermenting bed when you remove pickles).

If the pickles are too salty for your taste, soak them in cool water for a bit before slicing and serving.

If the fermenting bed becomes watery as vegetables release their own liquid into the bran, press a small bowl into the surface and scoop out and discard some of the water. Add a bit more toasted bran as necessary.

Supposedly the fermenting bed can last pretty much for eternity—Japanese cooks pass their rice-bran beds on to younger generations, and each family's has a particular flavor that depends on what vegetables are pickled in it regularly. Hisa-matsu says that when warm weather arrives you may empty the bed of pickles, put the bran mixture in a loosely closed plastic bag, and store it in the refrigerator, which will halt fermentation, until the fall returns and you can put it back in the crock for more fermenting action at cool room temperature.

Onigiri (Stuffed Rice Balls)

MAKES ABOUT 8 (½-CUP) *ONIGIRI*

FOR KIDS LEARNING THEIR GEOMETRIC SOLIDS—OVOIDS AND PYRAMIDS AND SUCH—THERE COULDN'T BE A BETTER LUNCHBOX STAPLE.

2 cups short-grain Japanese sushi rice
Pure kosher salt or fine salt
Diced *Nuka* (opposite), or any other sour or salty filling you can think of (see page 226 for a few ideas)
8 rectangles nori seaweed

Rinse the rice thoroughly by swishing it around in several changes of water. Put it in a medium saucepan with 2¼ cups water and let soak for 30 minutes. Bring to a boil over medium-high heat, then cover tightly, reduce the heat to medium, and cook for about 4 minutes, until the rice is level with the surface of the water. Turn the heat to the lowest setting and cook for about 10 minutes without lifting the lid, until the water is absorbed and the rice is tender. Remove from the heat and uncover; drape a clean kitchen towel over the pot (to absorb moisture) and let cool for 10 to 15 minutes.

While the rice is still hot, shape the *onigiri*: Line a teacup or small bowl with plastic wrap, leaving plenty of plastic hanging over the edge. Sprinkle the plastic inside the cup with water and salt, and fill with rice. Push about 2 teaspoons *nuka* into the center of the ball of rice and cover it completely. Gather up the edges of the plastic wrap and twist them together to wrap up the rice. Use your hands to shape it into a sphere, a triangular prism, or what have you. Let cool to room temperature, then refrigerate (or freeze) until ready to serve or pack in a lunchbox. Unwrap the *onigiri*, press a rectangle of nori onto the bottom of the shape and partway up the sides, and gently stick it to the rice. Serve at room temperature.

ONIGIRI FILLING IDEAS

* Any of the pickles in this book

* Tomato and Cashew Chutney (page 174)

* Slow-Roasted Tomatoes (page 175)

* Date and Lime Pickle Chutney (see page 249)

* Herb-Glazed Grilled Pork (page 192)

* Smoked salmon

* Rotisserie chicken

* Teriyaki beef

* ABOVE: **Onigiri (Stuffed Rice Balls)**. OPPOSITE: **Japanese-style lunch: Onigiri, panko-breaded baked chicken, Sweet Green Tomato Pickles (page 221), and fruit**

Pumpkin Chips

MAKES ABOUT 7 HALF-PINT JARS

RECIPES FOR PUMPKIN CHIPS APPEAR IN TURN-OF-THE-LAST-CENTURY COOKBOOKS PUBLISHED ALL OVER THE COUNTRY. One of the most workable recipes for this chunky, lemony sweetmeat or preserve appears in the California watercolorist Henrietta Latham Dwight's fascinating 1898 vegetarian tract *The Golden Age Cook-Book*. But these days pumpkin chips are mostly a hyper-local specialty of the past-worshipping South Carolina Low Country. They can be served on or alongside rich buttered biscuits or cakes, or as a "spoon sweet," a small but elegant treat at the end of a meal, similar to those served in the Middle East.

The recipe that follows is based also on one in Charlestonian commercial canner Stephen Palmer Dowdney's *Putting Up: A Year-Round Guide to Canning in the Southern Tradition* (see Further Reading, page 292). I've added spices (the star anise plays up the savory aspect of pumpkin, I think), but they're not traditional and are, of course, optional.

Though our forebears would put up jars of pumpkin preserves with impunity, as if it were a fruit, using only a boiling-water bath, it must be remembered that pumpkins are vegetables, and as such they're not actually acidic enough to safely can merely in boiling water, unless they're preserved in a very heavy syrup and are cooked in the syrup until translucent and completely saturated with sugar—that is, unless they're essentially candied. Don't rush the long simmer in the syrup.

4 pounds pie pumpkins (about 4 small)

5 cups sugar

2 cinnamon sticks

1 piece star anise

6 lemons

Cut the pumpkins in half and scrape out the seeds and stringy mess. Use a vegetable peeler to peel them, then cut each half into 4 pieces and cut them crosswise into 1/16-inch-thick slices. Layer in a wide, 6- to 8-quart preserving pan with the sugar, cinnamon, and star anise.

Cut the lemons in half and squeeze the juice through a sieve over the pumpkin mixture; reserve the lemon hulls. Toss to combine, then cover and refrigerate for 8 hours, or overnight.

Use a sharp knife or a spoon to scrape the membranes and flesh out of the lemon hulls, then cut the rinds into thin slices. Put in a small saucepan and cover with cold water. Bring to a boil, cook for 5 minutes, then drain. Repeat the boiling and draining 2 more times, then stir the lemon rinds into the pumpkin mixture.

Bring to a boil over high heat, then lower the heat and simmer briskly until the pumpkin slices are evenly translucent, about 1 hour and 15 minutes.

Prepare for water-bath canning: Wash the jars and keep them hot in the canning pot, and put the flat lids in a heatproof bowl. (See page 21 for details.)

Ladle boiling water from the canning pot into the bowl with the lids. Using a jar lifter, remove the hot jars from the canning pot, carefully pouring the water from each one back into the pot, and place them upright on a folded towel. Drain the water off the jar lids.

Ladle the hot pumpkin and syrup into the jars, leaving ¼ inch headspace at the top. Use a damp paper towel to wipe the rims of the jars, then put a flat lid and ring on each jar, adjusting the ring so that it's just finger-tight. Return the jars to the water in the canning pot, making sure the water covers the jars by at least 1 inch. Bring to a boil, and boil for 10 minutes to process. Remove the jars to a folded towel and do not disturb for 12 hours. After 1 hour, check that the lids have sealed by pressing down on the center of each; if it can be pushed down, it hasn't sealed, and the jar should be refrigerated immediately. Label the sealed jars and store.

FREEZING WINTER SQUASH

In late fall and through the winter, hard squashes are a staple on our table, and they tend to become a bit boring to me. But in late spring, and again toward the end of summer, when the temperature at night is just right (if only in my mind) and the days aren't quite as god-awfully muggy or as bitter as they could be in high summer or winter, I start to actually crave winter squash (and by winter squash I mean fall squash). Butternut squash soups, acorn squash risotto, pumpkin cupcakes with ginger-cinnamon cream cheese frosting, quick wonton-wrapper ravioli stuffed with winter squash and sautéed in brown butter and sage sauce with toasted bread crumbs, whipped potatoes lightened with pureed roasted squash—these seem like transitional foods to me, perfect for late-spring and late-summer dinner parties. Unfortunately, out-of-season hard squash is unbelievably expensive (for the price of an acorn squash I could be buying *meat*—or donuts!), and your choices are generally limited to the usual suspects, plus maybe a sad, shriveled Hubbard. So in the fall, when the prices plummet and the selection is interesting and colorful, I try to stock up on, roast, and freeze as much as I can for the off months.

Frozen roasted squash puree: Preheat the oven to 350°F. Cut the squashes in half lengthwise, scrape out the seeds, and put them, cut side up, on baking sheets or pans. If the squashes are very large, cut them into smaller pieces. There's no need to season them at this point, but you can rub the flesh with a bit of olive oil if you'd like. Roast for 35 minutes (for acorn or butternut squash) to 1½ hours (for firmer varieties like Hubbard), until tender. Scoop the flesh out of the skins into a food processor and process until very smooth. Transfer to small sealable plastic containers or freezer bags and freeze for up to a year. You can get a good 3 cups puree from 2 large acorn squashes.

Whole-Wheat Crespelle with Winter Squash

SERVES 4

A LOVELY MEATLESS SUPPER FOR A THROWN-TOGETHER END-OF-SUMMER DINNER WITH FRIENDS. *Crespelle* can be made a day in advance, wrapped in plastic, and stored in the refrigerator. They can be filled and laid out in the baking dish first thing in the morning, then covered and kept in the refrigerator until evening, when you're ready to bake them. Bring to room temperature, then pour the sauce over them just before baking.

The *crespelle* filling is very subtle and mild, and it works best with a very flavorful squash like Delicata or pie pumpkin.

For the *crespelle*:

3 large eggs

¾ cup whole-wheat flour (see Note)

½ teaspoon pure kosher salt

1 tablespoon minced fresh parsley

3 tablespoons unsalted butter, melted

For the filling:

1½ cups frozen roasted squash puree (page 229), thawed

½ cup Fresh Cheese (page 284) or ricotta

½ cup grated Parmigiano-Reggiano or other hard cheese

Generous grating of nutmeg

Pure kosher salt and freshly ground black pepper to taste

To bake:

Olive oil

1 pint All-Purpose Tomato Sauce (page 165), or other tomato sauce

1 tablespoon chopped fresh basil, plus more for garnish

¼ cup grated Parmigiano-Reggiano or other hard cheese

Make the crespelle: In a blender or food processor, combine the eggs, 1 cup water, the flour, salt, and parsley and blend until smooth. Let stand for 30 minutes; this will allow the gluten in the flour to relax and will result in a more tender *crespelle*. The batter should be thin and pourable, like heavy cream; add a bit more water if necessary.

Brush a small sauté pan with some of the butter and place over medium-high heat. Pour in a scant ¼ cup of the batter and tilt the pan so that the batter coats the bottom. Cook just until the top is dry, about 1 minute, then flip and cook the other side for about 20 seconds. Remove to a plate and cover with a clean kitchen towel or plastic wrap. Repeat with the remaining butter and batter to make at least 8 *crespelle*.

Make the filling: In a medium bowl, beat together all the ingredients.

Fill and bake the crespelle: Preheat the oven to 375°F. Lightly oil a 9-by-13-inch baking dish. Scoop about ⅓ cup of the filling onto each of 8 *crespelle*, roll them up, leaving the ends open, and arrange them, seam side down, in the prepared baking dish, fitting them snugly in one layer. Stir ¼ cup water and the 1 tablespoon basil into the tomato sauce, then pour the sauce over the filled *crespelle*. Sprinkle with the cheese and bake until the sauce is bubbly, about 30 minutes. Serve hot, garnished with more basil.

Note: If using coarse or stone-ground whole-wheat flour, you might have to add about ¼ cup all-purpose flour to thicken the batter a bit.

Pickled Greens with Fresh Chiles

MAKES ABOUT 7 PINT JARS

SERVE THESE ON SANDWICHES, OR FOLDED INTO A JAMAICAN-STYLE RICE-AND-PEAS COOKED WITH COCONUT MILK, OR JUST AS A SOUR SIDE DISH.

About 4 pounds kale or collard greens
3 tablespoons yellow mustard seeds
1½ tablespoons whole allspice
1 tablespoon green cardamom pods, lightly crushed
7 cups cider vinegar (5% acidity)
1 cup balsamic vinegar (6% acidity)
2 tablespoons pure kosher salt
2 tablespoons sugar
7 fresh chiles such as habanero
7 cloves garlic
1 small onion, cut into ½-inch-thick wedges

Wash the greens well, then pull off and discard the stems and thick rib in the center of each leaf. Roughly chop kale, or stack collard leaves and slice them crosswise into ¾-inch-wide strips. Put the greens in a clean pillowcase, go outside (or into the bathtub with the shower curtain closed), and swing it around to shake out excess water. In a small bowl, combine the mustard seeds, allspice, and cardamom. Set aside.

Prepare for water-bath canning: Wash the jars and keep them hot in the canning pot, and put the flat lids in a heatproof bowl. (See page 21 for details.)

In a nonreactive pot, combine the vinegars, 1 cup water, the salt, and sugar and bring just to a boil.

Ladle boiling water from the canning pot into the bowl with the lids. Using a jar lifter, remove the hot jars from the canning pot, carefully pouring the water from each one back into the pot, and place them upright on a folded towel. Drain the water off the jar lids.

Pack the greens, chiles, garlic, and onion wedges into the jars (tightly, as the greens will wilt when heated) and divide the spices among them. Ladle the hot vinegar mixture into the jars, leaving ½ inch headspace at the top. Use a chopstick to remove air bubbles around the inside of each jar. Use a damp paper towel to wipe the rims of the jars, then drain the water off the jar lids and put a flat lid and ring on each jar, adjusting the ring so that it's just finger-tight. Return the jars to the water in the canning pot, making sure the water covers the jars by at least 1 inch. Bring to a boil, and boil for 15 minutes to process. Remove the jars to a folded towel and do not disturb for 12 hours. After 1 hour, check that the lids have sealed by pressing down on the center of each; if it can be pushed down, it hasn't sealed, and the jar should be refrigerated immediately. Label the sealed jars and store.

Pickled Greens and Sweet Potato Tempura

SERVES 4

DESPITE MY (TENUOUS) SOUTHERN ROOTS, I'M NOT A HUGE FAN OF THE FRIED DILL PICKLE, WITH ALL ITS CRAZY WET DILL-PICKLE-NESS SQUIRTING OUT OF A HOT LITTLE PACKAGE OF BATTER-FRIED-NESS. But I wanted to at least point in its direction in this book, and here is where the fried pickled collards come in. In my opinion, Japanese tempura sits at the zenith of the fried-foods arc, so it was only natural that the greens should be fried tempura-style. Of course, sweet-potato tempura (a traditional part of *tendon*, or tempura *donburi*) fits the Southern theme just fine. And it turns out that the pickling liquid needs only the addition of some mirin to become a great approximation of the sauce drizzled over *tendon*. This may sound like a weird dish. It is. It also might be one of the best and most intuitive in this book.

One of the keys to good tempura is not to overmix the batter, so that the gluten in the flour doesn't have a chance to develop (stirring it with chopsticks will help keep you from overmixing). Another is to keep it cold in the refrigerator until just before you use it (the contrast between the cold batter and the hot oil will result in a puffier coating).

1 large egg
1 cup all-purpose flour
3 tablespoons cornstarch
1 teaspoon baking powder
1½ cups raw brown rice
1 pint Pickled Greens with Fresh Chiles (page 231)
½ cup mirin
Vegetable oil for frying
1 sweet potato, peeled, cut into ½-inch rounds

In a 2-cup or larger measure, beat the egg lightly with two chopsticks. Stir in ice water to make 1 cup liquid. Sift the flour, cornstarch, and baking powder together into a bowl, add the egg mixture, and stir until just moistened; there should be lumps—do not overmix. Set aside in the refrigerator.

Rinse the rice under cold running water, drain well, and put in a medium saucepan with 3½ cups water. Bring to a boil over high heat, then reduce the heat to low, cover, and cook for 25 to 30 minutes, until tender. Drain in a sieve, set the sieve over the hot saucepan, and cover to keep warm.

Drain the greens in a sieve set over a bowl. Put ½ cup of the pickling liquid and the mirin in a small saucepan, bring to a boil, then cover and remove from the heat. (Discard the whole spices.)

Preheat the oven to 200°F. In a heavy pot, heat 2 inches of oil to 350°F on a deep-frying thermometer. Working in batches, dip the sweet potato slices in the batter and carefully lower them into the oil. Cook, turning, for 4 to 6 minutes, until nicely browned and cooked through. Remove to a wire rack set over a baking sheet and keep warm in the oven.

Bring the oil to 375°F. Using your fingers, pick up a small tangle of pickled greens and dip the bunch in the batter. Carefully put the batter-coated greens in the oil and repeat until there are four or five clusters in the pot; cook until golden brown, 1 to 2 minutes. Transfer them to the baking sheet in the oven. Repeat with the remaining greens.

Scoop the rice into serving bowls, top with the sweet-potato tempura and greens, and sprinkle with sauce. Serve immediately.

Quick Lift (Middle Eastern Pickled Turnips)

MAKES 1 QUART JAR

◇◇◇

BEAUTIFULLY PINK, TART, AND SALTY *LIFT* ("LIF-IT") IS UBIQUITOUS AT THE MIDDLE EASTERN TABLE. It is wonderful served alongside falafel (chickpea fritters) or *mujaddara* (a Lebanese lentil-and-rice dish). My understanding is that traditional versions are fermented rather than pickled in vinegar—that is, the turnips are tossed with salt or submerged in a salt brine until bacteria have converted enough of the natural sugars in the turnips to lactic acid to make them sour and preservable. An excellent recipe for this slower process can be found in *Pickled*, a book of heritage recipes by Lucy Norris (see Further Reading, page 292). The method below, using vinegar, is more common now, as it comes together quickly and is usable within just a few days. The beet is added almost exclusively for its color; I use a few slices of pickled beets, since I always have them on hand, but cooked plain beets work fine too. You could even just drip some of the beet pickling liquid into the jar.

This pickle will last a month or more, but it must be stored in the refrigerator.

1 pound small turnips, peeled and cut into eighths

1 cup distilled white vinegar (5% acidity)

1 tablespoon pure kosher salt

½ small cooked peeled beet, sliced (or 3 slices Pickled Beets; page 55)

¼ cup chopped celery leaves

1 clove garlic, sliced

Heat the jar in a large pot of boiling water, then remove the jar to a folded towel on the counter. Return the water to a boil and drop in the turnips; after 1 minute, drain them in a colander and set aside.

In a nonreactive pot, combine the vinegar, 1 cup water, and the salt. Bring just to a boil.

Meanwhile, layer the hot drained turnips, beet slices, celery leaves, and garlic in the hot jar. Pour the hot vinegar mixture over the vegetables. Use a chopstick to remove air bubbles around the inside of the jar. Let cool to room temperature, then put the lid on the jar and store in the refrigerator for several days before using. The pickle will keep, refrigerated, for at least 1 month.

Cumin and Paprika Pickled Turnips

MAKES ABOUT 4 PINT JARS

ONE LATE AFTERNOON LAST FALL, MY FRIEND REGAN HUFF BROUGHT A BUNCH OF TURNIPS OUT TO THE HOUSE (SHE OFTEN BRINGS STUFF LIKE THIS OVER, AND WE THEN SPEND THE DAY COOKING IT IN VARIOUS WAYS). While my husband, Derek, and I chopped up some long-smoked barbecue pork shoulder we'd been tending since the early-morning hours, she whipped up a bowlful of cold diced turnips marinated in ground cumin, paprika, salt, fresh lemon juice, parsley, and cayenne. It was the best turnip dish I've ever had.

Smoky and a little spicy, tart, and pleasantly bitter, the following pickle is my attempt to bottle that wonderful day. Serve these turnips sprinkled with chopped fresh flat-leaf parsley. They make a good accompaniment not only to hickory-smoked pork but indeed to any slow-roasted or grilled meat. Or put them in a pita with some greens and a drizzle of tahini.

3 pounds turnips, peeled, quartered, and cut into
   ½-inch slices
¼ cup plus 1 teaspoon pure kosher salt
¼ cup strained fresh lemon juice
4 teaspoons cumin seeds, toasted
2 teaspoons paprika
¼ teaspoon ground cayenne
3 cups cider vinegar (5% acidity)

Put the turnips in a large bowl. Dissolve the ¼ cup salt in 1 quart water, then pour the brine over the turnips to just cover them. Set aside for 8 to 10 hours, or overnight. Drain and rinse the turnips, then toss them with the lemon juice, cumin seeds, paprika, and cayenne. Set aside.

Prepare for water-bath canning: Wash the jars and keep them hot in the canning pot, and put the flat lids in a heatproof bowl. (See page 21 for details.)

In a nonreactive pot, combine the vinegar, 1 cup water, and the remaining 1 teaspoon salt. Bring just to a boil.

Ladle boiling water from the canning pot into the bowl with the lids. Using a jar lifter, remove the hot jars from the canning pot, carefully pouring the water from each one back into the pot, and place them upright on a folded towel. Drain the water off the jar lids.

Working quickly, pack the turnips into the jars, along with any juice in the bottom of the bowl. Ladle the hot vinegar mixture into the jars, leaving ½ inch headspace at the top. Use a chopstick to remove air bubbles around the inside of each jar. Use a damp paper towel to wipe the rims of the jars, then put a flat lid and ring on each jar, adjusting the ring so that it's just finger-tight. Return the jars to the water in the canning pot, making sure the water covers the jars by at least 1 inch. Bring to a boil, and boil for 15 minutes to process. Remove the jars to a folded towel and do not disturb for 12 hours. After 1 hour, check that the lids have sealed by pressing down on the center of each; if it can be pushed down, it hasn't sealed, and the jar should be refrigerated immediately. Label the sealed jars and store.

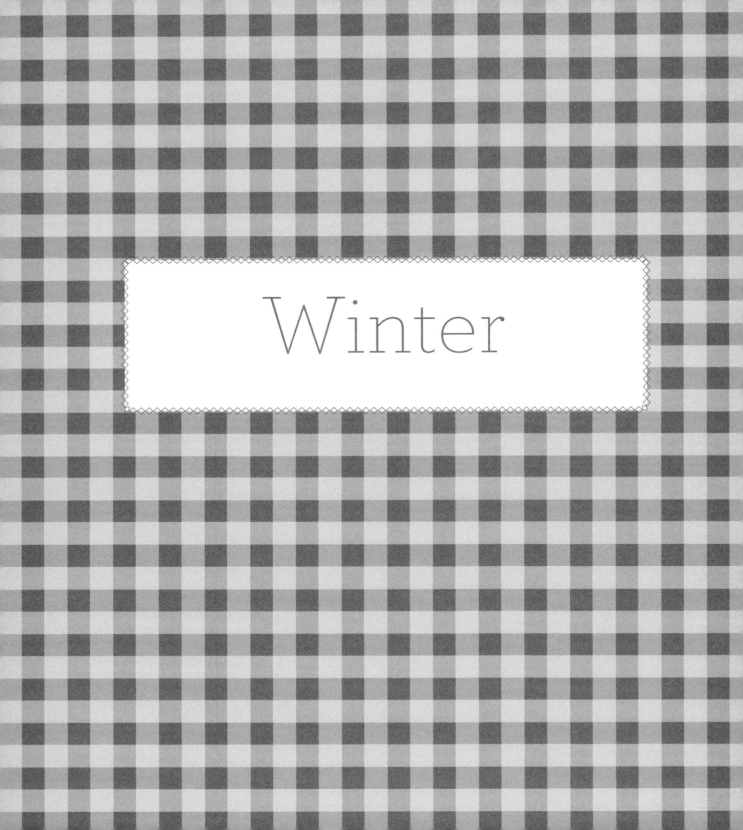

Winter

It's a lazy time, isn't it, winter—especially after the holidays. You toss something in a slow cooker, or roast a hunk of meat all afternoon, maybe adding some root vegetables in with it an hour before suppertime. Some evenings, you pull a jar of salsa verde out of the pantry and bake it into a bubbly dish of chicken enchiladas; or you stir-fry diced fermented long beans and some ground pork you found in a corner of the freezer with a bunch of scallions, drizzles of soy sauce and black vinegar, and a slick of orange-red chile oil. You might simmer hastily formed but still tasty meatballs in a bright, simple tomato sauce you put in jars or in the freezer over the summer; or you'll throw a handful of shrimp in a hot pan with a sweet-tart tamarind sauce. Perhaps, instead of anything fancy, for a weekend breakfast you toast sandwiches oozing fontina cheese in a cast-iron skillet and have them with spicy pickles and the Sunday paper, and maybe on busier weekdays you put a pot of oatmeal on in the morning when it's still dark out and open a jar of apple butter to stir into it. You might brighten everyone's gray afternoon with a summery cherry clafouti you threw together in a few minutes with a bag of frozen Bings; or, some days, you don't bother cooking anything at all and just slice a loaf of bread and an aged cheese (do you have a hard salami somewhere in the fridge too?) and set out little plates of homemade pickles and spoon sweets to go with them.

Or you make marmalade with winter's sunny gift of citrus. Jars and jars of it, in every variety, because you cannot get enough of the stuff and because the mere thought of it—bittersweet indeed—makes you swoon.

Or you do brilliant things with cabbage, stocking the fridge with fiery, bright-orange kimchi and starting a small crock of your own sauerkraut—this time maybe you'll add some grated turnips to the mix, next time apples.

And then there's all that green apple pectin stock you saved for downtimes like these. So you pick up a bottle of decent-but-not-too-decent wine, simmer it down, and make a jelly to tide you and yours over till the summer fruits come in.

WINTER FRUITS

Kumquat Preserves

MAKES ABOUT 4 HALF-PINT JARS

◇◇

KUMQUATS—TART AND OFTEN BITTER CITRUS FRUITS ABOUT THE SIZE OF PECANS—HAVE BEEN MUCH APPRECIATED BY THE MORE ADVENTUROUS CHEFS AMONG US FOR A DECADE OR SO. Unfortunately they're still none too popular outside Florida, where many folks have backyard (or patio) trees loaded with them in wintertime. Here, plump, shiny orbs, their bitterness tamed by blanching a few times in boiling water and a short soak in cold water, are nestled together in a thick syrup. Pitting the little suckers requires no small amount of patience, but it yields a very special preserve—this might be a good time to pull out the fancy Weck jars (you can get more quarter-liter jars' worth than half-pint jars' worth—all the better for doling out as gifts).

1½ pounds kumquats, scrubbed and patted dry
2¼ cups sugar

With a paring knife, cut 2 small slits in each kumquat. Put them in a saucepan and cover with cold water. Bring to a boil over high heat, boil for 5 minutes, then drain. Repeat boiling and draining 2 more times. Put the kumquats in a large bowl of cold water. Use a skewer or sharp chopstick to poke into each kumquat and lever out the seeds, working them out with your fingers as necessary; this is tedious, it's true, but entirely optional. Set aside.

Prepare for water-bath canning: Wash the jars and keep them hot in the canning pot, and put the flat lids in a heatproof bowl. (See page 21 for details.)

In a wide, 6- to 8-quart preserving pan, combine the sugar and 3 cups water and bring to a boil, stirring to dissolve the sugar. Add the kumquats and return to a boil. Skim off any foam, then lower the heat and simmer until the kumquats are translucent and glossy and the syrup is thick and reduced until it just covers the kumquats, about 30 minutes. Remove from the heat and stir gently for a few seconds to distribute the fruit in the syrup.

Ladle boiling water from the canning pot into the bowl with the lids. Using a jar lifter, remove the hot jars from the canning pot, carefully pouring the water from each one back into the pot, and place them upright on a folded towel. Drain the water off the jar lids.

Ladle the hot kumquats and syrup into the hot jars, leaving ¼ inch headspace at the top. Use a damp paper towel to wipe the rims of the jars, then put a flat lid and ring on each jar, adjusting the ring so that it's just finger-tight. Return the jars to the water in the canning pot, making sure the water covers the jars by at least 1 inch. Bring to a boil, and boil for 10 minutes to process. Remove the jars to a folded towel and do not disturb for 12 hours. After 1 hour, check that the lids have sealed by pressing down on the center of each; if it can be pushed down, it hasn't sealed, and the jar should be refrigerated immediately. Label the sealed jars and store.

Kumquat Knickerbocker

MAKES 1 GENEROUS COCKTAIL

ACCORDING TO DAVID WONDRICH, IN THE VERY WORTHWHILE *IMBIBE!*, THE KNICKERBOCKER, A COCKTAIL THAT WAS POPULAR IN THE 1850S AND '60S BUT NOT SO MUCH THEREAFTER, PROBABLY FIRST SHOWED UP IN NEW YORK (NO SURPRISE). Wondrich also throws out the possibility that the name might have come from the fact that, like knickerbockers the pants (which you'll remember, if you've ever been part of a theater troupe, are *short*), the drink itself is somewhat of an "abbreviated punch." With lime juice (as well as the squeezed-out lime hull, making it a drink after my own heart), rum, raspberry syrup, and curaçao, the original version could pass for, as Wondrich describes it, "the spiritual progenitor of the Tiki drink." More recent drinks bearing the Knickerbocker name are completely different, and are more like perfect Martinis garnished with strips of lemon peel.

This particular bastardization (admittedly originally concocted only because the name sounded cool) owes more to the earlier drink than the later.

¼ cup rum
Juice of 1 small lime
1½ tablespoons syrup from Kumquat Preserves
   (page 239), or to taste
1 preserved kumquat

Chill a stemmed cocktail glass in the freezer.

Fill a shaker with ice and add the rum, lime juice, and syrup. Shake well, then strain the drink into the chilled glass. Drop in the kumquat and serve immediately.

Cabernet Sauvignon Jelly

MAKES ABOUT 5 HALF-PINT JARS

◇◇◇

NOW, THIS IS MY KIND OF GRAPE JELLY: deep burgundy in color, sweet, tart, and winy. And, if you have the pectin stock on hand, no fuss; it's just a matter of reducing a bottle of wine to a concentrated base and then cooking it to a gelable syrup.

1 (750 ml) bottle Cabernet Sauvignon
3 cups Green Apple Pectin Stock (page 181)
¼ cup strained fresh lemon juice
3¼ cups sugar

Prepare for water-bath canning: Sterilize the jars and keep them hot in the canning pot, put a small plate in the freezer, and put the flat lids in a heat-proof bowl. (See page 21 for details.)

Pour the wine into a wide, 6- to 8-quart preserving pan. Boil over high heat until it has reduced to about 2 cups, about 20 minutes.

Stir the pectin stock, lemon juice, and sugar into the reduced wine. Bring to a boil over high heat and cook, stirring occasionally, until the mixture registers about 220°F on a candy thermometer or a small dab of it spooned onto the chilled plate and returned to the freezer for a minute wrinkles when you nudge it, 25 to 30 minutes.

Ladle boiling water from the canning pot into the bowl with the lids. Using a jar lifter, remove the sterilized jars from the canning pot, carefully pouring the water from each one back into the pot, and place them upright on a folded towel. Drain the water off the jar lids.

Ladle the hot jelly into the jars, leaving ¼ inch headspace at the top. Use a damp paper towel to wipe the rims of the jars, then put a flat lid and ring on each jar, adjusting the ring so that it's just finger-tight. Return the jars to the water in the canning pot, making sure the water covers the jars by at least 1 inch. Bring to a boil, and boil for 5 minutes to process. Remove the jars to a folded towel and do not disturb for 12 hours. After 1 hour, check that the lids have sealed by pressing down on the center of each; if it can be pushed down, it hasn't sealed, and the jar should be refrigerated immediately. Label the sealed jars and store.

Champagne Jelly

MAKES ABOUT 5 HALF-PINT JARS

◇◇

THE PARTICULAR DRYNESS OF CHAMPAGNE IS WHAT MAKES THIS GOLDEN JELLY SO APPEAL-ING. You don't have to use Champagne that's *too* special here, and you can even use any very dry white wine for a similar effect. The jelly is great on toast or biscuits, or, melted, as a glaze for roasted or grilled meats.

1 (750 ml) bottle Champagne or sparkling white or rosé wine
3 cups Green Apple Pectin Stock (page 181)
¼ cup strained fresh lemon juice
3¼ cups sugar

Prepare for water-bath canning: Sterilize the jars and keep them hot in the canning pot, put a small plate in the freezer, and put the flat lids in a heat-proof bowl. (See page 21 for details.)

Pour the wine into a wide, 6- to 8-quart preserving pan. Boil over high heat until it has reduced to about 2 cups, about 20 minutes.

Stir the pectin stock, lemon juice, and sugar into the reduced wine. Bring to a boil over high heat and cook, stirring occasionally, until the mixture registers about 220°F on a candy thermometer or a small dab of it spooned onto the chilled plate and returned to the freezer for a minute wrinkles when you nudge it, 25 to 30 minutes.

Ladle boiling water from the canning pot into the bowl with the lids. Using a jar lifter, remove the sterilized jars from the canning pot, carefully pouring the water from each one back into the pot, and place them upright on a folded towel. Drain the water off the jar lids.

Ladle the hot jelly into the jars, leaving ¼ inch headspace at the top. Use a damp paper towel to wipe the rims of the jars, then put a flat lid and ring on each jar, adjusting the ring so that it's just finger-tight. Return the jars to the water in the canning pot, making sure the water covers the jars by at least 1 inch. Bring to a boil, and boil for 5 minutes to process. Remove the jars to a folded towel and do not disturb for 12 hours. After 1 hour, check that the lids have sealed by pressing down on the center of each; if it can be pushed down, it hasn't sealed, and the jar should be refrigerated immediately. Label the sealed jars and store.

Hibiscus Jelly

MAKES ABOUT 4 HALF-PINT JARS

HIBISCUS, ALSO KNOWN AS JAMAICA OR SORREL (NOT THE SORREL GREENS USED IN SALADS AND SOUPS), IS WILDLY POPULAR THROUGHOUT LATIN AMERICA. There the fleshy, almost fruitlike calyces (the sepals below the blossoms) of the roselle variety of hibiscus are steeped to make cold, sweet-tart aguas frescas. Jelly made from it is luminescent red and pleasantly tart—it might almost (almost!) stand in for red currant jelly. Try brushing a bit of warmed hibiscus jelly on a turkey burger as it's grilling.

1 cup (2 ounces) dried hibiscus, or 6 ounces chopped
    fresh hibiscus
1 cinnamon stick
1 tablespoon whole allspice berries
2¼ cups boiling water
3 cups Green Apple Pectin Stock (page 181)
¼ cup strained fresh lemon juice
3¼ cups sugar

Prepare for water-bath canning: Sterilize the jars and keep them hot in the canning pot, put a small plate in the freezer, and put the flat lids in a heat-proof bowl. (See page 21 for details.)

Put the hibiscus, cinnamon stick, and allspice in a heatproof bowl and pour in the boiling water. Cover and let steep for 30 minutes.

Pour the hibiscus liquid through a very-fine-mesh sieve into a wide, 6- to 8-quart preserving pan, then add the pectin stock, lemon juice, and sugar. Bring to a boil over high heat and cook, stirring occasionally, until the mixture registers about 220°F on a candy thermometer or a small dab of it spooned onto the chilled plate and returned to the freezer for a minute wrinkles when you nudge it, 30 to 35 minutes.

Ladle boiling water from the canning pot into the bowl with the lids. Using a jar lifter, remove the sterilized jars from the canning pot, carefully pouring the water from each one back into the pot, and place them upright on a folded towel. Drain the water off the jar lids.

Ladle the hot jelly into the jars, leaving ¼ inch headspace at the top. Use a damp paper towel to wipe the rims of the jars, then put a flat lid and ring on each jar, adjusting the ring so that it's just finger-tight. Return the jars to the water in the canning pot, making sure the water covers the jars by at least 1 inch. Bring to a boil, and boil for 5 minutes to process. Remove the jars to a folded towel and do not disturb for 12 hours. After 1 hour, check that the lids have sealed by pressing down on the center of each; if it can be pushed down, it hasn't sealed, and the jar should be refrigerated immediately. Label the sealed jars and store.

Tea Jelly

MAKES ABOUT 3 HALF-PINT JARS

◇◇

USE ANY KIND OF TEA YOU'D LIKE! I've especially enjoyed jellies made with oolong and Earl Grey, but the possibilities are endless. Serve this jelly with toast or English muffins for breakfast or with your afternoon tea (preferably the same kind as the jelly).

6 tablespoons loose tea leaves
2¼ cups boiling water
3 cups Green Apple Pectin Stock (page 181)
¼ cup strained fresh lemon juice
3¼ cups sugar

Prepare for water-bath canning: Sterilize the jars and keep them hot in the canning pot, put a small plate in the freezer, and put the flat lids in a heatproof bowl. (See page 21 for details.)

Put the tea leaves in a heatproof bowl and pour in the boiling water. Let steep for 5 minutes, then pour through a fine-mesh sieve into a 6- to 8-quart preserving pan.

Stir the pectin stock, lemon juice, and sugar into the tea. Bring to a boil over high heat and cook, stirring occasionally, until the mixture registers about 220°F on a candy thermometer or a small dab of it spooned onto the chilled plate and returned to the freezer for a minute wrinkles when you nudge it, 25 to 30 minutes.

Ladle boiling water from the canning pot into the bowl with the lids. Using a jar lifter, remove the sterilized jars from the canning pot, carefully pouring the water from each one back into the pot, and place them upright on a folded towel. Drain the water off the jar lids.

Ladle the hot jelly into the jars, leaving ¼ inch headspace at the top. Use a damp paper towel to wipe the rims of the jars, then put a flat lid and ring on each jar, adjusting the ring so that it's just finger-tight. Return the jars to the water in the canning pot, making sure the water covers the jars by at least 1 inch. Bring to a boil, and boil for 5 minutes to process. Remove the jars to a folded towel and do not disturb for 12 hours. After 1 hour, check that the lids have sealed by pressing down on the center of each; if it can be pushed down, it hasn't sealed, and the jar should be refrigerated immediately. Label the sealed jars and store.

Lemon Curd

MAKES 3 SMALL (ABOUT-HALF-PINT) JARS

◇◇◇

CURD NEEDS TO BE REFRIGERATED, BUT IT WILL KEEP FOR WEEKS IF YOU TAKE CARE TO USE A CLEAN SPOON WHEN YOU SCOOP PORTIONS OUT. If you have sturdy glass jars you've saved from store-bought jams, salsas, Major Grey's chutney, or what have you, you can use them here; they don't have to be actual canning jars because they aren't processed.

Try this with The Best Gingerbread on page 68, or with the Rustic Almond Cake on page 277.

3 lemons
1 cup sugar
½ cup (1 stick) unsalted butter, cut into pieces
2 large eggs
1 large egg yolk

Put the jars in a large pot and cover with water. Bring the water to a boil over high heat and boil for 10 minutes to sterilize the jars. Keep the jars in the hot water while you prepare the curd.

Grate the zest of 2 of the lemons into a large heat-proof bowl. Juice all of the lemons into the bowl. Add the sugar and butter and set the bowl over a saucepan of simmering water; cook, stirring occasionally, until the butter is melted.

Meanwhile, in a small bowl, whisk the eggs and yolk until smooth. Pour the eggs through a fine-mesh sieve into the bowl with the lemon mixture, then cook, whisking constantly, until thickened to the consistency of melted ice cream, 6 to 8 minutes.

Using a jar lifter, remove the sterilized jars from the canning pot, carefully pouring the water from each one back into the pot, and place them upright on a folded towel. Pour in the hot curd. Let cool to room temperature, then put the lids on and store in the refrigerator for up to 3 weeks. Use a clean, dry spoon to scoop out the curd as you use it.

Preserved Lemons

MAKES 1 QUART

◇◇

THIS IS A CLASSIC NORTH AFRICAN STAPLE; THE FUNKY SALTED LEMONS ARE FEATURED IN TAGINES, SALADS, RICE DISHES, AND SO ON. To use the lemons, scrape off and discard the lemon flesh, leaving just the preserved peel.

5 lemons (about 1¼ pounds), washed
⅓ cup pure kosher salt
⅓ to ½ cup fresh lemon juice, as necessary

Pat the lemons dry and cut them lengthwise into eighths. Layer the wedges with the salt in a clean 1-quart jar, pressing them down with a wooden spoon handle to fit in the jar. Cover and set aside in a cool spot for 3 to 4 days. The juice will be drawn out and should cover or almost cover the lemons. Push the lemon wedges down so they are all submerged in the brine; if necessary, add more lemon juice to cover. Put the lid back on the jar and set in a cool spot for about 3 weeks, until the peel is soft.

The preserved lemons will keep, covered, in a cool spot, for at least 6 months; use a clean, dry utensil to remove the wedges, and make sure all the peel remains covered in brine. Discard any parts that exhibit mold.

• •

Fennel Salad with Preserved Lemon

SERVES 4 TO 6

◇◇

ANOTHER RECIPE FROM MY FRIEND REGAN HUFF, WHOSE MOM MAKES THIS SALAD OF MILDLY ANISE-FLAVORED FENNEL TOSSED IN A TANGY FRESH-LEMON VINAIGRETTE WITH A HINT OF SALTY-TART PRESERVED LEMON RIND. Bright, metallic cilantro brings everything together, but I also like it with mint or parsley.

Juice of 2 lemons
2 cloves garlic, minced
3 tablespoons olive oil
Pure kosher salt and freshly ground black pepper
2 medium bulbs fennel, trimmed, halved, and cored
1 wedge Preserved Lemon (above), flesh and pith cut off, rind minced
¼ cup chopped fresh cilantro

In a large bowl, whisk together the lemon juice and garlic, then whisk as you slowly drizzle in the oil. Season with salt and pepper to taste.

Using a sharp knife or a mandoline, cut the fennel into paper-thin slices. Add them, along with the Preserved Lemon, to the bowl with the dressing and toss to coat. Divide among 4 to 6 serving plates, sprinkle with the cilantro, and serve.

Indian Hot "Lime" Pickle

MAKES ABOUT 1 PINT

◇◇

THE LIME-LEMON CONUNDRUM THAT'S A BIG PART OF INTERPRETING INDIAN PICKLE RECIPES CAN GIVE ONE FITS. As far as I can gather, in India limes are smaller and perhaps juicier than the standard Persian limes sold here in the United States. I've tried to make lime pickle with U.S. limes, but they've been about as delicious as that edible-only-by-me "Shaker lime pie" Derek has never let me live down. Use lemons.

My friend Leda Scheintaub's mother-in-law, Marian Patel, was kind enough to share her lime pickle recipe with me. I've tried several other versions—it seems that every family in India has its own special way of making lime pickle—but this is the best I've made (or even eaten: It's fantastic!). The sugar tempers the heat of the cayenne a touch, and I find the balance of sweetish fenugreek and spicy mustard seeds to be most pleasant. Lime pickles are served with all manner of rice dishes, lentils, and dals, and as an all-purpose condiment much like a very potent chutney.

Be sure to dry the lemons, cutting board, knives, and all other utensils very well—no water can get into the pickle mixture, or it may spoil, as bacteria can thrive in the water.

7 lemons
½ cup pure kosher salt
2 teaspoons ground turmeric
½ cup sugar
2 to 3 tablespoons ground cayenne or other hot chile
1 teaspoon crushed fenugreek
1 teaspoon black mustard seeds
¼ teaspoon asafetida (optional; see Note)

Scrub the lemons and dry them thoroughly. Reserve 1 lemon and cut the rest in half on a dry cutting board with a dry knife. Cut each half into 6 wedges, then cut them crosswise into ¼-inch pieces. Put them in a clean, dry quart jar.

Add the salt and turmeric, put the lid on the jar, and shake well. Uncover and add the sugar and cayenne, then cover and shake again.

In a small skillet over medium heat, toast the fenugreek, mustard seeds, and asafetida, if using, until fragrant and a shade darker, about 2 minutes. Transfer to a spice mill and grind to a powder. Add the mixture to the lemons in the jar. Use a clean, dry chopstick or plastic or wood utensil to stir well. Put the lid on the jar and set it in a sunny spot for 3 to 4 weeks, shaking it occasionally to redistribute the lemons and juice, until the lemons are tender.

Using a clean, dry spoon, transfer the pickle to smaller clean, dry jars and store in a cool, dark spot. The pickle will keep for several months; be sure to use only dry utensils to scoop out the pickle as you use it, as it will spoil if any water comes in contact with it.

Note: Asafetida (pronounced "ass-uh-FEH-tih-duh," I think, though even among those in the know this is a subject for debate) is the dried and powdered gum resin of certain varieties of plants in the carrot family. True to its name, it smells positively repulsive (in my opinion), and I have to put the little jar of it in two sealed plastic bags to keep it from contaminating my otherwise sweet-smelling pantry, but used in very small amounts it adds something interesting to lime pickle, and to just about any dal, like the one opposite—an earthiness, perhaps, like garlicky mushrooms.

Lentils with Date and Lime Pickle Chutney

SERVES 4 TO 6

THIS SIMPLE STEW FEATURING THE LIVELY, SUMMERY COMBINATION OF FENNEL SEEDS, FRESH MINT, AND TOMATOES IS INSPIRED BY AN *URAD DAL* DISH IN YAMUNA DEVI'S *THE ART OF INDIAN VEGETARIAN COOKING.* I also like it with *chana dal*, but feel free to substitute yellow split peas or any other dal or lentil and adjust the cooking time as necessary. Add some chopped fresh greens with the mint, if you'd like, or add chunks of other seasonal vegetables.

For the chutney:
2 tablespoons Indian Hot "Lime" Pickle (opposite)
½ cup pitted dates
Grated jaggery or piloncillo, or brown sugar to taste
Ground cayenne to taste

For the lentils:
1 pound brown lentils, picked over and rinsed
1 cube frozen ginger-garlic paste (page 70), thawed,
   or 1 tablespoon each minced ginger and garlic
1 teaspoon fennel seeds
Pure kosher salt
3 medium tomatoes, diced
1 tablespoon ghee or vegetable oil
1 teaspoon cumin seeds
½ teaspoon crushed red pepper flakes
¼ teaspoon asafetida (optional; see Note, opposite)
¼ cup chopped fresh mint

Make the chutney: Combine all the ingredients in a mini food processor and pulse to make a paste; alternatively, grind them together with a mortar and pestle.

Make the lentils: In a large saucepan, combine the lentils, ginger-garlic paste, fennel seeds, 1 teaspoons salt, and 6 cups water. Bring to a boil, then lower the heat and simmer until the lentils are very tender, about 1 hour. Beat with a whisk or stir vigorously until the liquid is creamy and slightly thickened. Add the tomatoes and simmer until they are very soft, about 5 minutes. Season with salt to taste.

Meanwhile, in a small sauté pan, heat the ghee or oil over medium-high heat. Add the cumin seeds and red pepper flakes and cook until the cumin is fragrant and the pepper flakes are a shade darker, about 1 minute. Scrape the spice mixture into the lentils. Stir in the asafetida, if using, and the mint and simmer for 1 to 2 minutes longer, until heated through. Serve in wide bowls with a spoonful of the chutney on top.

Meyer Lemon and Rose Petal Marmalade

MAKES 4 OR 5 HALF-PINT JARS

THE MARMALADE-MAKING METHOD USED IN ALL THE CITRUS-MARMALADE RECIPES IN THIS BOOK IS BASED ON THE ONE USED AT THE VENERABLE JUNE TAYLOR JAMS IN SAN FRANCISCO AND DESCRIBED IN THE *NEW YORK TIMES MAGAZINE* A FEW YEARS BACK. It essentially involves removing all the tough and unpleasant membranes from the citrus while still taking advantage of the thickening pectin contained therein. It's not how my grandmother ever made marmalade (I imagine that, like my mom, she'd just finely chop the whole fruit), but the silky texture, with the occasional chewy chunk of bright lemon, is well worth the effort of segmenting. This is a marmalade to serve with silver spoons at afternoon tea with the queen of a small but important country.

2 pounds Meyer lemons (about 8), well scrubbed

1½ cups freshly squeezed regular lemon juice (from about 2 pounds lemons)

3 cups sugar

3 tablespoons dried untreated rose petals

Prepare for water-bath canning: Sterilize the jars and keep them hot in the canning pot, put a small plate in the freezer, and put the flat lids in a heat-proof bowl. (See page 21 for details.)

Cut the top and bottom off each Meyer lemon and cut the lemon into segments (see page 257), leaving the peel on and reserving the membranes and seeds. Cut the lemon segments crosswise into ¼-inch chunks and put them in a wide, 6- to 8-quart preserving pan. Add the lemon juice and 2 cups water.

Put as many of the lemon membranes and seeds in a jelly bag or 4 layers of cheesecloth as will fit, and tie the bag closed. Put the bag in the pan. Bring to a boil over high heat, then lower the heat and simmer until the lemon pieces are tender, about 30 minutes. Let cool until the bag can be handled. Squeeze as much of the juice as possible from the bag into the lemons in the pan, then discard the membranes and seeds.

Add the sugar and rose petals to the pan and bring to a boil over high heat. Boil, stirring occasionally, until the mixture registers about 220°F on a candy thermometer or a small dab of it spooned onto the chilled plate and returned to the freezer for a minute wrinkles when you nudge it, 35 to 40 minutes.

Ladle boiling water from the canning pot into the bowl with the lids. Using a jar lifter, remove the sterilized jars from the canning pot, carefully pouring the water from each one back into the pot, and place them upright on a folded towel. Drain the water off the jar lids.

Ladle the hot marmalade into the jars, leaving ¼ inch headspace at the top. Use a damp paper towel to wipe the rims of the jars, then put a flat lid and ring on each jar, adjusting the ring so that it's just finger-tight. Return the jars to the water in the canning pot, making sure the water covers the jars by at least 1 inch. Bring to a boil, and boil for 5 minutes to process. Remove the jars to a folded towel and do not disturb for 12 hours. After 1 hour, check that the lids have sealed by pressing down on the center of each; if it can be pushed down, it hasn't sealed, and the jar should be refrigerated immediately. Label the sealed jars and store.

Lime and Herb Jelly

MAKES ABOUT 4 HALF-PINT JARS

✧✧✧

FEEL FREE TO PLAY AROUND WITH THE COM-POSITION OF THE FRESH HERBS HERE. Basil and mint would be nice, maybe even rosemary (add minced rosemary, if you'd like, a few minutes before the jelly is ready to put into jars so the herb becomes tender), or lemon verbena and chamomile.

3 cups Green Apple Pectin Stock (page 181)
2½ cups sugar
1 cup strained fresh lime juice
2 large sprigs fresh tarragon
1 large sprig fresh mint
1 tablespoon each minced fresh tarragon and mint (optional)

Prepare for water-bath canning: Sterilize the jars and keep them hot in the canning pot, put a small plate in the freezer, and put the flat lids in a heat-proof bowl. (See page 21 for details.)

Put the pectin stock in a wide, 6- to 8-quart preserving pan, then add the sugar, lime juice, and herb sprigs. Bring to a boil over high heat and cook, stirring occasionally, until the mixture registers about 220°F on a candy thermometer or a small dab of it spooned onto the chilled plate and returned to the freezer for a minute wrinkles when you nudge it, 25 to 30 minutes. Fish out and discard the herb sprigs. Stir in the minced herbs, if using.

Ladle boiling water from the canning pot into the bowl with the lids. Using a jar lifter, remove the sterilized jars from the canning pot, carefully pouring the water from each one back into the pot, and place them upright on a folded towel. Drain the water off the jar lids.

Ladle the hot jelly into the jars, leaving ¼ inch headspace at the top. Use a damp paper towel to wipe the rims of the jars, then put a flat lid and ring on each jar, adjusting the ring so that it's just finger-tight. Return the jars to the water in the canning pot, making sure the water covers the jars by at least 1 inch. Bring to a boil, and boil for 5 minutes to process. Remove the jars to a folded towel and do not disturb for 12 hours. After 1 hour, check that the lids have sealed by pressing down on the center of each; if it can be pushed down, it hasn't sealed, and the jar should be refrigerated immediately. Label the sealed jars and store.

Lime Frozen Yogurt

MAKES ABOUT 1 QUART

◇◇

IS THIS CHEATING? I just adore limes so much, and I find it a shame that they don't work all that well in marmalades and the like (their rind is pretty tough, I've found, and becomes bitter, and this makes me sad). I love being able to pull this "preserve" of sorts out of the freezer—where it will keep, tightly covered, for months—for a hit or two of my favorite flavor. The beauty of this frozen treat is that it doesn't require an ice-cream maker; the fat in the yogurt, and the sugar syrup, keep the texture smooth and creamy.

1 cup sugar
1 quart Yogurt (page 287), preferably full fat
2 limes

Put the sugar and ½ cup water in a small saucepan over medium heat and cook, stirring, until the sugar is dissolved. Remove from the heat and let the syrup cool to room temperature.

While the syrup is cooling, put the yogurt in a colander lined with three layers of rinsed and squeezed cheesecloth to drain. Zest the limes with a fine grater held over a bowl, then squeeze the juice into the bowl.

When the syrup is cool, scrape the drained yogurt into a large stainless-steel bowl. Stir the syrup into the lime juice, then gradually add the mixture to the yogurt, whisking until smooth. Put the bowl in the freezer and freeze, whisking with a fork every hour or so if you can (it's not necessary), until firm, about 3 hours. Transfer to an airtight container; the yogurt will keep in the freezer for up to 3 months. Let it sit at room temperature to soften for 15 minutes before serving.

Navel Orange and Lemon Marmalade

MAKES 6 HALF-PINT JARS

◇◇

4 to 4½ pounds navel oranges (about 7), well scrubbed

2 lemons, well scrubbed

⅓ cup strained freshly squeezed lemon juice (from about 2 lemons)

3 cups sugar

Prepare for water-bath canning: Sterilize the jars and keep them hot in the canning pot, put a small plate in the freezer, and put the flat lids in a heat-proof bowl. (See page 21 for details.)

Use a vegetable peeler to cut the zest from 5 of the oranges, then stack the slices and cut them crosswise into thin julienne strips; you should have about 1½ cups zest. Use a sharp knife to segment all the oranges (see page 257), working over a bowl to catch the juice and reserving the membranes. Put the julienned zest and orange segments in a wide, 6- to 8-quart preserving pan. Strain the reserved juice into a measuring cup, add water to make 3 cups, and pour it into the pot. Cut the top and bottom off each lemon and cut the lemon into segments, leaving the peel on and reserving the membranes and seeds. Cut the lemon segments crosswise into ½-inch chunks and add to the pan, along with the lemon juice.

Put the orange and lemon membranes and seeds in a jelly bag or 4 layers of cheesecloth and tie the bag closed. Put the bag in the pan. Bring to a boil over high heat, then lower the heat and simmer until the zest is tender, about 30 minutes. Let cool until the bag can be handled. Squeeze as much of the juice as possible from the bag into the citrus in the pan, then discard the membranes and seeds.

Add the sugar to the pan and bring to a boil over high heat. Boil, stirring occasionally, until the mixture registers about 220°F on a candy thermometer or a small dab of it spooned onto the chilled plate and returned to the freezer for a minute wrinkles when you nudge it, 35 to 40 minutes.

Ladle boiling water from the canning pot into the bowl with the lids. Using a jar lifter, remove the sterilized jars from the canning pot, carefully pouring the water from each one back into the pot, and place them upright on a folded towel. Drain the water off the jar lids.

Ladle the hot marmalade into the jars, leaving ¼ inch headspace at the top. Use a damp paper towel to wipe the rims of the jars, then put a flat lid and ring on each jar, adjusting the ring so that it's just finger-tight. Return the jars to the water in the canning pot, making sure the water covers the jars by at least 1 inch. Bring to a boil, and boil for 5 minutes to process. Remove the jars to a folded towel and do not disturb for 12 hours. After 1 hour, check that the lids have sealed by pressing down on the center of each; if it can be pushed down, it hasn't sealed, and the jar should be refrigerated immediately. Label the sealed jars and store.

Grapefruit Marmalade

MAKES ABOUT 6 HALF-PINT JARS

◇◇◇

USE EITHER WHITE OR RUBY GRAPEFRUIT.
This makes a big batch, and the segmenting will
take some time; consider it a good excuse to call a
neighbor over.

6 to 6½ pounds grapefruit (about 9), well scrubbed

2 lemons, well scrubbed

4 cups sugar

Prepare for water-bath canning: Sterilize the jars
and keep them hot in the canning pot, put a small
plate in the freezer, and put the flat lids in a heat-
proof bowl. (See page 21 for details.)

Use a vegetable peeler to cut the zest from 3 of
the grapefruits, then stack the slices and cut them
crosswise into thin julienne strips; you should have
about 1 cup zest. Use a sharp knife to segment all
the grapefruits (see Note, opposite), working over
a bowl to catch the juice and reserving the membranes (save the peels for another use, such as
Candied Citrus Rind, page 259). Put the julienned
zest and grapefruit segments in a wide, 6- to 8-quart
preserving pan. Strain the reserved juice into a
measuring cup, add water to make 2 cups, and pour
it into the pan. Cut the top and bottom off each
lemon and cut the lemon into segments, leaving the
peel on and reserving the membranes and seeds.
Cut the lemon segments crosswise into ½-inch
chunks and add to the pan.

Put the grapefruit and lemon membranes and seeds
in a jelly bag or 4 layers of cheesecloth and tie the
bag closed. Put the bag in the pan. Bring to a boil
over high heat, then lower the heat and simmer
until the zest is tender, about 30 minutes. Let cool
until the bag can be handled. Squeeze as much of
the juice as possible from the bag into the citrus in
the pan, then discard the membranes and seeds.

Add the sugar to the pan and bring to a boil over
high heat. Boil, stirring occasionally, until the mixture registers about 220°F on a candy thermometer
or a small dab of it spooned onto the chilled plate
and returned to the freezer for a minute wrinkles
when you nudge it, 35 to 40 minutes.

Ladle boiling water from the canning pot into the
bowl with the lids. Using a jar lifter, remove the
sterilized jars from the canning pot, carefully pouring the water from each one back into the pot, and
place them upright on a folded towel. Drain the
water off the jar lids.

Ladle the hot marmalade into the jars, leaving
¼ inch headspace at the top. Use a damp paper
towel to wipe the rims of the jars, then put a flat
lid and ring on each jar, adjusting the ring so that
it's just finger-tight. Return the jars to the water in
the canning pot, making sure the water covers the
jars by at least 1 inch. Bring to a boil, and boil for
5 minutes to process. Remove the jars to a folded
towel and do not disturb for 12 hours. After 1 hour,
check that the lids have sealed by pressing down on
the center of each; if it can be pushed down, it hasn't
sealed, and the jar should be refrigerated immediately. Label the sealed jars and store.

Grapefruit Segments in Mint Syrup

MAKES 2 PINT JARS, OR 4 HALF-PINT JARS

◇◇

SERVE THIS WITH A VANILLA BEAN–SPECKED PANNA COTTA, OR WITH THE BEST GINGER-BREAD ON PAGE 68, OR THE RUSTIC ALMOND CAKE ON PAGE 277. It's also delicious with French Vanilla Ice Cream (page 288).

5 pounds grapefruit

1 cup sugar

¼ cup packed fresh mint sprigs, plus 1 small sprig for each jar

Prepare for water-bath canning: Sterilize the jars and keep them hot in the canning pot, and put the flat lids in a heatproof bowl. (See page 21 for details.)

Peel and segment the grapefruit (see Note), putting the segments in a medium bowl as you work. Holding back the segments, pour the juice that has collected in the bowl into a 2-cup measure. Add enough water to make 2 cups liquid. Put in a medium saucepan and add the sugar and ¼ cup mint. Bring to a boil over medium-low heat, stirring to dissolve the sugar. Fish out and discard the mint sprigs.

Ladle boiling water from the canning pot into the bowl with the lids. Using a jar lifter, remove the sterilized jars from the canning pot, carefully pouring the water from each one back into the pot, and place them upright on a folded towel. Drain the water off the jar lids.

Working quickly, fill the jars with grapefruit segments and a fresh mint sprig. Ladle in the boiling syrup, leaving ¼ inch headspace at the top for ½-pint jars or ½ inch for pint jars. Use a chopstick to remove air bubbles around the inside of each jar. Use a damp paper towel to wipe the rims of the jars, then put a flat lid and ring on each jar, adjusting the ring so that it's just finger-tight. Return the jars to the water in the canning pot, making sure the water covers the jars by at least 1 inch. Bring to a boil, and boil for 5 minutes to process. Remove the jars to a folded towel and do not disturb for 12 hours. After 1 hour, check that the lids have sealed by pressing down on the center of each; if it can be pushed down, it hasn't sealed, and the jar should be refrigerated immediately. Label the sealed jars and store.

Note: To segment citrus: Cut the top and bottom off of each fruit to expose the flesh. Set the fruit upright on a cutting board. If you want to save the rind for Candied Citrus Rind (page 259), use the tip of a sharp knife to score the rind from top to bottom in four or five places around the fruit, then carefully peel off the rind so it stays in large pieces. Set the fruit upright again and use the knife to shave off the layer of white outer membrane, exposing the segments separated by membranes. Otherwise, just cut off the rind and outer membrane, moving the knife from top to bottom following the curve of the fruit. Hold the fruit in one hand and cut right next to a membrane toward the center of the fruit, then pivot the knife and scrape it against the opposite membrane to lift out the fruit segment. Repeat until all the segments are removed. (Squeeze the empty membranes over a glass and take a juice break.)

Simple Dried Fruit Conserve

MAKES ABOUT 4 HALF-PINT JARS

SPOON A FEW PIECES OF SYRUPY FRUIT ONTO A CHEESE PLATE, OR OPEN UP A FEW JARS AND MIX THEM WITH SHREDDED FRESH APPLE FOR A QUICK, MEATLESS MINCEMEAT FILLING. Experiment with different combinations of dried fruits—raisins, prunes, apricots, peaches, nectarines, pineapple (low-sugar, if possible), guava, papaya, mangoes . . .

2 cups pomegranate or cranberry juice
1½ cups sugar
1 pound mixed dried fruit, diced if large (about 3 cups)
1 small navel orange, diced
½ cup walnut halves, toasted and coarsely chopped
½ teaspoon ground cinnamon (optional)

Prepare for water-bath canning: Sterilize the jars and keep them hot in the canning pot, and put the flat lids in a heatproof bowl. (See page 21 for details.)

Put the pomegranate juice, sugar, dried fruit, and orange in a wide, 6- to 8-quart preserving pan. Bring to a boil over high heat, stirring. Lower the heat and simmer, stirring occasionally, for about 30 minutes, until the fruit is very soft, the orange rind is translucent, and the liquid is syrupy. Stir in the walnuts and cinnamon, if using, and boil for 5 minutes more. Remove from the heat.

Ladle boiling water from the canning pot into the bowl with the lids. Using a jar lifter, remove the sterilized jars from the canning pot, carefully pouring the water from each one back into the pot, and place them upright on a folded towel. Drain the water off the jar lids.

Ladle the hot conserve into the jars, leaving ¼ inch headspace at the top. Use a chopstick to remove air bubbles around the inside of each jar. Use a damp paper towel to wipe the rims of the jars, then put a flat lid and ring on each jar, adjusting the ring so that it's just finger-tight. Return the jars to the water in the canning pot, making sure the water covers the jars by at least 1 inch. Bring to a boil, and boil for 5 minutes to process. Remove the jars to a folded towel and do not disturb for 12 hours. After 1 hour, check that the lids have sealed by pressing down on the center of each; if it can be pushed down, it hasn't sealed, and the jar should be refrigerated immediately. Label the sealed jars and store.

Candied Citrus Rind

MAKES ABOUT 6 CUPS

◇◇◇

THIS IS HOW PEOPLE WITH TIME ON THEIR HANDS CANDY CITRUS, AND IT'S REALLY THE BEST WAY TO DO IT. Sure, it's easy enough to quickly candy citrus *zest*, or just the outer colored layer of the peel, but here you use the whole rind—once-bitter white pith and all—so you get more candy bang for your fruit buck.

Peel from 5 pounds citrus, removed in large pieces (see Note on page 257)

5½ cups sugar

Cut the large pieces of peel crosswise into ½-inch-wide strips or long triangles, putting them in a bowl of cold water as you work. Drain and put the peel in a wide, 6- to 8-quart preserving pan. Cover with cold water, bring to a boil, then lower the heat and simmer for 10 minutes. Drain and repeat the blanching process two more times. Cover with cold water again, bring to a boil, then lower the heat and simmer until the peel is tender, about 30 minutes. Drain in a colander.

Put 5 cups of the sugar and 5 cups water in the pan. Bring to a boil, stirring just until the sugar is dissolved, then boil without stirring until the syrup reaches 220°F, about 15 minutes. Add the peel and simmer, without stirring, until the peel is translucent, about 45 minutes. Remove from the heat and let the peel stand in the syrup overnight, undisturbed, at room temperature.

Bring to a boil and cook, without stirring, until the syrup reaches 226°F, about 30 minutes. Remove from the heat and let stand for 2 to 4 hours. Bring to a boil again and cook until the syrup reaches 228°F, about 10 minutes (watch it closely, as it may come up to temperature more quickly depending on the size of your pan). Remove from the heat and let stand for 2 to 4 hours. Bring to a boil once more, then remove from the heat and set aside until just cool enough to handle. Fish out the peels with a fork and arrange them on wire racks set over baking sheets so that the pieces are not touching one another. Put the peels in a turned-off oven to dry for 24 hours.

Toss the peel with the remaining ½ cup sugar to coat them all over. Set on clean racks to dry again for 1 to 2 hours, then store in airtight containers. The peel will keep for about 2 months at room temperature.

Quince and Plum Jelly

MAKES ABOUT 5 HALF-PINT JARS

◇◇◇

IT'S DISTRESSING HOW INFREQUENTLY I'M ABLE TO GET SUPER-FRESH—THAT IS, JUST UNDERRIPE—QUINCE. (When will Americans start buying quince in quantities that will support a quince-growing industry? Please, folks, get on board! Quince has no substitute and is one of the most interesting and useful fruits in the world!) When I can't get them really fresh, I cut the quince with plums, which provide some needed acidity and also enhance the jelly's color.

2 pounds quince, cut into 1-inch chunks
2 pounds red-fleshed black plums, just underripe, pitted and chopped
9 cups water
About 4½ cups sugar
¼ cup strained fresh lemon juice

Put the quince and 4½ cups water in a wide, 6- to 8-quart preserving pan. Cover and bring to a boil. Boil, stirring occasionally, for 45 minutes. Add the plums and another 4½ cups water and return to a boil. Cook until the quince are very soft and easily crushed against the side of the pan with a spoon, about 30 minutes longer.

Set a large, very-fine-mesh sieve (or jelly bag) over a deep bowl or pot. Pour the fruit and liquid into the sieve and let drain for 30 minutes, stirring occasionally but not pressing down too hard on the solids; discard the solids (or make *Membrillo*, page 265). Measure the juice; you should have about 6 cups.

Prepare for water-bath canning: Sterilize the jars and keep them hot in the canning pot, put a small plate in the freezer, and put the flat lids in a heat-proof bowl. (See page 21 for details.)

Rinse the preserving pan and pour in the quince and plum juice. Add ¾ cup sugar for each cup of juice, then add the lemon juice. Bring to a boil over high heat and cook, stirring occasionally, until the mixture registers about 220°F on a candy thermometer or a small dab of it spooned onto the chilled plate and returned to the freezer for a minute wrinkles when you nudge it, 25 to 30 minutes.

Ladle boiling water from the canning pot into the bowl with the lids. Using a jar lifter, remove the sterilized jars from the canning pot, carefully pouring the water from each one back into the pot, and place them upright on a folded towel. Drain the water off the jar lids.

Ladle the hot jelly into the jars, leaving ¼ inch headspace at the top. Use a damp paper towel to wipe the rims of the jars, then put a flat lid and ring on each jar, adjusting the ring so that it's just finger-tight. Return the jars to the water in the canning pot, making sure the water covers the jars by at least 1 inch. Bring to a boil, and boil for 5 minutes to process. Remove the jars to a folded towel and do not disturb for 12 hours. After 1 hour, check that the lids have sealed by pressing down on the center of each; if it can be pushed down, it hasn't sealed, and the jar should be refrigerated immediately. Label the sealed jars and store.

Quince Slices in Cinnamon Syrup

MAKES ABOUT 4 PINT JARS

◇◇◇

3 pounds quince
2 cups sugar
4 cinnamon sticks

Peel, quarter, and core the quince and cut them into ½-inch-thick slices. Cook them in simmering water to cover until just tender. This could take as little as 10 minutes or up to 45 minutes, depending on the variety and how ripe the quince are. Drain.

Prepare for water-bath canning: Wash the jars and keep them hot in the canning pot, and put the flat lids in a heatproof bowl. (See page 21 for details.)

In a medium saucepan, combine 4 cups water, the sugar, and cinnamon and bring to a boil, stirring to dissolve the sugar. Lower the heat and simmer for 5 minutes.

Ladle boiling water from the canning pot into the bowl with the lids. Using a jar lifter, remove the hot jars from the canning pot, carefully pouring the water from each one back into the pot, and place them upright on a folded towel. Drain the water off the jar lids.

Working quickly, fill the hot jars loosely with the quince slices and put one of the cinnamon sticks in each jar. Ladle in the hot syrup, leaving ½ inch headspace at the top. Use a chopstick to remove air bubbles around the inside of each jar. Use a damp paper towel to wipe the rims of the jars, then put a flat lid and ring on each jar, adjusting the ring so that it's just finger-tight. Return the jars to the water in the canning pot, making sure the water covers the jars by at least 1 inch. Bring to a boil, and boil for 15 minutes to process. Remove the jars to a folded towel and do not disturb for 12 hours. After 1 hour, check that the lids have sealed by pressing down on the center of each; if it can be pushed down, it hasn't sealed, and the jar should be refrigerated immediately. Label the sealed jars and store.

Quince and Lamb Koresh

SERVES 4

◇◇

MY MOM'S FRIEND SHALAH WILLIAMS, FROM ISFAHAN, IRAN, SHARED HER AMAZING QUINCE AND APPLE *KORESH* RECIPES WITH US. I've been making variations on them for years because they're so simple, requiring no super-specialized ingredients or equipment, and yet they seem so different from ordinary meat stews. Incidentally, one thing I find charming about these rich, hearty, slightly sweet Persian stews is how they are named after the fruit they contain rather than the meat—though they tend to contain much more of the latter than the former. Sort of like Gullah recipes for vegetables and salads that, without fail, begin with some pork product or other.

2 tablespoons vegetable oil

2 onions, sliced

1 pound well-marbled lamb stew meat

Pure kosher salt and freshly ground black pepper

¼ teaspoon ground cinnamon

1 pint Quince Slices in Cinnamon Syrup (page 261),
    drained, syrup and cinnamon stick reserved

¼ cup red wine vinegar

⅓ cup yellow split peas

Large pinch of saffron threads, crushed and mixed
    with 1 tablespoon warm water (optional)

Steamed white rice, to serve

In a large skillet, heat the oil over medium-high heat. Add the onions and cook, stirring, until softened but not browned, about 10 minutes. Add the lamb and cook until the lamb and onions are browned all over, 5 to 8 minutes. Season with salt and pepper to taste and add the ground cinnamon. Put the reserved quince syrup and cinnamon stick in a large measuring cup and add water to make 3 cups; pour it over the lamb. Bring to a simmer, cover, and cook for 30 minutes, or until the lamb is just tender.

Add the vinegar, split peas, quince, and saffron water (if using). Bring to a simmer, cover, and cook until the split peas are soft, about 45 minutes. Taste and add more salt and pepper if needed, then serve hot with steamed rice.

Membrillo (Quince Paste)

MAKES ABOUT 8 (2½-BY-4-INCH) RECTANGLES

◇◇◇

DEEP ORANGE-RED *MEMBRILLO*, OR *DULCE DE MEMBRILLO*, IS UBIQUITOUS IN SPAIN AND PORTUGAL (WHERE IT'S CALLED *MERMELADA*), USUALLY PAIRED WITH SALTY, DRY MANCHEGO CHEESE OR EATEN WITH TOAST FOR BREAKFAST. Often the pieces of *membrillo* are stacked up, separated by bay leaves, for storage; my Georgia renditions are always too sticky to stack, so I just lay a leaf atop each piece for flavor and aesthetics and wrap in waxed paper.

If you live in a dry climate very much unlike Georgia, you can (I've heard) dry the paste in a turned-off oven—or any other cool, dark spot—for 3 to 5 days, until firm. I've had the best luck, though, drying it in a just barely warm oven.

Quince and plum pulp from making Quince and Plum
   Jelly (page 260)
Sugar
8 fresh bay leaves

Lightly oil a baking pan or quarter sheet pan and set aside.

Pass the quince pulp through a food mill fitted with the fine disk, or through a Squeezo strainer. Discard the cores and skins. Measure the puree. Put the puree in a wide, 6- to 8-quart preserving pan and add ¾ cup sugar for each cup of puree. Bring to a simmer and cook, stirring frequently with a long-handled spoon and being careful to keep the puree from boiling too vigorously (it can become downright magmalike, popping up out of the pan unexpectedly; cover the pan loosely with a lid if necessary), until it is very thick and dark colored, 30 to 40 minutes.

Preheat the oven to its lowest setting, about 170°F.

Carefully pour the puree into the prepared pan and use a spatula to smooth it into a rough rectangle about ½ inch thick. Put in the oven and let dry for several hours, until firm. Cut into rectangles and place a bay leaf on top of each. Wrap in waxed paper and place in an airtight container. The *membrillo* will keep at room temperature for at least 2 months.

WINTER VEGETABLES

Sauerkraut

MAKES ABOUT 8 PINT JARS

◇◇

ALTHOUGH IT MAY SEEM AS IF YOU'RE HAV-ING—AS MY HUSBAND SAID WHEN HE WALKED IN ON ME WITH MY ARMS ELBOW-DEEP IN A MASS OF PALE-GREEN SHREDS—"A DIFFICULT IMMIGRANT EXPERIENCE," SQUEEZING CAB-BAGE AND SALT TOGETHER TO MAKE SAU-ERKRAUT IS *FUN*. It's one of the most satisfying things you can do in the kitchen, and it always amazes me how these two cheap ingredients turn into something so delicious.

My dad, who as a kid worked in a Polish butcher shop in Gary, Indiana, and so has a deep under-standing of all things sausage-related (of course that includes sauerkraut), walked me through the squeezing part by phone years ago when, for some reason, I decided to make my own.

8 pounds green cabbage (about 5 large heads)
5 tablespoons pure kosher salt, plus more if needed
4 teaspoons caraway (optional)

Quarter, core, and thinly slice the cabbage. Working in batches, put some of the cabbage in—I'm going out on a limb here—*your largest bowl* and sprinkle in some of the salt. Use your hands to mix them together, then squeeze and knead the cabbage and salt until the cabbage is wilted and has released a fair amount of liquid, 15 to 20 minutes per batch. As you finish each batch, pack it tightly in a clean, straight-sided crock or bucket. If the liquid does not cover the cabbage (it should—keep squeezing!), dis-solve 1½ tablespoons salt in 4 cups water over low heat; let cool, then pour the brine over the cabbage. Set a plate or several large whole cabbage leaves directly on top and weight it down (a resealable plastic bag filled with water works well) so that the cabbage is submerged in the brine.

Place the crock in an out-of-the-way spot at room temperature and let the cabbage ferment for about 3 weeks, skimming any scum or foam from the surface every two days or so (scum will start to form after a few days) and replacing the plate or cabbage leaves with clean ones as necessary. The sauerkraut should taste sour and have softened slightly.

Prepare for water-bath canning: Wash the jars and keep them hot in the canning pot, and put the flat lids in a heatproof bowl. (See page 21 for details.)

Put the sauerkraut and caraway (if using) in a wide, 6- to 8-quart preserving pan and bring to a boil. Boil for 5 minutes.

Ladle boiling water from the canning pot into the bowl with the lids. Using a jar lifter, remove the hot jars from the canning pot, carefully pouring the water from each one back into the pot, and place them upright on a folded towel. Drain the water off the jar lids.

Spoon the hot sauerkraut and brine into the jars, leaving ½ inch headspace at the top. Use a damp paper towel to wipe the rims of the jars, then put a flat lid and ring on each jar, adjusting the ring so that it's just finger-tight. Return the jars to the water in the canning pot, making sure the water covers the jars by at least 1 inch. Bring to a boil, and boil for 10 minutes to process. Remove the jars to a folded towel and do not disturb for 12 hours. After 1 hour, check that the lids have sealed by press-ing down on the center of each; if it can be pushed down, it hasn't sealed, and the jar should be refriger-ated immediately. Label the sealed jars and store.

* CLOCKWISE FROM LEFT: Sauerkraut, Good Ketchup (page 173) on a good hot dog, Grandma Barron's Green Tomato Relish (page 220)

Small-Batch Fresh Sauerkraut

MAKES 1 QUART

TO GARNER THE FULL BENEFITS OF THE LIVE CULTURES FOUND IN FRESH SAUERKRAUT, DON'T CAN OR OTHERWISE COOK IT, AS THE HEAT KILLS THE GOOD BACTERIA. Here's a popular method for making a small batch of kraut (the quantities are from *So Easy to Preserve*; see Further Reading, page 292). Once it's fermented, the kraut will keep in the refrigerator for several weeks.

1 small head green cabbage (2 pounds)
4 teaspoons pure kosher salt

Quarter, core, and thinly slice the cabbage. Put it in a large bowl with the salt and mix and squeeze away. Pack it in a glass quart-size jar; it should all fit, and the brine that forms should just cover the cabbage when it's tightly packed. Use a chopstick to remove air bubbles around the inside of the jar. Fill a small heavy-duty resealable plastic bag with water and put it in the mouth of the jar to keep the cabbage submerged in the brine. Set the jar in a small bowl in case the brine overflows as it ferments. Let sit at cool room temperature for about 10 days, lifting the bag and skimming off any scum that forms, as necessary. When the bubbles stop appearing and the kraut tastes good, the fermentation is complete. Remove the bag, put the lid on the jar, and store in the refrigerator.

Spicy Kale with Chickpeas

SERVES 4

THIS MAY BE A PERFECT VEGETARIAN SUPPER. But that's not to say it isn't fantastic with a pork chop or bratwurst sitting next to it on the plate.

1 tablespoon olive oil
1 onion, finely diced
1 hot red chile, seeded and finely diced
1 teaspoon ground cumin
½ teaspoon crushed red pepper flakes
Pure kosher salt and freshly ground black pepper
1 (15-ounce) can chickpeas, drained and rinsed
1 sweet potato, peeled and finely diced
6 sun-dried tomatoes, diced
About 1½ cups frozen blanched kale (from about
    1 bunch, see opposite), thawed and drained

In a large sauté pan, heat the oil over medium-high heat. Add the onion and chile and cook, stirring frequently, until softened, about 5 minutes. Add the cumin, red pepper flakes, and salt and pepper to taste and stir for 30 seconds. Add the chickpeas and 2 cups water and bring to a simmer; simmer for 5 minutes. Add the sweet potato and sun-dried tomatoes and cook until the potato is just tender, 5 to 7 minutes. Fold in the greens and cook for 5 minutes, or until heated through. Season again with salt, if necessary, then serve hot.

Orecchiette with Broccoli Rabe and Sausage

SERVES 4

1 pound dried *orecchiette* pasta

Pure kosher salt

1 pound sweet Italian sausage, casings removed

1 teaspoon extra-virgin olive oil

3 cloves garlic, roughly chopped

1 cup chicken or vegetable stock

Generous pinch of crushed red pepper flakes

1 quart-size bag frozen broccoli rabe (below), thawed

Freshly ground black pepper

Freshly grated hard cheese (optional)

Cook the pasta in a large pot of boiling salted water until almost al dente.

Meanwhile, heat a large sauté pan over medium-high heat and add the sausage. Cook, stirring with a wooden spoon to break the sausage into little chunks, until lightly browned and cooked through. If there is a lot of fat in the pan, drain it off. Add the oil and garlic to the pan and cook, stirring, until the garlic is soft, about 5 minutes. Add the stock and stir to scrape up any browned bits from the bottom of the pan. Add the red pepper flakes and broccoli rabe and cook until it is very tender, about 5 minutes longer. Season with salt and pepper to taste. If the sauce looks too dry, tip in some of the pasta cooking water.

Drain the pasta and add it to the pan. Toss to combine, then let it cook in the sauce until just al dente. Spoon into pasta bowls and sprinkle with cheese. Serve immediately.

FREEZING WINTER GREENS

Frozen broccoli rabe: Bring a large pot of water to a boil over high heat. Fill a large bowl with ice water. Trim the bottom 1½ inches or so off the broccoli rabe. Cut the stems and leaves crosswise into 2-inch pieces, keeping the thicker stems in a pile. Drop the thick stems into the boiling water, return the water to a full, rolling boil, then add the leaves. Bring back to a boil and blanch for 1 minute. Drain in a colander, then immediately plunge the broccoli rabe into the ice water bath. When completely cool, drain again, shaking as much of the water out as possible. Lay a large handful of the broccoli rabe on a clean towel, gather up the corners, and swing the towel hard to remove more water. (Do this outside, or in the bathtub.) Repeat with the remaining broccoli rabe. Put into two quart-size resealable plastic bags, squeezing as much of the air out as possible and then sucking more air out one corner of the opening. Seal, label, and freeze for up to 6 months.

Other frozen greens: Wash the greens well in a sinkful of cold water, lifting them out into a colander. Bring a large pot of water to a boil and fill a large bowl (or the sink) with ice water. Add several handfuls of greens to the boiling water and cook for 30 seconds. Use a skimmer or large slotted spoon to transfer the greens to the ice water to cool. Drain well in a sieve or colander, pressing out as much liquid as possible, then put in small containers or freezer bags to freeze for up to 6 months.

Kimchi

MAKES ABOUT 1½ QUARTS

THERE ARE SO MANY VARIATIONS ON THIS KOREAN FERMENT THAT IT WAS DIFFICULT TO NARROW THE CHOICES DOWN TO ONE RECIPE. Basically, you can make kimchi out of anything: not only the usual Napa cabbage, but other kinds of cabbage or bok choy, grated turnips, daikon, apples, or even stone fruit! I don't think a Korean meal would be quite right without a small plate of bright orange-red folds of spicy, sour, pleasantly salty cabbage. It's fiber- and vitamin-rich and offers all the healthful benefits of fresh fermented foods.

Kimchi takes only about a week to reach its peak and then keeps for weeks in the refrigerator. It is almost infinitely versatile. Serve it as a side dish, but also drop some into broth along with cubed tofu, mince it and fold it into white rice, or use it in place of scallions in Chinese-style scallion pancakes.

Fermenting the kimchi in a half-gallon jar with a brine-filled plastic bag stuffed into the top is an idea that comes from the always brilliant Linda Ziedrich, who offers several intriguing kimchis in her *Joy of Pickling* (See Further Reading, page 292).

1 medium head Napa cabbage (about 1½ pounds)

6 scallions, trimmed and cut into 2-inch lengths

1 small daikon, peeled and cut into julienne strips (about 8 ounces)

¼ cup pure kosher salt

2 to 4 tablespoons Korean chile powder (see Note)

1½ inches fresh ginger, peeled and grated or minced

4 cloves garlic, minced

½ (2-ounce) can anchovy fillets in oil or salt, drained or rinsed and finely minced

Quarter and core the cabbage and cut it into roughly 2-inch squares. Put in a large stainless-steel bowl with the daikon and scallions and set aside.

In another large bowl or a half-gallon jar, combine the salt with 8 cups water, stirring to dissolve the salt. Pour the brine over the vegetables to just cover them, then put a plate on top of the vegetables to keep them submerged in the brine. Cover the container with a clean, heavy towel and let sit at room temperature for 8 hours, or overnight. Drain the vegetables, reserving the brine, and return them to the bowl.

In a small bowl, combine the chile powder, ginger, garlic, and anchovies, mashing with a fork to make a loose paste. Add the paste and the scallions to the cabbage and daikon and toss to coat thoroughly. Pack the mixture tightly into a half-gallon glass jar. Pour in some of the reserved brine if necessary, pressing down on the vegetables to make sure they're just covered with brine. Stuff a resealable plastic bag into the mouth of the jar, pour in enough of the remaining brine to keep the vegetables submerged in the brine, and seal the bag.

Let ferment at cool room temperature for about 1 week, until slightly sour and very tasty, then remove the bag and put a lid on the jar. Refrigerate and use as desired. The kimchi will keep in the refrigerator for several weeks, becoming gradually more sour.

Note: Korean chile powder, available in most Asian groceries, is much milder than the more common (in this country) ground cayenne—you certainly would not want to substitute the latter here in such quantity. If you can find ground dried New Mexico chiles, that would be the best alternative, but you could use part cayenne and part paprika for heat and color, respectively, though the paprika flavor will definitely change the character of the kimchi.

Kimchi and Pork Dumplings

MAKES ABOUT 46; SERVES 8 AS AN APPETIZER

THESE SIMPLE DUMPLINGS ARE DEEP-FRIED AT HIGH HEAT SO THEY STAY LIGHT AND CRISP AND NOT AT ALL GREASY. They're also good steamed or cooked briefly in simmering broth—a vegetable stock seasoned with a little soy sauce and chile paste, for example, or a miso broth with sliced shiitake mushrooms and scallions. The dumpling recipe is easily halved—or doubled: Freeze the extras, uncooked, in a single layer until hard, then put in freezer bags, where they'll keep for 6 months or so, ready to be dropped a few at a time straight into simmering broth to cook. A simple folding plastic dumpling press makes the filing step go quickly.

For the dumplings:
1 tablespoon vegetable oil
8 ounces ground pork
1 cup finely chopped Kimchi (opposite)
1 scallion, dark green part only, chopped (reserve the rest for the dipping sauce)
1 teaspoon soy sauce
About 46 (3½-inch-diameter) round *gyoza* (Japanese potsticker) wheat-flour wrappers
Vegetable oil for deep-frying

For the dipping sauce:
½ cup soy sauce
¼ cup rice vinegar
1 teaspoon sugar
1 inch fresh ginger, peeled and julienned
1 scallion, white and light green parts only, thinly sliced

Make the dumplings: In a medium skillet, heat the oil over high heat. Add the pork and cook, stirring, until no pink remains and the meat is browned and crisp in spots, about 5 minutes. Drain and put in a large bowl; let cool for 10 minutes. Add the kimchi, scallion, and soy sauce.

Lay the *gyoza* wrappers out on a work surface. Put a heaping teaspoonful of the kimchi mixture in the center of each. Dampen the edges of the wrappers with water, fold one half over the filling, and press to seal the edges. The dumplings can be made up to 1 day in advance; put them on a baking sheet or platter lined with waxed paper, cover with plastic, and refrigerate until ready to use.

Preheat the oven to 200°F.

In a heavy saucepan, heat 2 inches of oil to 375°F. Working in batches so you don't crowd the pan, carefully drop in the dumplings. Cook, turning with a slotted spoon, until well browned on both sides, 1 to 2 minutes. Remove to a rack set over a baking sheet and set aside in the oven to keep warm.

Make the dipping sauce: In a small bowl, combine all the ingredients and stir to dissolve the sugar. Serve in small bowls alongside the dumplings.

* Kimchi and Pork Dumplings

BAKED AND CREAMY THINGS TO PUT PRESERVES ON

Rustic Almond Cake

MAKES 1 (9-INCH) ROUND CAKE; SERVES 8 TO 10

1 cup almonds

¾ cup plus 2 tablespoons sugar

1½ cups all-purpose flour

2 teaspoons baking powder

1 teaspoon pure kosher salt

4 large eggs

Grated zest of 1 lemon

¼ teaspoon almond extract

¾ cup (1½ sticks) unsalted butter, melted

Preheat the oven to 325°F. Butter and flour a 9-inch round springform pan.

In a food processor, pulse the nuts with 1 tablespoon of the sugar until very finely ground. Transfer to a medium bowl and add the flour, baking powder, and salt. Whisk to combine. Set aside.

In a large bowl, using an electric mixer (with the whisk attachment if you have one), beat the eggs and ¾ cup sugar together until very light and fluffy and at least doubled in volume, about 3 minutes. Beat in the lemon zest and almond extract. In three batches, add the flour mixture alternating with the butter, beating after each addition until just incorporated. Scrape the batter into the prepared pan and sprinkle the top with the remaining 1 tablespoon sugar. Bake for 35 to 40 minutes, until nicely browned and starting to pull away from the sides of the pan; a toothpick inserted in the center will come out with damp crumbs clinging to it. Let cool in the pan on a wire rack for 10 minutes, then remove the springform ring and let cool to room temperature. Slice and serve.

Joe's Basic French Bread

MAKES 2 LOAVES

THIS METHOD IS BASED ON A RECIPE GIVEN TO ME BY MY HUSBAND'S BOSS, AND I INCLUDE IT HERE NOT TO FURTHER HIS CAREER BUT BECAUSE IT'S ONE OF THE EASI-EST AND MOST FOOL-PROOF WAYS I KNOW TO MAKE GOOD YEAST BREAD. Julia Child's instructions for folding, patting, and rolling to shape the dough in *Mastering the Art of French Cooking*, volume 2, are worth taking a look at, but if you don't have that book (yet), just pat the dough into a rectangle, then roll it up tightly and pinch the ends of the roll, and the seam along the length of it. Let rise seam side down.

1½ cups warm (not hot) water
1 scant tablespoon instant or active dry yeast
Pinch of sugar
3 to 4 cups unbleached bread flour
1 tablespoon pure kosher salt

Put the water in a large bowl and sprinkle in the yeast and sugar. Let sit until it bubbles a bit, about 5 minutes. Add 1 cup of the flour and the salt and beat with a wooden spoon for a minute or so. Add 2 to 3 cups more flour, to make a somewhat stiff dough; knead for 5 to 10 minutes, until no longer sticky. Lightly oil the bowl and return the dough to the bowl. Cover and set aside to rise in a warm spot until doubled in volume, about 2 hours. (If you have time, punch down the dough, cover, and let rise again until doubled in volume, about 2 hours.)

Cut the dough in half and roll each half into a loaf shape. Transfer to a baking sheet or perforated French bread pans and let rise for 45 minutes to 1 hour, until puffed up and tight-looking. Cut 3 deep diagonal slits in each loaf and let rest for 5 minutes. Put on the middle rack of a cold oven and set the oven temperature to 400°F. Toss 4 or 5 ice cubes onto the floor of the oven (or into a foil pan set on the oven floor). Bake for about 30 minutes, until golden brown; the bread should sound hollow when you tap the bottom of a loaf with your finger. Let the bread cool on a rack for 20 minutes before slicing into it.

Mom's Soft Rolls

MAKES 16

THESE LOVELY, LIGHT SOFT ROLLS ARE SIMPLE TO MAKE: You can put the bowl in the refrigerator overnight for the second rise, then shape and bake them the morning of your jam making. And they're just about the best thing to slather with warm jam scraped from the bottom of the preserving pan after the full jars have gone into the boiling-water bath. They make for cute little sandwiches and hamburgers, too, and store well in a resealable plastic bag.

I buy instant milk just for this purpose, but you can omit it and use warmed milk instead of the water.

4 to 5 cups all-purpose flour, plus more for dusting
¼ cup sugar
⅓ cup nonfat dry milk powder
1 tablespoon pure kosher salt
2 tablespoons instant or active dry yeast
2 cups warm water
⅓ cup vegetable or olive oil

In a large bowl, combine 2 cups of the flour with the sugar, milk powder, salt, yeast, and water. Stir for a minute, then stir in the oil. Gradually add the remaining flour, stirring well and adding a little more as needed to make a soft dough that isn't sticky. Knead on a lightly floured surface for 5 minutes, until smooth and elastic. Put in a lightly oiled bowl, cover with plastic wrap, and let rise in a warm spot until doubled in volume, about 1 hour. Punch the dough down to deflate it, cover, and let rise again until doubled.

Turn the dough out and cut it into 16 pieces. Shape each into a ball by rolling it around on an unfloured or very lightly floured surface. Put on baking sheets lined with parchment paper, sprinkle the tops with a little flour, cover with plastic wrap, and let rise until doubled, about 1 hour.

Preheat the oven to 375°F.

Bake for 20 to 25 minutes, rotating and switching the pans halfway through, until golden brown on top and bottom. Let cool on wire racks.

Regan's Oat Scones
MAKES ABOUT 22 SCONES

◇◇

MY FRIEND REGAN HUFF SAYS THIS RECIPE COMES FROM INA GARTEN OF *BAREFOOT CONTESSA* FAME. But Regan has made so many adjustments to it—for ease, convenience, clarity, and appropriateness for use with Cardamom Plum Jam (page 116)—that I'm not sure the contessa would recognize the resulting scones.

They truly are the best baked good you could possibly come up with to serve with a boldly spiced preserve: tender and refined (thank you, butter and eggs), but with character enough to complement rather than be overwhelmed by the strong flavor of the jam. I sometimes sprinkle the tops with crunchy crystals of raw turbinado sugar instead of the oats, and sometimes instead of oats I use a mixture of several flaked quick-cooking grains sold in the bulk section of my grocery store. Regan says that honey works just fine in place of the maple syrup, but I like the subtle breakfasty aroma that the maple imparts.

The scones stay fresh for several days in a resealable plastic bag and also freeze very well: a few seconds in a microwave oven or a minute in a toaster oven, and you've got a pretty fabulous afternoon snack. They're also great with Lemon Curd (page 245) or a spoonful of Sour Cherry Preserves (page 97).

3½ cups all-purpose flour

1 cup whole-wheat flour

1 cup quick-cooking (not instant) oats, plus extra for sprinkling

2 tablespoons baking powder

2 tablespoons sugar

2 teaspoons pure kosher salt

2 cups (4 sticks) cold unsalted butter, diced

½ cup Yogurt (page 287)

½ cup maple syrup or honey

5 large eggs

Preheat the oven to 400°F. Line two baking sheets with parchment paper.

In a large bowl, combine the flours, oats, baking powder, sugar, and salt. Using your fingertips, two knives held together, or a pastry cutter, cut in the butter until the largest pieces are the size of peas.

In a separate bowl, whisk together the yogurt, maple syrup, and 4 of the eggs. Pour the mixture into the flour mixture and stir until just incorporated; do not overmix. The dough will be somewhat sticky.

Turn the dough out onto a well-floured surface. Flour your hands, then pat the dough out ¾ to 1 inch thick. Cut into 2½-inch rounds and place at least 1½ inches apart on the prepared baking sheets. Gather up the leftover dough, handling it as little as possible, pat it out, and cut more rounds. If the kitchen is warm, put the baking sheets in the refrigerator for 30 minutes or so to firm up, so they don't spread too much in the oven. (The scones can be cut and refrigerated for a few days prior to baking.)

In a small bowl, whisk the remaining egg together with 2 teaspoons cold water and brush the tops of the scones with the egg wash. Sprinkle each scone with a half pinch of oats. Bake for 20 to 25 minutes, rotating and switching the pans halfway through, until deep golden brown. Remove the scones to wire racks. Serve warm or at room temperature, preferably split and spread with jam.

Clare's English Muffin Bread

MAKES 2 (9¼-BY-5¼-INCH) LOAVES

THIS IS HOW MY FRIEND CLARE ADAMS USES UP HER CHEESEMAKING WHEY. And given how wonderfully English muffins—in muffin or loaf form—go with many of the sweet preserves in this book, I could hardly not include her recipe. It's blessedly quick for a yeast bread, needing to rise only a little longer than it takes to preheat the oven, and the recipe is easily doubled: The loaves freeze very well. Try spreading the bread with Fresh Cheese (page 284) and Tomato and Basil Jam with Sherry Vinegar (page 176), or just about any other jam in this book.

Experiment with substituting some of the all-purpose with different types of flour—whole-wheat, of course, or just a touch of buckwheat or rye flour.

If you move straight from cheesemaking to bread baking, let the whey cool to lukewarm before you combine it with the yeast, and skip the heating step.

2 teaspoons cornmeal, plus more for the pans

1 tablespoon sugar

¾ cup warm water or whey from making Fresh Cheese (page 284)

1½ tablespoons instant yeast (see Note)

2 cups whey or milk

2 teaspoons pure kosher salt

6 cups all-purpose flour

¼ teaspoon baking soda

Grease 2 (9¼-by-5¼-inch) loaf pans and dust the bottoms and sides with cornmeal.

In a large bowl, stir together the sugar, water, and yeast; set aside.

In a heavy saucepan, combine the whey and salt and place over low heat until just lukewarm. Pour into the yeast mixture and stir to combine. Stir in 3 cups of the flour, along with the baking soda, then add the remaining 3 cups flour and stir well; the dough will be very wet and sticky.

Divide the dough between the prepared pans and smooth the tops as well as you can with a spatula. Sprinkle the top of each loaf with 1 teaspoon of the cornmeal and pat the surface to smooth it out a bit. Cover with a clean kitchen towel and let rise in a warm spot for about 30 minutes; the dough will rise almost to the tops of the pans.

Meanwhile, preheat the oven to 400°F. Bake in the center of the oven for about 30 minutes, until golden brown on top. Let cool on a wire rack in the pans for 5 minutes, then loosen the sides with a knife and turn out the loaves. Let cool completely on the rack before slicing. Wrap the loaves tightly to store, to prevent them from drying out.

Note: If using active dry yeast (not instant), let the sugar and yeast mixture stand for 10 minutes to proof—that is, become bubbly—before proceeding.

Jenny's Cream Biscuits

MAKES ABOUT 8

FROM THE HANDWRITTEN RECIPE NOTEBOOK DEREK GAVE ME BEFORE WE WERE MARRIED COME THESE PERFECT SOUTHERN BISCUITS. The recipe is from our friend Jenny Smith, of Atlanta. Officially, White Lily flour, made from soft winter wheat and much fluffier and finer than other brands, is essential in creating light-as-air biscuits. Off the record, these will still be great if you use another brand of all-purpose flour.

3 cups White Lily all-purpose flour

1½ tablespoons baking powder

2 tablespoons sugar

¾ teaspoon pure kosher salt

6 tablespoons unsalted butter, cut into bits

⅔ cup heavy cream

⅔ cup half-and-half, plus 2 tablespoons for brushing the tops

Preheat the oven to 375°F. Line a baking sheet with parchment paper.

In a large bowl, whisk together the flour, baking powder, sugar, and salt. Add the butter and use a pastry cutter, two table knives held in one hand, or your fingertips to cut it in until the largest pieces are the size of small peas. Make a well in the center and pour in the cream and the ⅔ cup of half-and-half. Stir with a wooden spoon until the dough comes together; do not overmix. Pick up small handfuls of dough (or use a spoon) and place them close together—with only about ¼ inch of space between them—on the prepared pan. Brush the tops gently with half-and-half. Bake until golden brown, about 20 minutes. Serve hot, warm, or room temperature, split if desired.

Fresh Cheese

MAKES ABOUT 2 CUPS CHEESE AND 6 CUPS WHEY

◇◇

THE WORD *RICOTTA*, AS YOU PROBABLY KNOW IF YOU'VE READ A COOKBOOK IN THE LAST TWENTY YEARS, MEANS "RECOOKED." It's made from proteins skimmed off reheated whey left over from cheesemaking, and because no starter is used, it's not technically a cheese. True ricotta isn't within my capabilities: I don't often have on hand the gallons of whey I'd need to make a cup of . . . *dairy product*.

But a good, easy, fast *approximation* of fresh ricotta? Hand me the cheesecloth already! I use the whey to make Clare's English Muffin Bread (page 282), which happens to pair very nicely with the fresh cheese that spawned it, especially when slathered in turn with marmalade or Slow-Roasted Fig Preserves (page 197).

½ gallon whole milk

1 cup heavy cream

½ teaspoon pure kosher salt

3 tablespoons strained fresh lemon juice

Line a fine-mesh sieve with 3 layers of rinsed and squeezed cheesecloth and set it over a bowl.

In a heavy saucepan, combine the milk, cream, and salt. Bring to a full foaming boil over medium-high heat, stirring occasionally to keep the milk from scorching. Drizzle in the lemon juice, lower the heat to low, and cook, stirring slowly in one direction, until the solid curds separate from the clear, yellowish whey, about 2 minutes. Pour into the sieve and let drain for about 30 minutes, or until the cheese is as thick as you'd like. Transfer the cheese to an airtight container and chill in the refrigerator. The cheese will keep for several days.

Clotted Cream

MAKES ABOUT 1 ¼ CUPS

✦✦

THE FIRST TIME MY THEN-FUTURE HUSBAND AND I LIVED TOGETHER, FOR ONE HOT SUMMER IN LOUISVILLE, I MADE CLOTTED CREAM. He was horrified that I would even think of leaving a dairy product out on the counter for two whole days. It didn't stop him from enjoying, in a way, the finished result: creamy, tangy, and as smooth as a contented sigh. Spread it on a crumpet, a biscuit, or a scone and silver-spoon some strawberry jam on top, and you'll swear you hear well-bred and well-fed British livestock mooing in the distance.

The draining makes a nice, thick clotted cream, but I remember having runnier clotted cream in England when I was a kid, so the extended draining isn't entirely necessary unless you want it extra-firm (and if you don't mind having, well, *less* of it).

1 quart whole milk
1 pint heavy cream

In a wide metal bowl, combine the milk and cream. Cover loosely with a clean towel or paper towel and set aside in a cool place (an air-conditioned house is fine), undisturbed, for 48 hours. Set the bowl over a pan of boiling water and heat to 175° to 190°F on a candy thermometer (it will take a long time to come to temperature over the water, but that's okay). Hold it at that temperature for 30 minutes—do not stir or jostle it. The surface of the cream will crinkle.

Remove the bowl from the pan and set it in a larger bowl of ice water to cool. When it has cooled to room temperature, use a slotted spoon to skim the cooled thickened cream into a fine-mesh sieve (or two, if you have them; otherwise, drain the clotted cream in 2 batches) set over another bowl. Put in the refrigerator and let drain for several hours or up to overnight, until it's as thick as you'd like it. Transfer to an airtight container and store in the refrigerator for up to 5 days.

Yogurt

MAKES 2 QUARTS

◇◇

I PROBABLY SHOULDN'T SAY THIS, BUT EVERY COUPLE WEEKS I BUY A HALF GALLON OF ALMOST-EXPIRED MANAGER'S-SPECIAL MILK SUPER-CHEAP (LIKE 50 CENTS CHEAP) AND THEN, UM, *PRESERVE* IT. I do this by making it into tons of smooth and delicious (not to mention packed-with-beneficial-bacteria) yogurt. No, I don't use fancy grass-fed, hand-squeezed farmhouse milk here; just supermarket milk. My kid eats *a lot* of yogurt, usually with a spoonful of preserves stirred in (or two, if I'm feeling weak) but sometimes with just plain fresh or frozen fruit, and I appreciate having it on hand to use in baked goods like scones and in Indian-style simmered or broiled meat dishes. Really, I'll put yogurt in or on just about anything.

The key to success in this very straightforward method is using the right yogurt as a starter. Check the ingredients list: The yogurt should contain only milk (maybe cream) and active cultures—nothing else: no pectin, no flavorings, no powdered milk. I most often use Chobani Greek yogurt, which is similar to Fage but less of an investment because the plain variety is available in small containers. For your second batch of yogurt, use your homemade yogurt as the starter. Every three or four batches, you'll probably have to buy another little cup of yogurt to use as a starter, as the homemade stuff tends to thicken the milk a little less with each successive batch.

½ gallon milk (low-fat is fine)

2 tablespoons plain yogurt with active cultures (and no pectin or other ingredients besides milk)

In a large saucepan, heat the milk over medium-high heat to 170°F on a candy thermometer, stirring occasionally. Remove from the heat and set the pan in a larger bowl of ice water. Let cool to 110°F, stirring occasionally.

Meanwhile, fill 2 glass quart jars with hot water to warm them; pour out the water. When the milk has cooled to 110°F, ladle a little of it into a small bowl and whisk in the yogurt; whisk the mixture back into the milk in the saucepan, then pour the mixture into the warmed jars and put the lids on tightly.

Set the jars in an insulated cooler, wrapping them with towels and tucking one or two jugs or bottles of hot water into the cooler with them if necessary to fill up space. Basically, make the jars cozy. Set the cooler aside in an out-of-the-way spot for 8 to 10 hours, or overnight, and be careful not to jostle or disturb it (the fermentation fairies greatly dislike being jostled and disturbed). The milk will thicken and become yogurt; at this point you can use it any way you'd use yogurt, but the consistency is better after it's been chilled in the refrigerator for at least 2 hours. In all likelihood your yogurt will be plenty thick to use as is, but if you want even thicker, Greek-style yogurt, put it in a sieve lined with a couple layers of rinsed and squeezed cheesecloth and let it drain in the refrigerator for a few hours. The yogurt will keep for at least 2 weeks in the refrigerator. Be sure to save 2 tablespoons of it to make the next batch.

French Vanilla Ice Cream

MAKES ABOUT 1 QUART

◇◇

MY GOOD FRIEND LEDA SCHEINTAUB QUICKLY BECAME AN EXPERT IN ALL THINGS ICE-CREAM-RELATED AFTER SHE WAS HIRED TO WRITE AND TEST RECIPES FOR A BOOK OF HUNDREDS OF GELATI AND SORBETTI. I really like the basic method she came up with, and it's how I make any classic ice cream now.

I use one of those machines that you need to put ice and rock salt in—I just find it easier than waiting for a gel canister to chill in the freezer overnight; usually the ice-cream making around here is rather spur-of-the-moment. For what it's worth, Leda says that the more expensive countertop machines, which don't require prechilled canisters because they have cooling apparatuses built in, are convenient and efficient.

This recipe can be doubled, and I'd suggest doing so if you're using a big crank machine with the drippy ice and all—makes it that much more worthwhile!

2 cups milk

1 cup heavy cream

1 vanilla bean, split, or 1 tablespoon pure vanilla extract

4 large egg yolks

⅔ cup sugar

Pinch of pure kosher salt

In a heavy saucepan, combine the milk and cream. Scrape in the seeds from the vanilla bean, if using (or add extract later), and heat over medium-low heat, stirring frequently, just until tiny bubbles start to form around the edges of the pan.

Meanwhile, in a large heatproof bowl, whisk the egg yolks and sugar together until the mixture is smooth and pale yellow. Very slowly pour in the hot milk mixture, whisking constantly. Return the custard to the saucepan and place over low heat. Heat, stirring frequently with a wooden spoon, until the custard is thick enough to coat the back of the spoon. Do not boil. Stir in the salt.

Pour the custard through a sieve into a clean bowl. Set the bowl in a larger bowl of ice water; let cool completely, stirring frequently. Cover and chill in the refrigerator for at least 4 hours, or overnight.

Whisk in the vanilla extract, if using, and freeze the custard according to the manufacturer's instructions. Transfer to an airtight container and freeze for at least 2 hours before serving—preferably with preserves.

Crème Fraîche

MAKES ABOUT 2 CUPS

CRÈME FRAÎCHE, WHICH IS BASICALLY FER-
MENTED CREAM, IS A PRESERVE IN ITS OWN
RIGHT. As beneficial bacteria take over the cream
environment and gently sour the mixture, they
crowd out the evil bacteria that will cause spoilage.
In France, crème fraîche is made with unpasteurized
(raw) cream alone, since it contains enough bacteria to get the ferment going. Here in the United
States most cream is pasteurized—that is, heated
to temperatures just high enough and for just long
enough to kill off all bacteria, good and bad—and
even the raw cream here (if you're lucky enough
to be able to get some, legally or not) supposedly
does not have enough of the necessary bacteria to
ferment properly. You can overcome these horrible
injustices of geography and government regulation
by adding a little buttermilk to the cream.

The double-fermentation method here was
detailed in a *Los Angeles Times* article a while back;
it's the method used by Colleen Hennessey, who
makes the crème fraîche at Suzanne Goin's restaurant, Lucques. It does indeed result in a thicker
and tastier cream, and is worth the extra time if you
have it.

A mere spoonful of crème fraîche on a plate next
to an equal amount of good preserves will satisfy
me, but you can also try it as a dollop for pies and
cobblers, perhaps whipped together with a pinch
of sugar; or as a spread under especially sweet preserves that would benefit from a tart counterpoint;
or thinned and swirled into winter squash or asparagus soup; or in any dish that features smoked or
unsmoked salmon; or on top of fresh sliced cucumbers with rose petals scattered on top. You can also
whisk it with salt, pepper, and a squeeze of lemon
juice and toss boiled waxy potatoes, fresh lovage,
and sweet onion in the dressing for a simple salad.
And it makes superb *rajas con crema* (page 152).

2 cups heavy whipping cream (at least 36% butterfat,
  pasteurized but preferably not ultrapasteurized)
4 tablespoons cultured buttermilk

In a medium saucepan, combine the cream and buttermilk. Place over medium heat and bring to 100°F
on a candy thermometer. Immediately pour the
mixture into a stainless-steel bowl, cover with plastic wrap, and set aside in a warm spot for 24 hours.
The cream should have started to thicken.

Put the bowl in the refrigerator for 8 hours or
overnight, then put it in a warm spot for another 24
hours. Transfer to an airtight container and store in
the refrigerator for up to 2 weeks.

Acknowledgments

Thanks first to Luisa Weiss, my editor, who read a rambling and incoherent email of mine and saw in it a book, and to the amazingly talented Rinne Allen, for making this volume look as good as it does (and my food look better than it usually does). The pictures for the book were shot in and around Athens, Georgia; many thanks to the smart, with-it Athenians Lucy Allen Gillis and Chrissy Reed, Hugh Acheson, and Hillary Brown for their contributions to the effort. And thanks to the copyeditor, Elizabeth Norment, and the proofreader, Erin Slonaker. I owe a huge thank you to Kate Norment, who read and reread this book countless times as she shepherded it through production. I am also very grateful to Alissa Faden, the designer, for her thoughtful and intelligent work here. She, along with Kate and Natalie Kaire, made what could have been a difficult process an absolute pleasure. I also very sincerely thank Patty Catalano for her close reading of some of the more science-y sections of the book.

Warmest thanks to Marisa Bulzone, for her generous and invaluable publishing-industry-type advice, as well as her stash of vintage canning guides and her stories about canning, the Ball company, and her family's toxic-seeming, fluorescent-green Christmas pickles. Which I swear I'm going to make . . . soon.

Thank you, too, to all the friends who gave me old and new family recipes to pore over and pointed me to this or that interesting preserve here and there. I'd especially like to thank David Centner, a.k.a. Father Kitchen, who has been a constant source of ideas, inspiration, and encouragement from the very beginning of this long project. I'm very sorry I wasn't able to develop a recipe for the *mostarda di frutta* of his dreams; perhaps when Americans discover the wonder that is quince and start growing it like they mean it, I can take another crack at it. Clare Adams has also been an enormous inspiration to me: When she isn't dehydrating, canning, pickling, and fermenting everything in sight, she's giving it all away. Thanks, too, to my generous neighbors Cecilia Underwood and June Hawkins. And thank you to Athens's own Jane Kobres for sharing so many brilliant ideas, tips, and leads that I was tempted to start a spreadsheet and filing system to keep track of them.

Heidi Butler deserves much of the credit for helping me develop the idea for this book. It was, in fact, a jar of her parents' Michigan sour cherry jam that tipped me off to the fact that, despite what the authorities say, one *could* make preserves with less sugar and more intense fruit flavors. Also thanks to Leda Scheintaub, who read early drafts of many of these recipes and offered invaluable advice and smart suggestions.

Special thanks to my dear friend Regan Huff, whose influence on my way of thinking about food in general and preserving in particular, as well as about books and writing and things that are beautiful, can be seen on every page of this book. I can't thank her enough for all she's done for me and my family.

Finally, as always, thank you to my parents, Diana and Dave Fredley, who it's clear would do anything to help me with anything. And most of all, I thank Derek and Thalia, my husband and daughter and my best friends.

Sources

Canning and Preserving Supplies
Everything you need for basic canning and preserving—the preserving pan, canning pot, jar lifter, wide-mouth funnel, jars and lids, and everyday colanders and sieves—can usually be found in hardware stores and big-box emporiums. For more specialized tools, look in restaurant-supply stores and online.

All Seasons Homestead Helpers
Most of the stuff on this site is purely aspirational for someone like me—that is, it's serious equipment, and seriously expensive—but it makes for entertaining browsing. The store is affiliated with the maker of Squeezo and carries several different models of Squeezo and Squeezo-like strainers, food mills, and "sauce makers." Also a few dehydrators, plus a fancy, heavy-duty, large cw pot if you feel you need one.

homesteadhelpers.com
44 Lamoille View Lane #101
Jeffersonville, VT 05464
Tel: 800-649-9147

Canning Pantry
Pretty much anything you need to start canning, dehydrating, fermenting, and so on. Jars, crocks, dehydrators at different price points, freezer containers, vacuum-packing equipment, food mills, and Squeezo strainers.

canningpantry.com
Highland Brands
19 N. 100 W.
Hyrum, UT 84319
Tel: 800-285-9044

Leeners
A treasure trove of goodies for big projects in the kitchen. Not only canning supplies but also equipment for brewing and winemaking, fermenting, cheesemaking, meat curing, and candymaking, as well as quirky instructional books for all of the above (and more). Leeners carries citric acid, which you might need for tomato canning (look for it in the cheesemaking section).

leeners.com
9293 Olde Eight Road
Northfield, OH 44067
Tel: 800-543-3697

Omega Engineering
Relatively economical handheld pH testers and buffer solution. If you plan to make up recipes for your own pickles, you really should invest in a tester and 4.0 buffer solution (which is what you dip the tester into in order to calibrate it). See below for a source for pH test strips.

omega.com
1 Omega Drive
Stamford, CT 06907
Tel: 800-622-2378

Sanitation Tools
Source for pH test strips in the 2.5 to 4.5 range; the paper test strips, while much cheaper than a pH meter, are quite difficult to interpret with any degree of accuracy, but they're fine for determining the pH of, say, tomatoes if you want to be extra-certain that they're acid enough to can safely in a boiling-water bath.

sanitationtools.com
Sanitation Strategies
P.O. Box 485
Williamston, MI 48895
Tel: 877-494-4364
info@sanitationstrategies.com

Simply Natural
Fermenting crocks, Japanese tsukemono pickle presses, dehydrators.

simply-natural.biz
Discount Natural Foods
146 Londonderry Turnpike #10
Hooksett, NH 03106
Tel: 888-392-9237
sales@discountnaturalfoods.com

Weck
The most elegant and graceful canning jars you'll ever see are made by Weck. While they're a bit hard to find in stores, they can be ordered the old-fashioned way, over the phone. Drool over the photographs on the website, then call up the friendly folks in Illinois to place an order.

weckcanning.com
450 Congress Parkway, Suite E
Crystal Lake, IL 60014
Tel: 815-356-8440
info@weckcanning.com

Further Reading

These are a few of the sources I found most helpful and inspiring when writing this book. They're all well worth seeking out.

Books

Bone, Eugenia. *Well-Preserved: Recipes and Techniques for Putting up Small Batches of Seasonal Foods*. New York: Clarkson Potter, 2009. Appealing, modern preserves (boiling-water-bath canning and pressure canning, plus low-impact smoking and curing) and recipes for using them.

Bullwinkel, Madelaine. *Gourmet Preserves Chez Madelaine*. Chicago: Surrey Books, 2005. Lower-sugar jams and sensible techniques. Also includes lots of recipes for accompaniments to fruit preserves—various scones, cakes, and so on.

Cooperative Extension Service, University of Georgia. *So Easy to Preserve*, 5th ed. Copies usually available at: uga.edu/setp. One of the bibles of home preserving. Comprehensive and complete.

Dowdney, Stephen Palmer. *Putting Up: A Year-Round Guide to Canning in the Southern Tradition*. Layton, UT: Gibbs Smith, 2008. The only canning book I've seen that explains the methods required by the FDA for small-scale commercial canners. The recipes are not the easiest to use—no processing times are given because it's assumed you will follow the guidelines and take the internal temperature of the jar contents as it heats in the boiling-water bath—but the description of the method in the introduction is valuable.

Ferber, Christine. *Mes Confitures: The Jams and Jellies of Christine Ferber*, trans. Virginia R. Phillips. East Lansing: Michigan State University Press, 2002. Some of the most exquisite-sounding jam recipes you'll ever see in print. A truly inspiring read.

Hisamatsu, Ikuko. *Quick and Easy Tsukemono: Japanese Pickling Recipes*. Tokyo: JOIE, 2005. Japanese pickles, but also some Korean and other Asian techniques. Full-color step-by-step photographs are very helpful, especially when unfamiliar ingredients are used. The book is available online.

Hupping, Carol, and the staff of the Rodale Food Center. *Stocking Up*, 3rd ed. New York: Fireside, 1990. The classic homesteader's tome. Not a whole lot of canning, but after flipping through this book you'll want to dehydrate the universe. And then freeze it for good measure.

Fun Ingredients

Kalustyan's

One of the best sources for good, fresh spices, specialty grains and beans, rice, nuts, honey, extracts, puffy Indian snack foods, and more. Kalustyan's carries citric acid—look for it under the name "lemon salt."

kalustyans.com
123 Lexington Avenue
New York, NY 10016
Tel: 800-352-3451
sales@kalustyans.com

Penzey's Spices

Very good Vietnamese ground cinnamon, as well as tons of other spices. Also vanilla.

penzeys.com
16750 W. Bluemound Road
Brookfield, WI (and other retail locations)
Tel: 800-741-7787

Pomona's Universal

The most popular all-natural sugar-free low-methoxyl pectin.

pomonapectin.com
Workstead Industries
P.O. Box 1083
Greenfield, MA 01302
Tel: 413-772-6816
info@pomonapectin.com

Vanilla Products USA

This reputable eBay seller offers excellent Tahitian, Bourbon Madagascar, and other varieties of whole vanilla beans, vanilla bean paste, and extracts at almost unbelievably good prices.

stores.shop.ebay.com/Vanilla-Products-USA

MacRae, Norma M. *Canning and Preserving without Sugar*. Seattle, WA: Pacific Search Press, 1982. Out of print, but available online. Lots of clever ideas for reducing sugar content of preserves and pickles: concentrated fruit juices, alternative sweeteners, and others.

Norris, Lucy. *Pickled: Preserving a World of Tastes and Traditions*. New York: Stewart, Tabori & Chang, 2003. Traditional recipes and techniques from all over the world.

Plagemann, Catherine. *Fine Preserving*, ann. M.F.K. Fisher. Berkeley, CA: Aris Books, 1986. Fun read, as you can imagine, and the recipes are actually sort of workable! Not up to current USDA standards, but you can use them for inspiration and adjust your process as required.

Ziedrich, Linda. *The Joy of Pickling*. Boston, MA: Harvard Common Press, 1998. The bible of pickling. Ziedrich is a national treasure, and this book is absolutely brilliant, comprehensive, informative, and do-able. If you're at all interested in furthering your pickling repertoire after trying some of the recipes in the present volume, please get hers.

Websites

Altitude Finders
maps.google.com

You can contact your local county extension office to find out your approximate altitude, or use an online tool, but probably the easiest thing to do is to type your address into Google Maps and use the "Terrain" view, which overlays topographic lines.

Ask-a-Scientist on MadSci Network
madsci.org

Not canning-specific, but a surprisingly useful website. If you have a science question, submit it on the "Ask-a-Scientist" link, and a scientist in the related field will write back with an answer. I've been impressed by the quality and timeliness of the responses.

Ball's Fresh Preserving
freshpreserving.com

Lots of recipes (some goofy, some good), tips, forums, and so on from the makers of Ball jars.

Chest of Books
Cookbooks
http://chestofbooks.com/food

Public domain cookbooks from way back. Lots and lots of old preserving recipes, though of course techniques described are not up to date with modern science and recipes should be taken with a grain of salt.

Food and Drug Administration
http://www.fda.gov/Food/FoodSafety/FoodborneIllness/
FoodborneIllnessFoodbornePathogensNaturalToxins/
BadBugBook/ucm122561.htm

If you don't know whether a food has a pH below 4.6, the cutoff for canning in a boiling-water bath, check this list of pH levels of various foods on the FDA website.

Local Harvest
localharvest.org

Type in your zip code and find local farmers' markets, CSAs, co-ops, and small produce and meat farms.

National Center for Home Food Preservation
uga.edu/nchfp

This is the definitive, official source of information and recipes for home canners. The NCHFP publishes *So Easy to Preserve*, one of the most comprehensive canning and preserving books out there.

PickYourOwn.org
pickyourown.org

Impressive international directory of pick-your-own farms and orchards, updated regularly and reader-annotated.

The Pickle Bibliography
http://fsweb2.schaub.ncsu.edu/USDAars/html/Fflbiblio1.htm

Links to peer-reviewed papers about everything to do with pickles. Papers range from 1938 to the present. Fascinating stuff.

Conversion Charts

Weight Equivalents: The metric weights given in this chart are not exact equivalents, but have been rounded up or down slightly to make measuring easier.

Volume Equivalents: These are not exact equivalents for American cups and spoons, but have been rounded up or down slightly to make measuring easier.

avoirdupois	metric
¼ oz	7 g
½ oz	15 g
1 oz	30 g
2 oz	60 g
3 oz	90 g
4 oz	115 g
5 oz	150 g
6 oz	175 g
7 oz	200 g
8 oz (½ lb)	225 g
9 oz	250 g
10 oz	300 g
11 oz	325 g
12 oz	350 g
13 oz	375 g
14 oz	400 g
15 oz	425 g
16 oz (1 lb)	450 g
1½ lb	675 g
2 lb	900 g
2¼ lb	1 kg
3 lb	1.4 kg
4 lb	1.8 kg

american	metric	imperial
¼ tsp	1.2 ml	
½ tsp	2.5 ml	
1 tsp	5.0 ml	
½ Tbsp (1.5 tsp)	7.5 ml	
1 Tbsp (3 tsp)	15 ml	
¼ cup (4 Tbsp)	60 ml	2 fl oz
⅓ cup (5 Tbsp)	75 ml	2.5 fl oz
½ cup (8 Tbsp)	125 ml	4 fl oz
⅔ cup (10 Tbsp)	150 ml	5 fl oz
¾ cup (12 Tbsp)	175 ml	6 fl oz
1 cup (16 Tbsp)	250 ml	8 fl oz
1¼ cups	300 ml	10 fl oz (½ pint)
1½ cups	350 ml	12 fl oz
2 cups (1 pint)	500 ml	16 fl oz
2½ cups	625 ml	20 fl oz (1 pint)
1 quart	1 liter	32 fl oz

oven mark	f	c	gas
Very cool	250–275	130–140	½–1
Cool	300	150	2
Warm	325	170	3
Moderate	350	180	4
Moderately hot	375	190	5
	400	200	6
Hot	425	220	7
	450	230	8
Very hot	475	250	9

Index

About the Author

Liana Krissoff is the author of STC's *Secrets of Slow Cooking* and *Hot Drinks for Cold Nights*. She worked in the editorial departments of Rizzoli and HarperCollins, and has been a freelance recipe tester, editor, and writer for more than a decade. She lives with her husband and young daughter in Georgia.

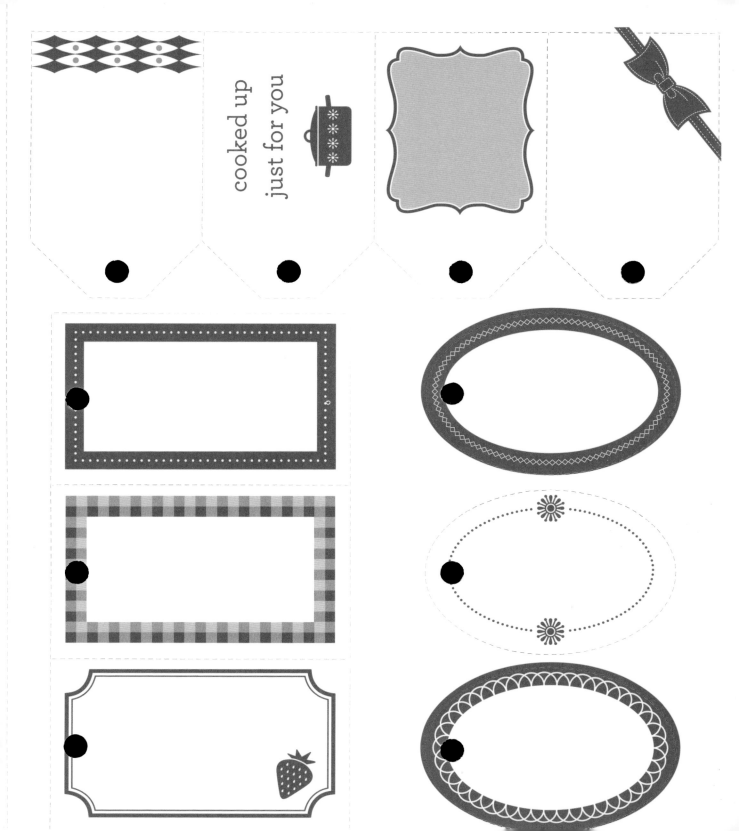

cooked up
just for you

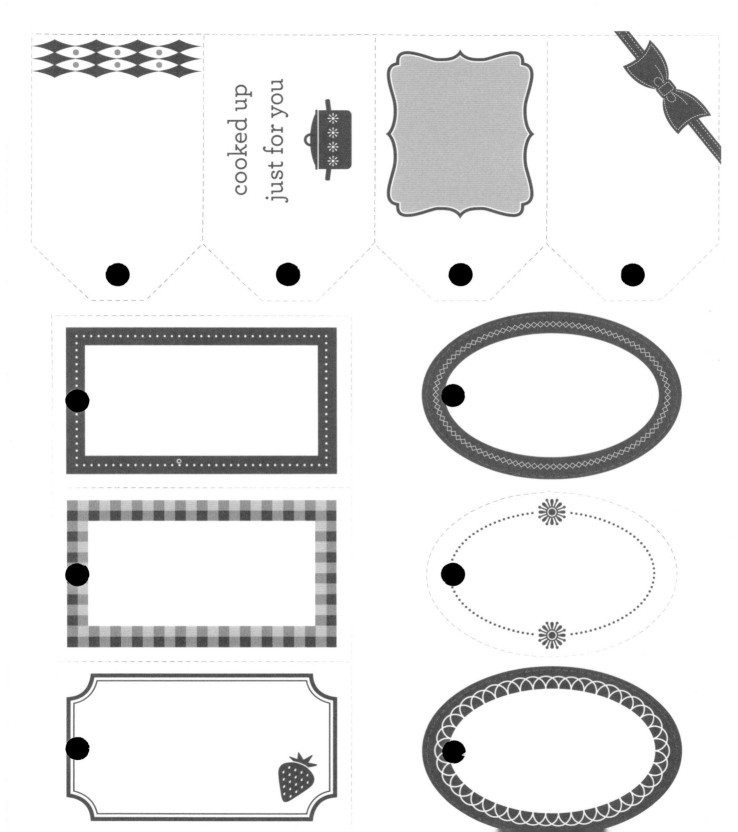

cooked up
just for you

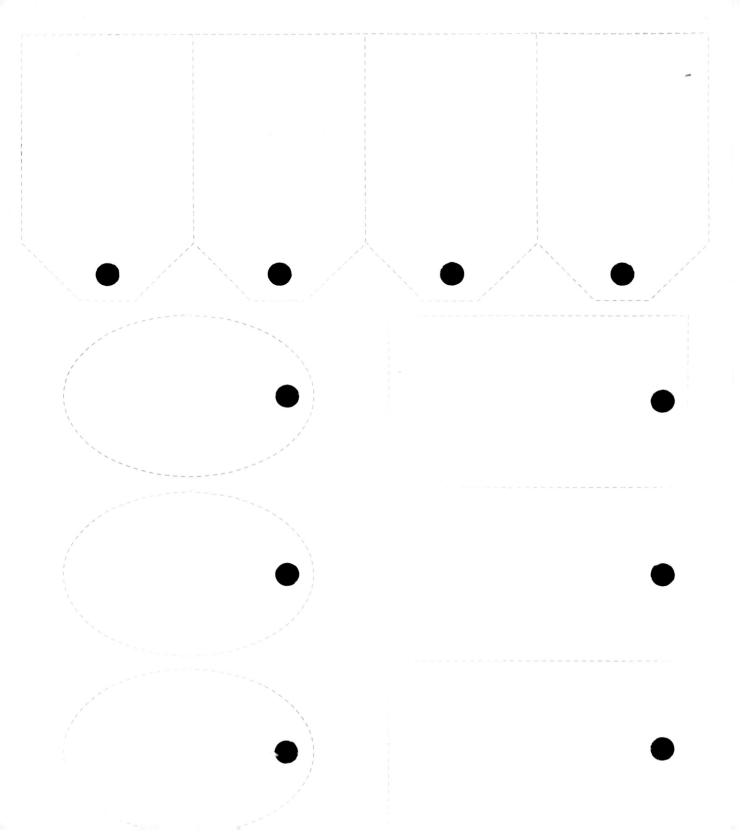

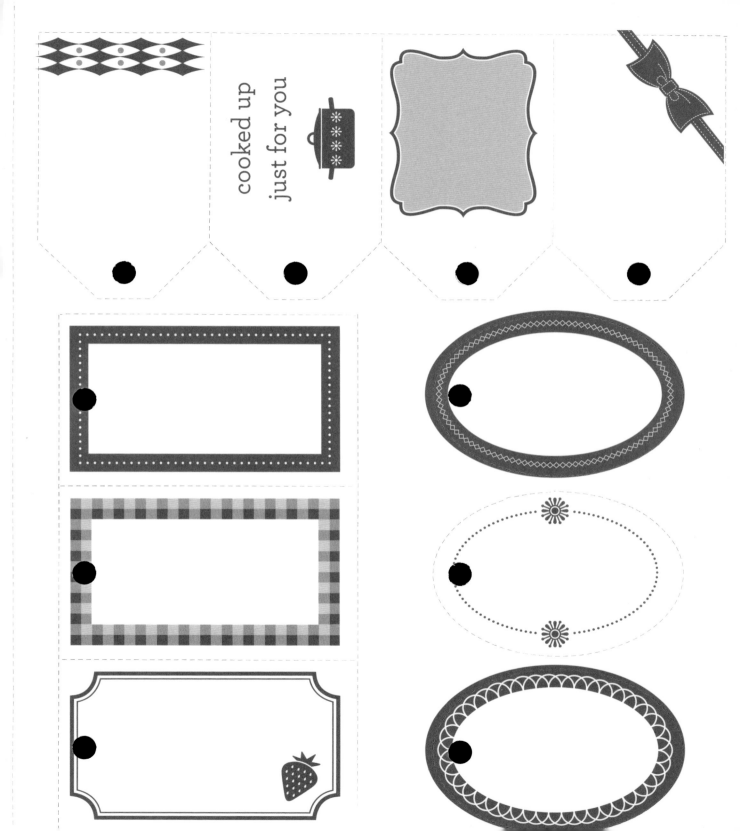

cooked up
just for you

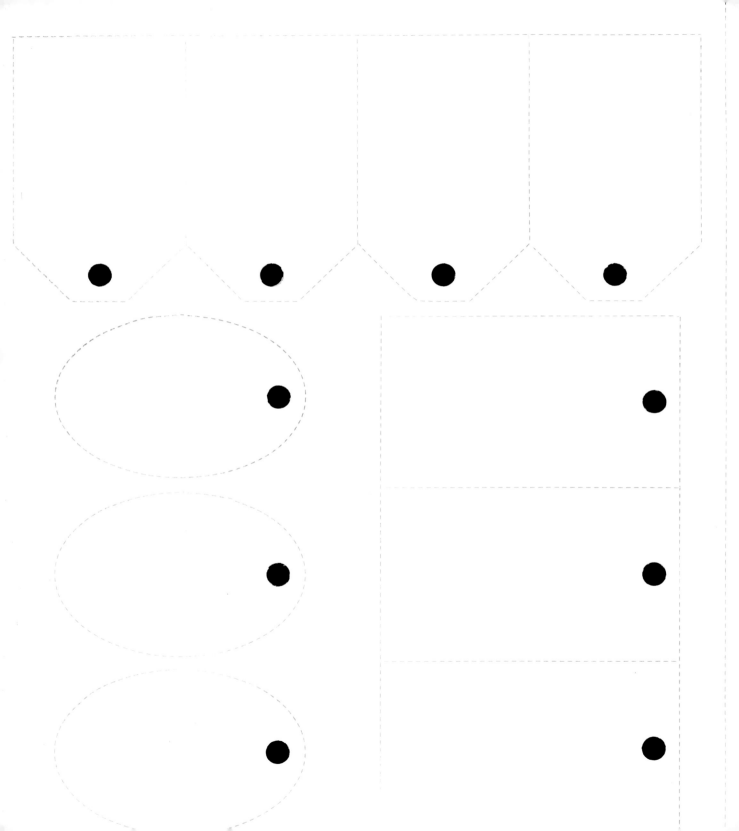